WITHDRAWN

STUDIES IN THE RUSSIAN ECONOMY BEFORE 1914

STUDIES IN THE RUSSIAN ECONOMY BEFORE 1914

OLGA CRISP
Reader in Russian Economic History
University of London

M

in association with the
School of Slavonic and East European Studies
University of London

First edition 1976
Reprinted 1978

Published by
THE MACMILLAN PRESS LTD
London and Basingstoke
Associated companies in Delhi Dublin Hong Kong
Johannesburg Lagos Melbourne
New York Singapore Tokyo

ISBN 0 333 16907 7

Printed in Great Britain by
LOWE AND BRYDONE PRINTERS LIMITED
Thetford, Norfolk

In memory of

R. R. Betts

1903–1961

Masaryk Professor of Central European History
School of Slavonic and East European Studies
University of London

1946–1961

Contents

Tables

Abbreviations

AN	*Archives Nationales*
DDF	*Documents Diplomatiques Français*
O.S.	Old Style
PSZ	*Polnoye Sobraniye Zakonov Rossiyskoy Imperii*

Acknowledgements

I owe many lasting debts of gratitude to my academic colleagues here, in France and the USA, and to the staffs of the archives and libraries in London, Paris and Helsinki for their counsel and assistance. In particular I wish to express my warmest appreciation to Professors François Crouzet and Pierre Léon of the Sorbonne, for inviting me to participate in the most stimulating international *Colloque* on European industrialisation at Lyon in October 1970, to Professor Maurice Lévy-Leboyer of Nanterre for asking me to attend the French Economic History Conference in Paris in October 1973, and to Professor Rondo Cameron of Emory University, Atlanta to whom I owe the honour of taking part in a conference of eminent banking and monetary specialists at the Villa Serbelloni, Bellagio, Italy. Three of the essays in this book had started as papers for the above conferences.

I wish to express my thanks to the Oxford University Press, New York, to the Centre National de la Recherche Scientifique, Paris, to the editors of *Business History, Economic History Review, Slavonic and East European Review, Slavic Review* and *Soviet Studies,* for their permission to use material originally published by them, as indicated in the text.

Introduction*

The bulk of the essays here printed have appeared in various journals and symposia over a number of years. No excuse, it is felt, need be offered for republishing them. Some of the studies were published in journals or symposia read as a rule by economic historians only, while others were printed in journals the readership of which is confined mainly to students of Eastern Europe. It is hoped that their publication in book form will make these studies accessible to a wider range of readers. Several sections have been restructured or expanded, and a new essay is added.

Neither the evidence nor the findings here recorded have been superseded by works which have appeared since their original publication. More often than not the few closely related studies in English by for example T. H. von Laue, J. P. McKay, and more recently by R. Girault in French, have amplified or added a further dimension to our interpretation, as indicated in the review appended to the relevant chapters.

These essays lay no claim to comprehensiveness. They do not add up to an economic history. They are in the main studies in depth of certain aspects of the economy or broader studies of certain salient features of economic development and policy. It is felt that such studies are more appreciated by students for essay writing and examination purposes than are general histories or large monographs. Four of the essays are largely based on unpublished sources from French archives; the rest drew extensively on Russian official publications and on articles and monographs by Russian and Soviet scholars, not as a rule accessible to the general economic historian.

The literature in English on the Russian pre-revolutionary economy is very sparse, though some of it is of high quality. A. Gerschenkron's brilliant conceptual approach to the study of economic backwardness derived from the Russian model, though not acceptable in its entirety,

* For works mentioned in the Introduction see the Bibliography.

has nevertheless been a constant inspiration and point of departure in our approach to the study of Russia.

Arcadius Kahan's articles, precise and scholarly, have set the highest standards in quantitive research on the Russian economy. He has justly reproached students of Russia for their preoccupation with acts of governments as distinct from the examination of the workings of economic forces.

M. Falkus's short and lucid account of the industrialisation of Russia and Blackwell's more comprehensive monograph on the early nineteenth century are good introductory and background studies, as is the erudite monograph on landlords and peasants, spanning nine centuries, by J. Blum. The two chapters on Russia in the Cambridge Economic History by A. Gerschenkron and R. Portal are in the same category.

Though the above enumeration does not exhaust the literature in English on the Russian economy published within the last two decades (to mention only Pintner, articles by Rimlinger and von Laue on labour, Garvy on banking, by Gregory on the structure of industry and Falkus on Russia's national income), the record in terms of quantity alone is singularly unimpressive, especially if compared with the amount of written work available on the Soviet economy, on Russian politics, and on economic history in general. It is a measure of the scarcity of work on the Russian economy in English that a translation from Russian of a study of the Russian factory by M. Tugan-Baranovsky, originally published as early as 1898, and the reissue of M. Miller's book on Russia's economic development between 1905 and 1914, which came out originally in 1926, still meet a real need both of the student of Russia and for comparative study.

'The new economic history', sometimes called econometric history or cliometrics implying the use of economic theory and mathematical methods to test largely counter-factual hypotheses, which burst upon the academic community in the USA towards the end of the 1950s and became more or less universally acclaimed there in the 1960s and to a much lesser extent and with less alacrity in this country, has not as yet very significantly affected the study of the Russian economy. J. Metzer's study of railway development in Tsarist Russia, based on the methods used by R. W. Fogel and A. Fishlow and Barkai's article on the cost of the adoption of the gold standard are so far the only ones known to us.

Though the choice of topics was largely determined by the author's special interests the problems discussed are significant aspects of the evolution of the Russian economy, essential for its understanding. These aspects are the rôle of serfdom, the position of the state in the economy, the interaction between government policy and market forces, the contribution to and the influence of foreign capital on the Russian economy, monetary and banking policies, and the structure of industry. A great deal of conventional wisdom has amassed over the years around these topics, sometimes traceable to one or a few sources.

Much pre-revolutionary Russian historical writing had an inbuilt anti-government bias; it was more often than not in the nature of an ideological debate in which economic facts were used as ammunition, or a literature of 'social lament'. Political, legal, and institutional factors were given prominence in explaining economic phenomena. Much of this approach was taken over by Western historians, partly because they shared the dislike of the despotic tradition of the Russian state and partly because the momentous events of the October Revolution and the creation of the Soviet state had the effect of confirming the existing and inducing a few new biases in the interpretation of past history. Aspects of pre-revolutionary history began to be studied, implicitly or explicitly, almost entirely from the angle of their effectiveness or otherwise in deterring revolution.

Our aim is not to refute accepted views, but to induce some doubt by indicating disconfirming evidence. To give one example : Serfdom has been looked upon as a constraint on economic improvement, as the prime cause of the backwardness of the Russian economy in the nineteenth century. This assumption is challenged by an attempt to find out whether those sections of the economy or society where serfdom was less influential fared better than the rest. The essay on state peasants, who made up nearly half of the peasant population, shows that despite better land provision, lesser taxation burdens, and greater freedom of choice, no significant economic advance was made by them. Indeed, progressive change in the sense of industrial growth seems to be more frequent in areas where both landlordism and serf densities were well pronounced and of long standing. Another instance of disconfirming evidence is to show that while it was true that stagnating Ural industries were based on serf labour in the main as against the modernising textile industries which had almost a wholly hired labour force, the sugar beet industry which was also using serf labour in the main was nevertheless an innovating industry.

The first chapter is much broader in scope than the title implies. It examines the differential elements in Russia's backwardness and the manner in which they affected institutions and policies over time. It provides the framework within which the bulk of the remaining chapters, which deal with more specific self-contained issues, can be studied. Chapter 2 is a composite review of books dealing with industrial developments and policies under serfdom. It has been used as a vehicle for our views on the course of Russia's economic development before the emancipation of the serfs and as a background for the chapters which follow and which mainly relate to the post-1861 period.

1 The pattern of industrialisation in Russia, 1700–1914*

By the commonly accepted criteria of industrialisation Russia in 1914 was not yet an industrialised country. Agriculture was still the most important sector, accounting in 1913 for nearly two-thirds of the population and for at least 45 per cent of the national income. Over the whole period since 1860 agricultural production grew by about 2 per cent annually (of which half only on account of higher yields), which, given a population growth rate of about 1·5 per cent, was not more than ½ per cent per head. Manufacturing and mining accounted for not more than one-fifth of the national income and employed not much over 5 per cent of the entire labour force. This sector grew at an approximate rate of 5 per cent per annum, if both factory and handicraft industry are included, which gave a comparatively high rate of per capita increase of 3½ per cent. For the economy at large, including transport, trade and services as well as industry and agriculture, the total volume of output grew at 2½ per cent per annum or only about 1 per cent per head. Real income per head in 1913 was only half that of Germany, one-third that of the USA and Britain, and approximately equal to that of Italy.[1] Not more than about 18 per cent of the population of some 170 million lived in urban centres in 1916.

The only impressive feature of the above recital was the high growth rate of manufacturing and mining. In the view of Alexander Gerschenkron this is the most significant indicator of successful industrialisation in conditions of backwardness. He singles out the decade of the 1890s and the years 1910–13 as most significant, the first giving an annual growth rate of over 8 per cent and the second 7·5 per cent. Gerschenkron argues against the use of aggregates such as national in-

* Originally published in *L'industrialisation en Europe au XIXe siècle*, published by the Centre National de la Recherche Scientifique edited by P. Léon, F. Crouzet and R. Gascon, (Paris, 1972). Reprinted with modifications, by permission.

come rates, because however significant the initial spurt, in a backward country it cannot possibly render the product of industry bulky enough in absolute terms to affect national income rates.[2]

Also with regard to such criteria of industrialisation as urbanisation for example, it is clear if only from the experience of the heir to Imperial Russia that however considerable and rapid the rates of investment and growth in industry and notwithstanding the 'vigorous', to say the least, policies on the agrarian and handicrafts industries front in the 1930s, it was not till 1961 that the urban population in the USSR topped the 50 per cent mark; in 1969 it was only 56 per cent despite a very slow overall population growth. Notwithstanding Stalin's forced draft industrialisation and the massive substitution of machinery for labour in agriculture and the pricing policy which undervalued food, the share of agriculture was still 54·4 per cent of employment and 30·7 per cent of the GNP in 1937. It only gradually fell to become 30·1 and 15·3 per cent, respectively, in 1965.[3] Russia's experience shows how great was the effort needed to shift the weight of so massive an agricultural sector as the Russian and in general, how, despite the obvious advantages from the opportunity to borrow technology, inhibiting was the legacy of past backwardness.

Nevertheless by 1914 Russia had already a substantial social overhead capital and an important modern industrial sector,[4] which though relying to a significant extent on foreign capital and foreign technology was not a 'colonial' type of growth but in many intrinsic ways part of the total economic body gradually affecting its 'metabolism', to use Landes' felicitous expression.

It is not the intention of this paper to give a full account of Russia's industrialisation path; some aspects such as population, agriculture, wages, urbanisation, education, training and foreign trade have either not been covered at all or only alluded to. The intention here is to highlight, question, reinterpret and on occasion amplify certain aspects of the Russian industralisation process which tend to be considered peculiarly Russian : the weakness of autonomous forces, the rôle of the state, the place of heavy industry, and the pressures upon the consumption standards of the peasantry consequent upon the specific industrialising policies of the state.

THE NATURE OF RUSSIA'S BACKWARDNESS

Studies of industrialisation of Western European countries tend to assume implicitly or explicitly that all pre-industrial economies and societies were on broadly comparable levels in that they were all traditional, in that in all of them only short-run growth could be achieved because of the Malthusian checks which sooner or later set in. In stressing this point the intention is to emphasise the breakthrough made possible by the industrialisation process. The consequence however is often to underestimate the differentials in development or backwardness, depending which way one looks at it, of the individual 'traditional' societies, differences which though not quantitatively measurable were frequently as important as those separating contemporary advanced and developing countries.

Russia, we would argue, was backward relatively to most Western European countries at any given point of time and remained so at the terminal point of our enquiry. Before attempting a discussion of the industrialisation process we propose to dwell a while on the main differential elements of the Russian environment as it evolved historically, for it is our contention that Russia's backwardness was historically cumulative, layers of backwardness reinforcing each other, a diminution of backwardness in one aspect meaning frequently a deepening of it in another.

Poor natural endowment was among the elements of Russia's environment which affected her economic development. Though she has one of the best stretches of black earth in the world she came into the ownership of it only in the course of the sixteenth and seventeenth centuries. Moreover this rich area was poorly provided with waterways so that agricultural producers could not benefit from the demand of other regions while relatively marginal regions had to grow food because they could not be sure of supplies. By the end of the eighteenth century half of the country's supply of food came from the less rich soils while the excellent harvests of the central agricultral region often found no outlets.

The vast stretches of the steppe to the south-east, which Russia gradually colonised but which remained sparsely populated until the second half of the nineteenth century when the railways and the opportunity to export grain through Black Sea ports attracted settlers, were subject to considerable harvest fluctuations because of low rainfall and dry winds from the Central Asian deserts.[5]

The location of mineral resources on the peripheries inhibited their utilisation prior to the building of railways and made for high costs subsequently. Furthermore most of the resources were not available to Russia till the eighteenth or nineteenth century, by which time elements of backwardness which made their subsequent utilisation difficult had already set in.[6]

Size compounded by climate and the direction of rivers made the year-round utilisation of rivers impracticable, accentuated the seasonal rhythm of economic activity, and made for slow commodity circulation and high costs. Canal and road building as well as their maintenance was prohibitive in terms of costs. Connections by sea with foreign countries, acquired as late as the eighteenth century, at a time when Russia's poverty had already become a chronic feature to which incidentally the effort involved in acquiring them had made its distinct contribution, while undoubtedly of immense importance economically and culturally (without them Russia would have remained an Asiatic backwater), suffered from the same inadequacies of distance and climate. Contacts between ports within Russia were wasteful of time and prohibitive in cost.

The poor quality of Russia's resources made for slow population growth until the second half of the eighteenth century, so that Russia suffered from a constant imbalance between the size of her territory and the size of her population making for difficulties of labour supply and putting a strain on the thinly spread administration and other skills. This was the more important as the base from which expansion began in the sixteenth century was very poor and the new acquisitions could become an asset in the course of time only. From every point of view except perhaps the defence angle in the event of invasion, size was a liability for Russia.

All the above mentioned factors which accounted for Russia's poverty, to which should be added distance from the main international trade arteries which had since the sixteenth century been centred on the Atlantic as well as her cultural isolation from the West during the latter's most fertile periods (the late medieval and the sixteenth century), made for very tenuous trading relations and an underdeveloped market. If one were to single out one factor in Russia's resource endowment, the quality of which inhibited development, it would be that which made for difficulty of communications.

The geopolitical was the second differential element in Russia's environment considered historically. Since the very beginning of her statehood she had been open to repeated onslaughts of nomadic peoples who poured in through the open gateway between the Urals and the Caspian killing, looting, and breaking up carefully built up networks of trade.

Pechenegs in the tenth century, Kumans in the eleventh and twelfth, finally the hordes of Jenghiz Khan who in the thirteenth century laid waste what was then a network of wealthy cities and caused the displacement of the Russian people from the fertile Dnieper area.[7]

Between the thirteenth and sixteenth centuries a stunned and decimated Russian people, deprived of its most productive elements through slaughter or abduction, sought security in the swamps and forests of the Volga–Oka triangle, only a handful of the great ancient cities having escaped the holocaust. Opinions differ as to the actual damage of two and one-half centuries of Tartar domination, though all are agreed upon the devastating effect of the initial onslaught. We personally have no doubt that from the economic point of view the Russians became reduced to a most primitive form of existence, with a marked decline in commerce, a very primitive form of agriculture, and a drastic fall in population. To this should be added the financial strain of the Tartar tribute, of the gifts and fines and of the repeated punitive expeditions into the interior in which the horrors of the initial onslaught were repeated.

The most important effect of the Tartar yoke in our estimation however was that the trauma produced by it put a premium on concern for military security in Russian thinking. This was the more pronounced as the euphoria resulting from the formal renunciation of Tartar sovereignty at the end of the fifteenth century soon gave way to fear of the military superiority of Russia's Western neighbours. Furthermore, the Tartar menace did not end in 1480, for the heirs of the Golden Horde, along the Volga, in the Urals, and in the steppes of southern Russia continued to harass the Muscovites, often in alliance with her Western neighbours or Turkey, the Russians paying back with vengeance.

The consequence was a savage concentration on the search for resources to ensure security, a subordination of all interests to the task of holding and then gradually pushing back the frontiers to the east, south and west, 'gathering the Russian lands', groping for natural frontiers and sea outlets, imperceptibly passing from defence to attack and great power status. From the sixteenth to the late eighteenth century the Russians were almost constantly in a state of emergency, developing the now familiar 'siege mentality'. In the process the power of the state increased out of all proportion.

Partly this was owing to the relative weakness of the autonomous social forces (a result of poor-quality resource endowment), which meant feeble resistance to the encroachment by the state, partly because state action already at this stage was a form of 'substitution' for missing or inadequate factors of production. Then as later the main motivating force of government action was 'the national interest', though at the earlier stage it might be more appropriate to speak of 'national survival', or so it appeared to Russia's rulers.

The institutional and fiscal system was another differential element of the Russian environment which, though causally connected with the other two, became an important feature of Russia's backwardness. Faced by tasks the cost of which was far in excess of what the impoverished, largely natural economy could provide, the rulers of Russia gradually evolved an institutional and fiscal structure which enabled them to claim a larger share of the country's output than warranted by the producers' incomes.

However such a tax system, to be effective in a country with open frontiers, where the taxpayers could and did 'protest with their feet' and where whole communities even in the nineteenth century could exist in forest clearings unbeknown to the authorities, required an effective form of control. This was provided by a system of collective responsibility of rural and urban communities alike, by fixing both peasants and townsmen to their place of residence, and finally by enlisting landowners, more often than not endowed with land by the state which assumed a *dominium supremum* over all land and resources, for tax collecting and policing functions. In return the state gave its sanction to the use of serf labour and offered its aid in claiming fugitive peasants.

That serfdom, as it was instituted in the seventeenth century, was a state measure connected with the state's need for control over the financial and human resources for military purposes rather than a privilege granted to the nobility (who had had a species of economic serfdom *via* debt bondage and a variety of contractual arrangements for centuries) is evident from the fixing of the townsmen and from the use of collective responsibility and fixed residence in the crown villages where no labour services obtained (at least not as a rule).[8]

It was in such a way that the familiar, undifferentiated social structure of Russia had emerged : a pyramid with a broad mass of largely self-sufficient atomised peasant households at the base, followed by a narrow layer of people with commercial functions rather than interests (the state used successful merchants as farmers of crown monopolies, tax collectors on markets, etc., and these in turn used a species of mutual guarantee in undertaking business transactions on behalf of or with the state) and a slightly broader layer of service gentry with military and administrative functions rather than farming interests (at least till the second half of the eighteenth century) in the middle, and above them all, pressing down heavily, the onion-dome of the state.[9]

Between the sixteenth and eighteenth centuries Russians evolved what Professor Hicks describes as the 'Bureaucratic Revenue State', which existed in embryo elsewhere[10] but which reached in Russia the dimensions and duration unique in Europe because there was, or the rulers could claim that there was (given the 'siege mentality' mentioned above), almost a continuous state of emergency and because a market and autonomous centres of power within society were slow in forming to enable the state to relax its hold and leave certain functions to autonomous forces.

It should be emphasised however that the system which had evolved in Russia, which in its political aspect is sometimes described as 'oriental despotism', could assume the forms it did because Russia lacked the political traditions and concepts of law which restrained despotic rulers elsewhere and because she had missed the liberalising influences of the Renaissance and the Reformation.

From the long-term point of view the system was proving self-defeating in that it sapped the vitality of the people and blunted their response to economic opportunity. It led to deviousness in business conduct, to concealment, crudity and outright dishonesty. Townsmen were even more affected, as control in cities was easier, the bureaucrats nearer, and the money incomes more coveted. The Soviet historian Ryndzyunsky provides a great deal of illustrative detail indicative of the reasons why the towns failed to become growth centres, pointing to the weakness and unreliability of the commercial elements and the stifling effect of bureaucratic controls, and indicative of a specific philosophy underlying the bureaucracy's attitude to the mercantile classes – an anticipation of fraudulent behaviour unless hedged about by restrictions.[11] Similar attitudes prevailed in relations between merchants : the essential element of trust, reinforced by due processes of law, was entirely absent.

BEGINNING OF INDUCED DEVELOPMENT

This lengthy excursion into history is designed to underline Russia's backwardness and to highlight the unique position of the Russian state *vis-à-vis* the economy and society as a background to Russia's pattern of industrialisation in the nineteenth and twentieth centuries. All Russia's past had prepared the state for its specific functions in the industrialisation process following the Russian defeat in the Crimean War and the diplomatic discomfiture at the Congress of Berlin in 1878. All the prerequisites were there : experience in mobilising the nation's resources, motivation in the single-minded concern for protecting national sovereignty which could be broadly interpreted in view of the wide ramifications of Russia's international position, finally the prestige as a great power which could be utilised to bring financial dividends. All this equipped the Russian state for its rôle as industrialiser, a rôle which, whatever the degree of backwardness, could not be easily undertaken by the state in say Bulgaria or Italy.

This rôle was already incipient in the sixteenth and seventeenth centuries but especially under Peter the Great, when the state directly and indirectly provided a market, capital and a labour force for the mining, metallurgical, armaments and textile industries which it brought into being and which undoubtedly yielded a very high annual growth rate.[12]

In his Cambridge lectures Gerschenkron implies that the introduction of the serf variable into the industrialisation equation determined its inability to be successfully sustained.[13] Tugan-Baranovsky similarly singles out the use of serf labour as the limiting factor in Peter's industrialisation experiment. He stresses the low productivity of manufactured goods produced by serf labour, which made them in the eyes of Russian merchants very imperfect substitutes for imports both as regards quality and price.[14] (Tugan does not mention that this was also the case a century and one-half later when free men worked in Russian, often highly mechanised, factories).

However Peter Struve's diagnosis seems to me the more correct one, namely that the various methods of fixing workers to factories and plants practised by the Russian government in the eighteenth century clearly show that it 'is impossible to organise [large-scale] production in a society with a natural economy other than on the basis of personal dependence'. The accent is on the weakness of the market which had produced most of the social anomalies. There is no evidence of state peasants or townspeople volunteering for factory work; the former had to be ascribed to factories for a variety of ancillary jobs, and as late as 1807 a law was issued making all people engaged in work in mines forever attached to them.[15]

It is noteworthy that by the first decade of the nineteenth century non-nobles were no longer interested in special rights to buy serfs for factories. By then there was already a labour market from among privately owned serfs paying money rents and from among state peasants seeking cash earnings. Indeed owners of so-called *possessional factories* who by law were not allowed to curtail their labour force, whatever the state of business, began to petition the government to allow them to dismiss the workers and their families. Though the law of 1840 which met their wishes entailed considerable money outlays as endowment for released workers, the vast majority of the owners availed themselves of the law.[16]

AUTONOMOUS DEVELOPMENT BEFORE 1860

Nevertheless in the eighteenth century autonomous growth came clearly into evidence. Moreover there are indications that it was not unrelated to the gigantic effort of modernisation under Peter the Great, who had undoubtedly created conditions facilitating the growth of a market.[17] Though in David Landes's telling phrase 'the greatest asset of a port is a productive hinterland', in Russian conditions the acquisition of the

Baltic ports under Peter and the Black Sea ports under Catherine II, the construction of roads and the digging of canals, whatever the cost in human lives and suffering, were slowly piercing the blanket of self-sufficiency and rendering the hinterland productive. Furthermore, however inefficient and costly Peter's factories, they acted as training ground for skills and managerial talent in the long run. However reluctant the Russian nobles to acquire the educational minimum 'prescribed' by Peter, educational attainment soon became a must, and the taste for a better life a stimulus for securing the wherewithal to acquire it.[18]

Thus from the second half of the eighteenth century there was un-doubtedly an autonomous growth stream as well as the continuation in a somewhat modified form of the inducing policies of the state. The autonomous stream had by the time of the emancipation of the serfs in 1861, a date normally considered as the landmark separating modern or 'capitalist' from traditional or 'feudal' Russia, reached sufficiently large dimensions to suggest to some scholars, notably S. G. Strumilin, that Russia had experienced an industrial revolution in the second third of the nineteenth century. While Strumilin's viewpoint illustrates a somewhat narrow interpretation of the term 'industrial revolution', it is nevertheless true that modern technology was beginning to play a significant part in transforming the cotton spinning and sugar beet industry during the forties and fifties and that the growth of these and other consumer goods industries had been propelled by largely auton-omous forces right up to 1914, only indirectly affected by government policies.

The tariffs of 1822, 1824 and 1841 were undoubtedly important but they were motivated by mainly fiscal and monetary considerations and the consequent substitution of home production for imports of first fabrics and in the forties of yarn was a by-product of tariffs. The main propelling forces were first the cheapness of British yarn and after 1842 the machinery imports and British entrepreneurship and skill as personified in the person of Ludwig Knoop, who helped to finance, equip and man the majority of Russian cotton mills. British demand for Russian grain contributed to the availability of foreign exchange and to increased purchasing power. The stabilisation of the rouble by Kankrin during 1839–44 and the law of 1840 releasing the *possessional* workers were also of some importance in stimulating the autonomous stream.[19]

It is noteworthy that both the cotton and the sugar industries developed within a serf environment. In the former both workers and entrepreneurs originated from privately owned serfs of the so-called central industrial region consisting of some eight provinces including

Moscow. The region had poor soil but greater population densities and better transport connections by water than other regions of Russia, and consequently exchange relations and responsiveness to economic opportunity were less inhibited here than elsewhere.

Gentry entrepreneurship developed largely in the middle of the eighteenth century, mainly in distilling and the manufacture of cloth for uniforms and linen for which the raw material was on the spot, to meet the growing cost of their 'European' way of life. It was further encouraged by their growing indebtness due to the losses sustained during the Napoleonic invasion of Russia and the falling grain prices of the 1820s.[20] By specialising in different products and working for a different market, gentry manufactories did not on the whole compete with peasant entrepreneurship. On the contrary landlords nurtured the latter, at least in the initial stages, by offering their serfs protection from the arbitrariness of the fiscal and police authorities as well as guaranteeing their solvency *vis-à-vis* creditors. This may explain among other things why there were more entrepreneurs of serf origin than from among state peasants or townsmen. Needless to say, the gentry in encouraging the industrial activities of their serfs and in helping them to acquire skills were pursuing their own self-interest in that they could claim higher rents from the larger incomes of their serfs.

On the whole the growth of rural as distinct from urban entrepreneurship was due to the relatively lower costs of the former : raw material was often available on the spot, subsistence was derived from agriculture which cushioned falling demand for manufactured products, the peasant producers usually paid no industrial or commercial taxation until their business had reached a certain scale. Given the landlord's protection it could be kept secret for a considerable length of time, during which it could consolidate and accumulate profits for further expansion.

This may explain among other reasons why so many successful entrepreneurs came from among sectarians. The habit of secrecy, the mutual trust and shared hostility to and persecution by the authorities, made it possible for their businesses to reach considerable dimensions without having to declare their income to the authorities, or to fear denunciation. More than a century of persecution and poverty had given them the habit of thrift, not a common feature of the Russian character.

Commercial elements from the towns began to take an interest in industry after 1860, especially in the two capitals, but Soviet historians ascribe their relative passivity in this field to the high profits which could be derived from commercial operations and their unwillingness to face risks. The success of the rural producer can also be explained by the profitability of his commercial operations; it has been said that at least two-thirds of the difference between the cost of materials and the selling price of the manufacturing commodity was commercial gain and one-third industrial.[21] As he usually had his own transport, or simply walked, and operated within a much smaller radius, his costs of marketing must have been minimal. This may account for the successful emergence of entrepreneurs among calico printers, who being involved in the final process were in contact with the consumer directly, unlike the spinners or weavers. Finally the relative lack of successful entrepreneurs of urban origin may also be due to the greater opportunity available to the ablest among them to climb into the bureaucracy and even to personal nobility, *via* Peter I's Table of Ranks.

The Ivanovo district of the province of Vladimir to the east of Moscow was the birthplace of serf entrepreneurs among cotton bleachers, dyers and printers, many of whom became founders of cotton mill dynasties which survived until 1917. The skills were apparently disseminated by peasants who worked in *possessional* factories in Moscow and who began to practice in their villages following the destruction of Moscow in 1812, the 'French Year' marking the rise of many self-employed *'kustars'* to owners of manufactories.[22]

Initial capital requirements were low, technical equipment simple, and linen canvas gave way to cotton because the latter lent itself better to the bright dyes and prints for which the Russians had acquired a taste from their contacts with the Eastern peoples, and because cotton combined cheapness with warmth. Transition to factory production began to take place in the 1830s because of the high wages which calico printers were demanding. Schultze-Gaevernitz maintains that French prisoners of war, probably from Alsace, contributed greatly to improved technique, as did specialists in dyes and chemicals imported from abroad. Weaving was done by hand either by independent peasant weavers who bought yarn and sold unbleached fabrics, or by weavers working in special sheds consisting of five, ten or twenty hand looms, who were supplied with yarn by the owners or agents of the cotton printing factories.[23]

While cotton weaving remained till the 1880s only partly mechanised though part of the factory system, cotton spinning was acquiring predominance gradually integrating the other processes. However there were also many instances of backward integration in the factories owned by the Ivanovo cotton printers. The evidence on this point is somewhat obscure, Soviet sources tending to stress native while Gaevernitz emphasises the contribution of foreign entrepreneurship. He argues that when Russia began to import raw cotton and yarn the expertise of the importer, his knowledge of markets, and his credit availability became all important, and he subordinated all processes in the industry to spinning. As fas as one can judge, the foreign importer performed an important function as banker and transmitter of technology while entrepreneurship was largely Russian. The need to advance fairly long-term credit, which given currency fluctuations involved a double risk, in the absence of commercial banks till the 1860s made the banking functions of the importer particularly vital.

Moreover, to judge by the career of Ludwig Knoop, the importer acted as a link between British suppliers of plant and the Russian cotton mills, and as guarantor of solvency. This rôle could be gradually relinquished when Russian firms began to be known abroad and began to establish direct contact with foreign banks, and when a second or even third generation of Russian entrepreneurs with financial expertise, technical knowledge and foreign languages made its appearance. This was certainly the case among the 'elite' of Moscow mill owners.[24]

Whatever the case might have been, by 1860 over 90 per cent of the cotton yarn consumed in Russia was of home production. The share of domestic spinning jumped from 32·6 per cent on the average during 1836–40 to 44·1 per cent during 1841–5 and 73·5 per cent during 1846–50. The industry worked entirely for a civilian market, and consumption per head was an estimated 7½ *arshins* (5·75 yards). However it still accounted for a much smaller share of the market than flax and hemp products, much of which however was for export. Its relative success is to be attributed to its relative cheapness made possible by the technical advances in Britain and by its newness and hence lower resistance to change.[25]

The second industry which had adopted modern technology before 1860 was the sugar industry that developed in the Ukraine. Steam driven factories began to appear in the 1840s; by 1853–4 they accounted for 56 per cent of the total refined sugar produced, and by 1860–1 for as much as 85 per cent.[26] The success here was due to the considerable capital resources at the disposal of local landowners, many of them Polish, and the better quality of entrepreneurship (at least Witte thought so), though the labour force was practically all serf and the factory owners 'feudal' owners of *latifundia*.[27] The greater strength in this region of the Jewish element and the semi-banking as well as commercial functions which they performed, may also have been contributory. The evidence for a later period indicates much lower interest rates in these former Polish provinces.[28] Anyhow the success of the sugar industry shows that the historian must look more critically at the so-called institutional rigidities arising from serfdom and the gentry labour monopoly.

THE EMANCIPATION AND ITS EFFECTS

It is accepted to look upon the second quarter of the nineteenth century in Russia, which coincided with the reign of Nicholas I, as one of stagnation or as static at best. Soviet historians often describe it as the 'crisis of the serf economy', during which in Marxian parlance the forces of production had come into conflict with the system of social and legal relations.

However it was during this period that significant changes were taking place in the Russian society and economy, which have suggested to a recent historian of Russia's early industrialisation the idea of describing the period as 'preparatory'.[29] This interpretation is rejected by Gerschenkron, who stresses elements of discontinuity.[30] While not accepting the term 'preparatory' as accurately describing the nature of the changes involved, I would argue that where consumer goods industries were concerned the element of continuity across the watershed of the emancipation, if a watershed it be, and across the revolutionary 1890s, is much more in evidence. It is railway construction rather than the abolition of serfdom which clearly demarcates the two periods, though even here one might argue that construction which started in 1836 would have continued, and that by and large railways during the 1860s and 1870s aimed mainly at opening markets for agriculture and that industrial growth which followed it was a by-product of this policy. However, the effect of the railways was truly revolutionary in that they stimulated an internal and foreign market for grain.[31]

Gerschenkron had made a careful analysis of the provisions of the Emancipation Act which emphasised their defects from the point of view of industrialisation. In particular he stressed those elements in the emancipation settlement which had negatively affected the peasants' purchasing power and hence the market for industry, and those which had affected his mobility and hence the formation of a labour force.[32]

Effects of the Act on purchasing power

The first factor needs qualification. The redemption payments were in excess of the market value of the land at the time and contained a concealed redemption of the peasant's freedom, which was resented by him. The payments, however, were not higher and were often lower than the average rents payable by the serfs before 1861.[33] There was hardship in areas where peasants had hitherto performed labour services because cash was difficult to obtain at least until the railways brought the market closer and because hitherto the landlord cushioned the impact of cash tax payments. Above all there was disappointment because the peasants believed that that land was theirs and that they should not have been asked to pay for it.

Ryndzyunsky has shown that in the first two decades after the emancipation peasants were buying land in small individual plots,[34] a sign that effective purchasing power or private credit was available. Moreover though there has been no significant change in the system of agriculture there was a great deal of slack to be taken up, which stimulated by the appearance of a market, especially a foreign market thanks to railways and the need for cash to pay redemption and to buy land, led to increasing marketability of Russian agriculture. Before the arrival of railways there were regions in Russia where harvests of several years were accumulating, prey to the weather and rats. In some years harvests were just left in the fields in sheaves. In some areas landowners abandoned cultivation, leaving all land to the peasants.[35]

Thus even without any improvements in yields, increased marketings by the peasants need not have meant any pressure upon levels of consumption, especially as grain prices in Russia rose substantially between the end of the the 1850s and the beginning of the 1880s. The price of rye doubled. Tugan-Baranovsky ascribed the flight of workmen from factories to the fall in real wages during the 1860s and 1870s and the attraction of agricultural pursuits.[36] The fall in international grain prices was not felt in Russia immediately because the downward fluctuations of the rouble cushioned the price and because the building of railways often meant that spot prices actually rose. Moreover yields had also been growing steadily if not spectacularly, and more slowly in peasants' than in landlords' fields, only half of the growth being due to the extension of arable land.[37] It is not quite true therefore that one can speak generally of pressures on consumption standards or about the negative effect of the provisions of the Emancipation Act upon peasant purchasing power, at the worst the impact was neutral.

Already Tugan-Baranovsky held that stationary and even falling agricultural output need not be a bar to industrial growth as long as the marketable part of the product grows, in Russia's case as a result of the penetration of exchange relations into agriculture. He also maintained that where agriculture was not yet fully commercial production levels need not be affected by price falls.[38] I shall return later to the question of peasant consumption standards in connection with indirect taxation in the 1880s. For the present we shall make a few points on the second aspect.

The effect of the Act upon the formation of the labour force*

There is no doubt that communal ownership of land and the collective responsibility for redemption payments and direct taxation were a qualification of the peasant's newly won freedom. This was old Muscovite practice kept alive, and its potential consequences especially on mental attitudes no less insidious than serfdom, and on occasion more. But life has a way of by-passing laws where conditions favour it, and there is no evidence that the commune had really impeded mobility wherever and whenever there were attractive earning opportunities, to judge by the number of passports for 'going away' work issued.[39]

It is a matter of speculation whether abolition of communal ownership in 1861 would have led to a supply of cheap labour for industry, which would have encouraged industrial promotion. Given the availability of land for colonisation, gentry land which the peasant expected sooner or later to be his, and much of which he was already buying or renting, it needed a much greater *demonstration effect* of factory work or outright expropriation to drive the peasants *en masse* into factories. By the end of the century the demonstration effect was beginning to play a part, but by and large the 'push' from the village was still rather gentle and the 'pull' of the factories not great enough. Moreover local industrial work as an independent or semi-independent *kustar* offered greater attractions undoubtedly until the 1880s and to a large extent right up to 1914, as the average estimated incomes of independent *kustars*, allowance being made for the seasonal nature of their occupation, are said to have compared favourably with the average real factory wage.[40]

The above is not intended to give the impression of an absolute labour shortage. The emancipation meant the severance of the already tenuous links with the land of some 2·6 million people, according to Lokhtin, which could practically meet the actual requirement of manufacturing and transport in as late as 1897.[41] Furthermore with emancipation the former serfs who before 1861 performed labour services, who were in the majority (70 per cent according to some estimates, and if allowance is made for mixed services, certainly over half), found that half their time or half their labour force hitherto applied to work on the estate was redundant. There was certainly a potential labour pool from members of peasant families rendered idle.[42] Some Russian scholars argued that the land shortage which

* The problem of labour supply is discussed fully by this author in a chapter on Labour and industrialisation in the forthcoming 7th volume of the Cambridge Economic History.

made itself felt after 1861 was often not so much shortage relative to consumption needs but relative to the household labour supply. Zak maintained that the potential factory labour pool was larger than industry could absorb and that the instability of the factory labour force was due less to the pull of agriculture or rural industry than to fluctuations in demand on the part of factory industry.[43] A recent writer argues that supply of agricultural labour to industry usually exceeded demand. If the demand for labour rose, migration from the village to the town tended to rise still faster.[44] This explains the curious phenomenon that in Russia hidden unemployment often increased simultaneously with a rise in visible employment, a phenomenon which one economist of underdevelopment described as 'hidden unemployment of expansion'.[45]

It is debatable whether it was communal ownership and collective responsibility which contributed to the seasonal nature of the Russian labour force and to its tendency to float, a feature which has been described as 'industrial nomadism'.[46] It is certain that wages were lower in winter and that the most modern firms tended to concentrate the bulk of their labour intensive activities during the period of low wages. Zak maintains that complaints of employers notwithstanding, this practice enabled them to reduce the share of wages in the cost of production and keep wage rates low.[47] There were provisions in the Emancipation Act for departure from or the dissolution of the commune under certain circumstances and if the peasant did not avail himself of these it was, among other things, due to the obvious value he attached at this stage to the commune, which whatever its insidious effects upon agricultural techniques and economic motivation, afforded him a measure of security.[48]

Before the railways and the banks had helped the money economy along, it is very doubtful whether the abolition of the commune in 1861 would have had the desired effect. The reality if not the law of the commune would have persisted, as in many areas pseudo-serf relations had continued, until by way of formal education and more importantly education by the market and by the experience of the fair operation of the law collectivist mentality began to give way to individualism.[49] In this respect too, institutional arrangements and mental attitudes were the outward manifestation and product of economic backwardness.

Even after 1906, despite over forty years of land buying by peasants, a practice which according to *Zemstva* observers was gradually eroding the old concept of land as a 'free gift' and increasing marketability of peasant agriculture (by 1914 peasant grain accounted for 78 per cent of the marketings as against a much smaller proportion in

1861),[50] there was still much opposition on the part of peasants to the abolition of the commune by Stolypin's legislation. There is also no evidence of mass selling of land by peasants following Stolypin's reform. The relatively weak response to the abolition of 'compulsory ownership' would indicate that the pool of reluctant owners was not all that large.[51]

On the whole the practice of combining agriculture with subsidiary earnings in industry either as *kustars* or factory workers was a reflection of backwardness of both industry and agriculture in Russia. Industry was not in a position to develop fast enough to cope with the infinite variety of commodities needed by a market of the Russian size and type, so that rural industries filled an important gap. Where agriculture was concerned there was its nature, as largely a monoculture, with a very short vegetation period and the almost simultaneous ripening of grains over the whole expanse of the sprawling empire, making for a high peak labour demand. Then there was a very restricted use of labour saving machinery because of capital shortage and the availability of labour either migratory or local in a species of arrangements reminiscent of serf labour services but which seemed more economic in the short run.[52] It basically reflected the very heavy weight of the agricultural sector and the large scope within it for extensive development and for absorbing population increase without actually introducing labour saving techniques.

Consequently what was happening in Russia right up to 1914, and in particular up to the mid-1880s, was a gradual erosion of the subsistence economy, which took the forms of increased marketability of agriculture, of land becoming a commodity (though peasant allotment land was not yet in this category till 1906), of an increasing variety of cash earning activities in construction, carting, hawking, river transport, domestic and other services, and finally increasing industrial work as *kustars* or factory labourers. Though allotment land was not marketable, peasants were active in the land market. Between 1863 and 1905, peasants accounted for 21·3 per cent of all land purchases and for 7·8 per cent of all sales. During the period 1883–92 alone they accounted for nearly 52 per cent of the 8 million desyatinas purchased.

The development discussed above was in the first half of the century confined to a few areas only. With the railways it extended horizontally and also developed in depth. The Emancipation Act had affected this development indirectly by contributing to a rise in the urban market on account of the impoverished gentry and by contributing to liquid capital by way of realised redemption bonds advanced by the state which amounted to just under 900 million roubles nominal.[53]

There is no study of the use of redemption bonds which only gradually entered the market as and when agreements were reached between landlords and peasants. As the redemption transaction was tied up with the recall of mortgage debts and as all state banks were dissolved in 1859 and no other official credit source was available, the pressure of supply of bonds for realisation on the money market led to a very reduced effective yield, especially as this was also a period of intensive promotion of railway bonds.[54] One can assume that those most severely afflicted were the small and medium owners who could least afford to hold out.

In a large number of cases the repayment of former debts to state banks swallowed up all that was due from redemption payments.[55] The vast majority of medium and small owners often, upon deduction of debts, did not have enough left to modernise their estates and simply spent what was left on everyday living in the city, or tried to modernise and failed. Some indulged in a short lived spree of 'conspicuous consumption'.[56] Given, however, the structure of Russian gentry landownership on the eve of emancipation with some 3·6 per cent of all owners owning over 40 per cent of all serfs, and a mere 1 per cent of owners accounting for 29 per cent of the total number of serfs, fairly large sums must have been due to large owners upon redemption.[57] Even if one assumes that their debts were correspondingly large as banks lent on security of serfs, a significant residue was undoubtedly available for investment either on modernisation of estates or in joint stock companies, even when allowance is made for the bonds' depreciation. Witte intimated that only landlords from the western provinces used redemption payments for estate improvement.[58] It was therefore to a large extent from the top 3 or so per cent of the landowners that many of the shareholders of the St Petersburg banks and railway companies were recruited. Many of these were usually also high aristocrats and dignitaries whose status added prestige to the boards of directors of the newly formed companies.

GOVERNMENT INDUCING POLICIES

Though the Emancipation Act was prompted by political motives in the main, those responsible for framing it had certain vague economic notions. Basically these were notions of economic liberalism, of the need to create conditions within which private initiative could develop and lead to a modernisation of the economy as a prerequisite for the maintenance of great power status. This attitude was reflected in the attempt to found a central bank on the model of the Bank of England, in encouraging private banks, railway and industrial companies, in Reutern's refusal to provide state mortgage credit for the gentry, and in the tariffs of 1857 and 1868 which abolished some and drastically reduced other import duties on manufactured goods.

One could argue that this liberalism was simple common sense because the treasury and the State Bank were weighed down by the cost of financing the emancipation, liquidating the old banking system, and making good the cost of the Crimean War, and had little to spare for investment in the economy; and that the liberal tariffs were needed to enable the speedy construction of the essential minimum of railways and for equipping of industries without the encumbrance of heavy duties.[59] There seems to be no doubt however that the liberalism of those responsible for government policy during this period was not just opportunism but a genuine if short-lived attempt to allow autonomous forces free sway. The specialist on Russian finance, Professor Migulin, even spoke of 'doctrinaire laissez faire' of the Russian government from the 1850s to the 1870s.[60]

However one by one these liberal policies were abandoned. The central bank became the State Bank and till the mid-1880s practically a treasury department. The joint stock banks were left to private initiative, but there was a large measure of initial inducement and much careful nursing and assistance later, and right up to 1914 there was a special relationship between banks and the State Bank and treasury.[61] The financing of railway construction was coming increasingly *de facto* if not yet by law within government orbit on account of the guarantees of interest on railway bonds and often also on shares. By the 1880s the state began to build railways for its own account and also to take over private lines and to impose a uniform tariff policy to encourage movement of goods over long distances. At first this state intervention was due to the inability of private companies to float the necessary capital on reasonable terms, their competition for funds on European bourses which negatively affected the state's credit standing, and the reluctance of private capital to go into railways without government guarantee because of the lack of certainty that the lines would be remunerative, which they rarely were, so that government guarantee was usually invoked.[62] The negligent and frequently wasteful policies of railway companies and public criticism of the government's alleged favouritism and squandering of public money for the benefit of railway tycoons, gradually induced the government to take over the railway economy and administration and to evolve a concept that railways need not be looked upon as profit yielding assets but as instruments of economic policy. However in practice 'even under Witte' there was still some confusion in government thinking in this respect, and often the strictly financial aspect of the railway economy was emphasised. The 'liberal' commercial policy also gave way in a piecemeal fashion as from 1877, usually not as change in principle but prompted by *ad hoc* considerations : monetary difficulties, budgetary deficits, and finally the consequences of increased indebtedness on account of the Russo-Turkish war.[63]

The diplomatic defeat at the Congress of Berlin was undoubtedly an important event which added urgency to the need for more specific and committed policies on the part of the government. For one it was realised that the railway network was far from sufficient from the military point of view, though during 1865–78 as much as 11,744 miles of line were built.[64] Secondly Russia's diplomatic position in Europe became more complicated, and the need to build strategic lines to the west and the south became a matter of urgency. Finally increased foreign indebtedness and the fall in agricultural prices made the balance of payments and the budgetary situation a cause of anxiety.[65]

On the whole when speaking of the industrialisation-inducing policies of a government of the Russian type, it is difficult to say to what extent one deals with a consciously designed and collectively agreed policy or simply with personal policies of individual ministers who succeeded in imposing their views. There is much evidence throughout of a great deal of conflict and of a certain dichotomy. Throughout, though the finance ministry had become something in the nature of a ministry of national development, its competence reaching into every sphere of national life, so that Izvolsky could describe it as 'a state within the state', narrowly financial matters were still its primary concern and more often than not considerations of revenue or concern for protecting the exchange value of the rouble or the funds took the upper hand over general economic interests. In other words fiscal considerations prevailed over macroeconomic needs. Moreover though successive finance ministers had gradually devised a pattern for mobilising resources by imaginative and novel devices, they basically believed in financial orthodoxy and often tried to gloss over or conceal their unorthodoxy.[66] Usually this was necessary in a world of financial orthodoxy and in view of Russia's dependence on foreign money markets.

No one would deny that Reutern and Witte were industrialisers by confession; one an integrationalist, believing in principle in an open-ended economy, the other more of an economic nationalist desirous of drawing as cheaply as possible upon the capital and skills from abroad to speed up the modernisation of Russia and to render her self-sufficient and even able to play the imperialist game of 'peaceful economic penetration' of the markets of China and Persia.[67] It would be absurd however to assume that the neat pattern of interrelated policies in the budgetary, tariff, railways and monetary spheres which emerged in the mid-1890s, was from the start devised consciously with industrialisation in view. It is truer to say that just as elsewhere private individuals and firms in pursuing the aim of maximising profits effected an industrial revolution, so the Russian government in pursuing general financial and political aims had created conditions within which industrialisation could proceed more rapidly and within which certain industries for the products of which there was great demand in connection with railway construction could be induced.

During the period 1870–9 domestic production met only 41 per cent of internal demand for iron and steel.[68] There was undoubtedly scope for import substitution but autonomous investment was unlikely to take place because of the cheapness of foreign metallurgical products and because of the scale of capital requirement and risk involved. A variety of individual measures of inducement during the 1860s and 1870s proved ephemeral or abortive. The success of John Hughes' South Russia Company incorporated in 1869 is frequently mentioned to show that autonomous development in this area was possible, but whatever the expertise and perseverance of the plucky Welshman and his colony of Welsh workmen in the Russian steppe, he enjoyed privileges, assistance and subsidies unthinkable in his home environment, and his success might have remained isolated or short-lived had it not been for the vast railway programme and the tariffs.[69] During 1891–1902 about 17,000 miles of line were laid, of which nearly 5400 were in Asiatic Russia.[70] As Raymond Goldsmith's study has shown, industry grew very slowly during the 1860s and 1870s. The consumer goods industries, notably the textile industry, which had significantly increased their capital equipment and output, failed to activate the rest of industry. This may bear out Hirschman's contention that in backward countries textile industries, because of the few backward linkages and complementarities, are not successful in introducing what he calls 'Direct Economic Activities'.[71] There is no question that the impressive and concentrated growth of the 1890s with mining and metallurgy leading was made possible by the massive injection of capital by the state into the economy and by special policies of inducement in the form of tariffs, currency stabilisation, long-term orders, subsidies and bonuses.

Government expenditure

During the six years of Vyshnegradsky's administration expenditure on railway construction was only 309·6 million roubles or 51·6 million annually. Between 1893 and 1900 the state put at the disposal of the railway economy 2226·6 million roubles of new capital or 278·3 million roubles annually.[72]

Various outlays in connection with the introduction of the state spirit monopoly meant an estimated 260 million roubles of new capital during 1893–1900. Extraordinary expenditure on ports and ships in 1893 and 1894 involved a sum of 237·8 million roubles, so that the total injection of net capital into the Russian money market directly through the agency of the government was around 2800 million roubles.[73]

In addition the government put at the disposal of the economy by way of the banking system 229·6 million roubles between 1892 and 1900. Finally, by stabilising the currency and introducing convertibility (1894–7) and a variety of other promotion measures, it encouraged an influx of foreign capital into Russian joint stock companies, which between 1893 and 1902 meant a minimum of 400 million roubles of new capital.[74]

Thus the total of new capital which entered the Russian market on account of government policies had reached the enormous sum of over 3000 million roubles, a sum exceeding the value of the war indemnity which the Germans received from France in 1870.

Budgetary policy

The significant features of Russia's budgetary policy since the 1880s were firstly the general growth of budgetary revenue from around 960 million roubles in 1890 to over 2000 million at the end of Witte's term of office in 1903 (and to over 3000 million in 1914);[75] secondly the appearance of surpluses since 1888 and their continuation, after a few years interval after the Russo–Japanese War, up to 1914. The net surpluses from the ordinary budget were used together with yields from credit operations both internal and abroad for capital investment through the extraordinary or below-the-line budget, or as reserve. Under Witte the surpluses are estimated to have reached about 1800 million roubles.

The policy of surpluses on the ordinary budget was subject to much attack as a doubtful accountancy trick designed to conceal the overall deficit, which was made good by resort to borrowing. (The net deficit on both budgets under Witte amounted to 2500 million roubles). Actual receipts nearly always exceeded estimates, a phenomenon similarly the target of attacks (Witte being accused of deliberately underestimating receipts for advertisement purposes). In 1907 when the duma began to participate in budgetary work, the two budgets were amalgamated for overall results, but when surpluses again appeared so did, to the confusion of all concerned, the excess of receipts over estimates.[76] This phenomenon was undoubtedly connected with the next two features of the budget, the increased weight of revenue from indirect taxation which could not be accurately assessed as it depended upon demand for goods and services taxed, and of revenue from the government owned economic assets; and the growing relative weight of commercial and industrial sources of state revenue.

By the end of Witte's term of office direct taxes accounted for only 17 per cent (in 1910 for only 12 per cent) of budgetary revenue. There was also a definite shift in the weight of direct taxation since Bunge (1881-7) from agriculture to industry and commerce. Under Witte, a fact not commonly known, this tendency had been reinforced, so that the relative weight of rural taxation, i.e. redemption payments (which were not strictly speaking taxes) and the land tax, fell substantially because of the increase in the incidence and yield of taxes coming from commercial and industrial sources. However indirect taxation was the most important source of revenue yielding together with government assets 78 per cent of revenue (80 per cent in 1910).[77] The most important revenue producing items were the taxes on commodities such as sugar, spirits, kerosene, matches, tobacco and on imported goods on account of tariffs. Customs duties provided one-third of ordinary revenue, and income from vodka sales another third, almost meeting the entire expenditure of the war ministry in 1897.[78] However the counterpart of part of the income were government outlays on running the monopoly. It was this feature of the Russian budget which gave rise to views that the capital accumulated by the state for investment purposes was at the expense of the peasantry and that the inducing policies of the state were effected by pressing down consumption standards of the Russian village. There was undoubtedly a rise in the incidence of taxation on the various items mentioned, but the revenue increase was to a much greater extent due to the increased demand for the goods and services taxed.[79]

In an interesting article in the *Russian Review* in 1912, Babkov argues that there was a close correlation between national finances and the economic evolution of Russia. He demonstrates that since 1896 there had been a close correspondence between budgetary income and industrial fluctuations, and practically none between revenue and harvests.[80] This explains why the budget committee of the duma were puzzled when in anticipation of a poor harvest in 1911 they reduced the estimated budgetary revenue relative to the previous year to find that the effective receipts exceeded the estimate. This also explains the strange phenomenon of receipts usually exceeding budgeted surpluses.

Evidence from various studies of rural life shows that the taxed commodities were only sporadically consumed by peasants while for the urban population they were articles of necessity. Even the consumption of spirits, the *per capita* consumption of which was incidentally lower in Russia than elsewhere in Europe, was in the village occasional rather than regular, which may account for the effect it tended to produce.[81] Professor Ozerov in his *The reverse side of the Russian Budget* (Moscow, 1911) sums up : 'The town population of Russia consumes far more than the rural, of some products ten to twenty times as much; of vodka three or four times, of kerosin twenty times; our progress is [that] of our urban Russia, and the growth of consumption can be to a considerable extent explained by the growth of the town population'. Even a 15 or 18 per cent urban element (in 1897 and 1916, respectively) meant a consumer market of a fair sized country, especially as the effective urban market was larger on account of the seasonal residents. However the rural market also grew if only on account of numbers, and there were rural areas in Russia where patterns of consumption were similar to the urban.[82]

It is legitimate to argue that the high price of the taxed articles made them into luxury items for the majority of the peasants, but it is incorrect to assume, as it often is, that the budgetary policies of the 1880s and 1890s were the cause of agrarian distress. It is also highly doubtful whether low prices would have significantly increased rural demand at this stage because of the evident preference of peasants to use cash for land purchase. Two further points need to be made in connection with the budget. Between 1878 and 1904 Russia had two and one-half decades of peace, hence no unproductive expenditure to replace destroyed war equipment, no legacy of wartime budget deficits, currency depreciation or indebtedness. Further Witte had procured by way of foreign loans capital at a relatively low price, and the debt conversion policy meant a lower weight of interest and amortisation payments in budgetary expenditure.[83] Without foreign loans the strain on consumption standards would have been undoubtedly severe, if politically possible. As it was, it can be said that the budgetary policies were at worst neutral *vis-à-vis* the rural sector. Witte argued that the railway deficits were a substantial subsidy to the agricultural sector, though of course in lowering the cost of freight his concern was not for agricultural incomes but for the balance of payments.[84]

Tariff Policy

In addition to providing or facilitating capital investment the government pursued a variety of policies which were designed or had the effect of procuring markets for industry, in particular mining, metallurgy and railway equipment.

The Tables 1.1 and 1.2 sum up neatly the magnitude of the change in commercial policy by 1891 :[85]

TABLE 1.1   Tariffs, 1868 and 1891 (kopeks per pood)

	1868	1891
Pig iron	5	25–52½ depending whether imported by sea or by land
Iron	20–50	90–150
Rails	20	90
Machinery (copper excepted)	30	250
Locomotives and other engines	75	300

TABLE 1.2   Customs duties as percentage of the total value of imports[86]

Year	Percentage
1851–6	24·3
1857–68	17·6
1869–76	12·8
1877–80	16·1
1881–4	18·7
1885–90	28·3
1891–1900	33
1902	40

An interesting feature of the tariff policy as it emerged in the 1890s was the increasing proportion of duties relative to value levied on raw materials and semi-manufactured goods, exceeding those levied on finished products as Table 1.3 shows, as well as the continuation of high duties on foodstuffs, mainly exotic and luxury foods, but also on tea and sugar, for purely fiscal reasons.[87]

This change was partly due to the modification of the tariffs on manufactures in the Russo–German treaty of 1894 following a tariff war, but it also reflected the 'concern of the Russian government for the most intensive possible development of all branches of the national effort' and the attainment of the 'national economic task of making Russia entirely independent of foreign markets in all that is essential for her existence'.[88] It undoubtedly helped to develop the coal and

iron industry, but it also significantly increased the costs of manufacturing especially in the Baltic and Polish regions which hitherto relied
on cheap foreign imports and were inconveniently placed relatively
to the South Russian mining industries. Schultze-Gaevernitz argued
that the Russian government overpaid during 1884–95 about 100
million roubles, the equivalent of the cost of 1333 miles of line.[89] The
fiscal and monetary elements in the tariff (even after 1897) remained
strong. The tariffs on foodstuffs were certainly of a fiscal nature entirely,
as were those on raw materials. The duty on raw cotton which grew
steadily till it reached 4·15 roubles per pood (3d per lb.) was at first
purely fiscal. Subsequently it became of importance as a measure of
protection for cotton growing in Central Asia so that by 1914 Russia
met more than half her cotton requirements from domestic sources.[90]

TABLE 1.3   Duties on various categories of imports

	Foods %	Raw mat. & semi-manuf. %	Manufactured goods %	All goods %
1894	73	24	27	31
1896	72	27	25	32
1898	80	33	28	37
1900	81	25	25	33
1902	96	31	28	40

By 1912 the duty on raw cotton alone yielded one-fifth of the
customs revenue. However the tariff on raw cotton and machinery
meant that prices of Russian cotton fabrics remained high despite
increases in productivity and that the differential between British and
Russian prices for equivalent products actually widened.[91] The higher
prices for raw materials were said to have hit the kustar industry. They
were certainly pushing out the hand weaver, who as he was losing
ground tended to try to make good by cheating, which still further
accelerated transition to factory weaving.[92] Duties on rubber, as well
as on coal for St Petersburg and Poland, were undoubtedly fiscal and
partly political in nature; so were duties on complex machinery as
there was no chance for it to develop domestically in the foreseeable
future. They were too low anyhow to deter imports, but revenue from
them, given large imports, was large.

Furthermore, duties imposed as temporary measures remained, and
on the whole government policy was not flexible enough to make adjust-
ments in accordance with shifts in productivity or with price changes

abroad. Tugan-Baranovsky argued that the iron industry no longer needed such strong protection in 1910 but that the government had become timid and over-protective especially after the depression. Consequently the tariff policy tended either to blunt the competitiveness of Russian manufacturers or fail in the very purpose for which it was introduced. The commonly held view that it also led to very high profits of manufacturers who passed on the cost to the consumer may be partly true of the cotton industry, but it is not borne out by the evidence of profits in the mining (except oil) and metallurgical industries.[93]

One point should be made at this stage. There is a widespread belief that the growth of manufacturing due to protection was achieved at the expense of agriculture. The agricultural population paid its share of tariffs, though a much lesser share than its numbers would suggest, but it is not well known that the industrialiser Witte actually exempted from duty complex agricultural machinery and reduced substantially duties on simple machines as from 1898 and that duties on such raw materials as wool, flax, tallow, hops, etc. gave valuable protection to agricultural interests.[94]

Provision of markets

In addition to tariffs the government widened the market by way of long-term orders to domestic industry which included an element of subsidy, by way of bonuses, and outright subsidy. Measures were taken to ensure that government orders were placed internally and that new railway lines purchased rails exclusively from domestic sources. During 1890–1900 domestic production satisfied 73 per cent of demand as against 41 per cent in the 1870s. The Trans-Siberian was almost entirely constructed out of and equipped with Russian material and products. It has been estimated that the Russian government had purchased during the 1890s hardware for the railways to the tune of 116 million roubles out of a total value of the metallurgical and machine building output (not counting agricultural machinery) of 259 million in 1897. A. A. Radtsig estimated that the railways alone accounted during 1893–9 for 37 per cent of the entire market for pig iron. The railway market was particularly vital for the new foreign owned industries of South Russia which specialised almost entirely in railway material.[95]

In other ways too the government tried to secure markets for industry. It facilitated flotation of municipal loans and simultaneously insisted that orders be placed with Russian industry. The government had potent levers for enforcing its wishes. Thus in 1892 when the munici-

pality of Warsaw was contemplating ordering a mechanical earth
scoop abroad, the governor of Moscow was instructed to intimate to
the persons concerned that unless the order was switched to Kolomensk
or any other Russian firm, there would be no relief with transportation
costs or import duties.[96] Side by side with municipal, there was private
urban development supported by urban banks with the active encouragement of the finance ministry. The value of real estate mortgaged
with various banks increased during 1894–1900 by 70 per cent as
against only 17 and 13 per cent, respectively, during the two preceding
periods, 1888–94 and 1882–8, though there was a previous significant
increase of 60 per cent during 1876–82.[97]

The powerful inducing policies of the 1890s had their effect. They
contributed to a significant increase in capital invested in industry : in
joint stock companies alone by 200 per cent. Particularly impressive
was the growth of investment in the metal group, mining, building and
chemicals. Foreign companies increased investment by 389 per cent
overall. The percentage increase in textile and food industries was
much smaller. Correspondingly the mining, metallurgical and building
industries gave the highest rates of growth of output and food industries relatively modest ones. In absolute terms, according to V.
Varzar, between 1890 and 1900 the number of factories and works
increased from 32,254 to 38,141, the value of output from 1,502·6
million to 3,438·9 million roubles, and the number of workmen from
1,424,800 to 2,373,400.[98] These figures do not include artisans and
kustar workshops or works employing exclusively hand labour.

The behaviour of the cotton industry was partly due to its longer
history of growth and partly to its different rhythm, geared as it was
to a much greater extent than other industries to the consumer and
especially the rural market. The cotton industry was only very slightly
affected by the slump at the turn of the century and continued to grow
during the prolonged period of depression following the slump.[99] The
behaviour of the cotton industry explodes the myth that the crisis and
depression which followed the boom of the nineties were due to the
'exhaustion of the base' produced by the strain imposed by the industrialisation policies upon the rural market. There was undoubtedly a
close correspondence between grain prices and the market for cotton,
and though consumption per head grew uninterruptedly since the
1850s, it slowed down during the 1880s and 1890s, though of course by
Western European standards per capita consumption was very low.[100]
The autonomous growth stream had certainly continued across the
revolutionary changes of the 1890s, and the textile and food industries
remained the two largest industries in terms of value of their output.

Some riders

The inducing policies of the state bear out Gerschenkron's thesis on the rôle of the state in conditions of backwardness, but not without some qualifications. The inducing policies proved by and large successful because by the 1890s there was already in Russia a fair sized market, a firm monetary system and financial institutions which had gradually evolved during the preceding decades, a skeleton of transport and educational facilities, and most importantly a pattern of commercial and financial relations abroad, backed by the prestige of the Russian state and its excellent record as a debtor. Mobilisation of resources *via* the budget may look like the well tried Muscovite practice of fleecing the taxpayer whatever his means, but the novel feature was its operation through the market. However undemocratic indirect taxation may be, in Russian conditions its effect was educative or at least it did not have the disincentive effect of the repartitional taxes of the past. The stabilisation of the rouble and its circulation as coin satisfied the hoarding instinct of the peasant and gradually induced savings banks deposits, especially during the 1890s, which made it possible to place loans internally.[101]

The success in developing the South Russia metallurgical base by largely foreign capital was in part due to luck and to the publicity given to early successes of foreign investors. There is no doubt, whatever the subsequent performance, that it was somewhat in the nature of a leap in the dark, without a clear realisation of the difficulties involved. Once a fair amount of capital was sunk there was nothing for it but to put in more to make it work. It is fair to say however that Witte and the State Bank did a great deal to help, especially when the crisis came at the turn of the century.[102] It is most unlikely that even with government help native entrepreneurs would have been able either to secure the capital of the dimensions needed in view of the many external diseconomies which the firms had to internalise, or that they would have had the staying power. Gindin quotes instance upon instance of failure in this field of Russian entrepreneurs despite backing by the State Bank.[103] This may indicate that capital shortage was an important factor in the slow growth of autonomous forces, and the success of the textile and food industries might have been due to the smaller capital requirements, at least in the initial stages. Furthermore, these industries developed in fairly well populated areas and were less dependent on access to raw materials and were therefore less hampered by external diseconomies.

In Gerschenkron's scheme there is a difference between the period of the 1890s and that from 1909 to 1914. There was undoubtedly a difference in quality in the latter phase, a kind of coalescing of the two streams and a reorientation of the heavy industries towards the private consumer market stimulated by the improvement in terms of trade in favour of agriculture and by a series of good harvests. The state however was still very much in evidence.[104] Money was being injected into the economy, by way of the budget in which indirect taxation and surpluses figured prominently, and through the State Bank, but this time into the agrarian sector. The need for the State Bank to undertake a programme of building grain elevators in 1911 is a measure of the weakness of the autonomous forces and a significant pointer to the still vital role of the public sector.[105] The shift once more towards railway construction by private companies was less a matter of principle than a necessity in view of the many claims on budgetary resources and the somewhat battered foreign credit standing, at least for a while. More than ever before, government guarantees of not only the debenture but also of the share capital were necessary to induce investment. Heavy protection was still maintained in all branches of domestic industry.[106] Even the role of banking, which in Gerschenkron's scheme indicated diminishing backwardness in the second or sub-phase, was often more in the nature of a channel for government inducement than an independent agent. However this role of the banks applied more to foreign capital, and by and large the banking system had become a strong autonomous force, accepting government assistance out of convenience rather than necessity. It should be added however that banking had played an important rôle already during the inducing policies of the 1890s.[107]

INDUSTRIAL STRUCTURE

Relative shares of industries

The structure of industry remained even by 1914 characteristic of an immature industrial economy. In terms of output value and of employment the textile industries continued to be in the lead throughout the period under consideration. They accounted for 28 per cent of the total output value of industry and for 30 per cent of the factory labour force in 1914. They showed remarkable steadiness in their relative position across the changes of the 1890s, when resources were directed mainly into mining, metallurgy and metal processing. In 1908 textiles made up 29·7 per cent of the value of output and 36·5 per cent of the labour force. If we add the food industries which had a 22 per cent share in the total output value and employed 13 per cent of the labour force in 1914, the joint relative weight of the two main light industries working for a mass consumer market was 50 per cent of the output value and 43 per cent of the labour force. Even in terms of steam power as measured in horsepower, the two light industries stood up well to the machine building, metal working and heavy metallurgy group. Their share in the total steam power used in industry was 38 per cent as against a 39 per cent combined share of the latter group.

The data for mining, metallurgy and metalworking industries are more difficult to handle and are not easily compared over periods of time. The indications are that the relative share of the machine and metal working group rose from an estimated 9·8 per cent of the total output value to 15 per cent between 1899 and 1913. Mining and metallurgy accounted in 1914 for only 14 per cent of the value of industrial output and for about 21 per cent of the labour force.[108] Only in St Petersburg was there a change in the distribution of industries in favour of the metal working group, as reflected in Figure 1.1.[109]

The structure of Russian industry in this respect was certainly in contrast to the German, which it allegedly resembled, in that in Germany the weight of the heavy industry groups in the labour force

FIGURE 1.2 Growth of factory employment in St Petersburg

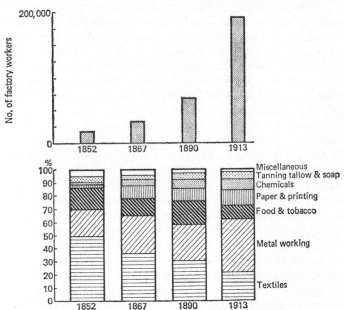

was in 1907 over 43 per cent and in energy equipment 52 per cent, as against 27 per cent on both counts in the textiles and food groups jointly. In absolute terms German industry's energy equipment was nearly three and one-half times that of Russia's, and in the machine building industry seven and one-half times greater. Only in the textiles group was it approximately comparable.[110] Thus the customary assertion that Russia's pattern of industrialisation in terms of employment and output value was different from that of early industrialising countries, where industrialisation affected first of all consumer goods industries and only later by way of backward linkages metal and machine construction industries, is not borne out by the evidence.

Where capital investment is concerned, mining and metallurgy had the highest nominal foundation capital.[111] However, the textile industries were not far behind, accounting for one-fifth of global investment in corporate industry.[112]

Industrial concentration

Soviet economic historians lay great stress on the high level of industrial concentration in Tsarist Russia. Such emphasis has strong ideological implications. The reasoning goes : though the modern industry sector was by 1917 still relatively small, it nevertheless developed all the most advanced forms of industrial organisation characteristic of monopoly capitalism from which transition to socialist ownership and management was but a natural progression. Furthermore, the reasoning continues, though the factory labour force represented less than 5 per cent of the labour force and was of recent ancestry, concentrated as it was in large numbers in individual concerns, it did early become class conscious and open to revolutionary propaganda and a worthy leader of the toiling masses in the revolution.

The criteria commonly used to indicate a high degree of industrial concentration are the average size of the foundation capital and of the labour force per concern. The use of these criteria gives a somewhat false picture of the real industrial structure in Russia with its predominance of small units.

By using foundation capital as a criterion of concentration, sight is lost of the large number of industrial units which did not take corporate form and which tended to be relatively small. Moreover size of foundation capital did not always correspond to the effective capital invested or to the scale of the firm's productive operations or its output value. Expansion of foundation capital could be dictated by a variety of reasons, among which company and taxation laws were most important. There is little doubt that the acceleration in the

TABLE 1.4 Distribution by industry of industro-commercial companies in Russia[a] (1 January)

Branches of industry	1861 A	1861 B	1875 A	1875 B	1881 A	1881 B	1893 A	1893 B	1900 A	1900 B	1908 A	1908 B	1914 A	1914 B
I Industrial companies	54	34·5	232	193·7	356	330·8	414	501·8	960	1,507·8	1,014	1,694·8	1,621	3,223·6
Mining	–	–	21	32·5	31	48·2	45	97·9	83	274·1	168	492·9	271	791·0
Metallurgical, mechanical, including construction	2	1·2	17	28·1	30	39·8	38	40·6	210	486·0	156	305·1	262	858·6
Processing of mineral products	3	0·7	5	0·9	11	5·0	9	8·1	65	61·6	54	46·7	92	124·0
Chemicals	3	1·5	14	8·2	25	13·6	17	16·0	69	69·4	74	103·1	107	153·8
Processing of fibres	25	24·6	59	55·6	93	112·4	136	219·6	226	384·1	237	486·5	315	713·0
Food processing	10	2·2	87	57·8	132	92·6	124	90·8	217	160·7	234	184·6	373	389·6
Processing of animal products	3	1·2	7	2·2	10	5·4	10	8·1	11	9·9	17	21·5	34	43·4
Timber processing	1	0·1	3	0·5	4	0·8	13	6·6	25	18·7	30	24·5	83	67·4
Paper, printing	7	3·0	19	7·9	20	13·0	22	14·2	54	43·3	44	29·9	84	82·8
II Commercial concerns	6	8·1	15	17·3	16	18·3	18	36·0	49	51·1	76	99·8	214	203·0
TOTAL	60	42·6	247	211·0	372	349·1	432	537·9	1,009	1,588·9	1,090	1,794·6	1,835	3,426·6

A=Number of companies. B=Nominal share and debenture capital in millions of roubles.

[a] As a large number of industrial companies also sold their own production, Shepelev included them in a compound group, singling out (under II) those specifically formed for purposes of commerce, without industrial output of their own.

Source: L. E. Shepelev, 'Aktsyonernoye uchreditel'stvo v Rossii', in Akademya Nauk, Iz istorii imperializma v Rossii (Moscow–Leningrad, 1959) pp. 152–3.

expansion of foundation capital of individual firms after 1899 and after 1906 had a great deal to do with the change in the laws governing taxation of company profits.

Where the labour force was concerned, the large average size of the labour force was due to the tendency of Russian official statistics to understate or altogether omit to record smaller units. *Kustar* industry was not statistically recorded at all. Urban artisan industry (*remeslo*) was as a rule recorded only for large cities. The factory inspectorate usually took into account units with over twenty workers each, and for 1913 over thirty each. In its report for 1900 the inspectorate cited only 18,000 firms, which suggested a work force of 93·6 per plant, while the unofficial business directory, *Vsya Rossiya*, covering the period 1898–1901 cited 142,000 firms giving only about twelve workers per firm on the average.[113]

Industrial censuses, though fuller in geographical coverage and more comprehensive, also under-recorded smaller firms. In 1900 they took into account firms with sixteen hands upwards and in 1909 probably only those with twenty upwards. Consequently the average size of the labour force in plants under factory inspection fluctuated between 102 and 131 during 1902–12. The average on the basis of industrial censuses was 42·7 in 1887, 53·8 in 1897, and 67·2 in 1908.

The average for Germany on the basis of industrial censuses was twenty-six and thirty-five workers per unit in 1895 and 1907, respectively; for the USA – 37·3 in 1914. However the data for both Germany and the USA were based on a much greater spread of industrial units. German statistics took into account units with upward of five workers each; the USA recorded all units with six or more wage earners.[114] It would appear that where the share of employment is concerned the bulk of the labour force in manufacturing was by 1914 in small units. Even on the basis of data provided by Soviet labour historian A. G. Rashin, who though he records *kustars* under-states their number, as much as 60 per cent of the labour force in manufacturing was in small units by 1914. Moreover it also appears from his data that the number of hands in what is imprecisely defined as 'small industry' was growing faster than employment in factory industry between 1860 and 1914.[115]

The growth of small units is also evident from the data provided by the Russian statistician A. V. Pogozhev for 1903. Even during the 1890s, which was a period of extensive promotion of companies and of conversion of family firms into companies, 40 per cent of the newly founded concerns were in the category employing less than fifty hands each.

If therefore real industrial concentration as measured in terms of

TABLE 1.5 Russian companies according to the size of their nominal share capital in 1911

Branches of Industry	Up to 0·5		From 0·5 to 1·0		From 1·00 to 2·0		From 2·0 to 5·0		From 5·0 to 10·0		Over 10·0		Total	
	A	B	A	B	A	B	A	B	A	B	A	B	A	B
I Industrial concerns	360	124	344	264·1	226	352·1	200	653·3	75	540·5	23	346·1	1,228	2,280·1
Mining and metallurgical	31	11·4	50	40·7	38	59·7	58	193·1	37	263·9	17	238·1	231	806·9
Metal products and machine construction	58	19·6	41	30·7	19	29·2	22	73·5	10	62·4	1	30·0	151	245·4
Brick and cement industry	22	7·0	24	17·0	8	10·6	10	25·1	1	5·0	–	–	65	64·7
Chemical	36	12·2	18	13·2	15	23·5	8	24·7	2	15·0	1	18·0	80	106·6
Textile	36	14·7	75	59·7	68	109·2	72	245·6	19	152·6	3	45·0	273	626·8
Food	107	37·2	104	77·2	48	70·9	20	57·3	4	25·6	1	15·0	284	283·2
Meat products	15	5·0	5	4·1	7	11·4	5	16·9	1	6·0	–	–	33	43·4
Timber products	26	8·2	10	8·2	9	15·5	3	11·0	–	–	–	–	48	42·9
Paper, printing	29	8·7	17	13·3	14	22·1	2	6·1	1	10·0	–	–	63	6·02
II Commercial concerns	63	19·7	53	44·9	31	47·4	5	16·1	6	50·4	–	–	158	178·5
TOTAL	423	143·7	397	309·9	257	399·5	205	669·4	81	590·9	23	346·1	1,386	2,458·6
As percentage of total	30·4	5·8	28·8	12·5	18·5	16·2	14·8	27·3	5·9	24·1	1·6	14·1	100	100

A = Number of companies. B = Nominal capital in millions of roubles.
Source: Shepelev, *Aktsyonernoye uchreditel'stvo v Rossii*, Table 7, p. 157, based on the *Statistical yearbook for 1914* (St Petersburg, 1914), pp. 306–7.

average capital employment per concern has been over-stated, it is
nevertheless true that Russian industry was characterised by a relatively
high number of giant concerns employing over 1000 workers each
and disposing of a foundation capital of over 5 million roubles, or
around £500,000 each.[116] Data relating to these so-called giants are
also subject to some qualification.

Some of the *giants* in terms of foundation capital could be cut to
much less impressive size if all the data were available as to the
accountancy procedures used by firms to inflate their nominal share
capital to reduce their tax burden. Fred Carstensen of Chicago University, in a paper presented to a conference of the French Economic
History Society in Paris in October 1973, gave several instances of
such procedures.[117]

Where employment is concerned size was often a function of low
productivity of labour; of the underdevelopment of supporting and
service industries so that their functions had to be carried out within
the framework of the concern; of hoarding of labour for various reasons
and of apportioning employment among a larger labour force to
avoid dismissal for social or political reasons; of the relatively low
technological level of the majority of concerns; of the use of unskilled
hand labour for preparatory or ancillary jobs as complementary to
capital intensive processes; of intensive use of machinery which required
more labour for shift work, making good defects caused by intensive
use of machinery and for maintenance work.

Contemporaries were not in doubt that capital was expensive in
Russia relative to labour, at least in the short term, and that the cost
of installing a piece of machinery was so inflated by transportation
costs, tariffs, high interest rates and social costs on the infrastructure,
that these costs could only be recouped by very intensive working of
machines and by resort to much hand labour on various levels of the
industrial process. There was a kind of dualism not only as between
large-scale modern industrial complexes and small units using mainly
hand labour, but also within the large concerns in which sophisticated
technology in one process could exist side by side with very primitive
processes and methods. In mining for example the shovel and pick-axe
method of extracting coal, often by peasants working seasonally only,
went on hand in hand with elaborate modern methods of utilising
coal residues, electric winding, and conveying. In the cotton mills
unskilled manual labour was used in cotton mixing, scutching, carding,
piecing and packing. In order to increase the annual output per spindle
and to distribute costs of depreciation per spindle over a large amount
of output, manufacturers tended to have recourse to night as well as
day work. Till the 1890s the average working day per spindle was 17·3

hours, which gave around 5000 spindle hours a year. Even in 1910 spindles continued to be used more intensively in Russia than in Western Europe and Japan, the average being nearly 4200 hours per year as against 3000 on the average elsewhere.[118]

The above discussion throws doubts on the assertion that a large labour force in a concern was evidence of mature capitalism; one may venture to suggest that it was indeed an indication of insufficient capitalism. Large enterprises in terms of employment were already a characteristic feature of Russia's industrial structure before 1861. In *possessional* factories and in state owned plants, where the labour force was attached to the factory, and in many estate factories where the estate's own serfs were employed, there was often wasteful use of labour not justified by the needs of the production process. However firms set up by foreigners in the 1840s and 1850s and factories owned by serf entrepreneurs, employing mechanical power and salaried labour, tended also to be large, and the foreign ones were large from the start. In the cotton industry as early as 1866 26 per cent of the labour force were in nineteen concerns employing over 1000 workers each. Concentration of workers in huge enterprises was not as elsewhere a product of the gradual evolution of modern industry, the consequence of substitution of capital for labour and of specialisation. In Russia concentration was not accompanied by specialisation but by creating complexes combining as in textiles all processes, or as in the south of Russia mining with metallurgy, metal working and mechanical construction. In addition large concerns had their own machine repair shops, workers' houses, hospitals, baths, schools, slaughter houses, bakeries, etc. Many firms had their own marketing agencies.

The German specialist of the cotton industry, commenting in 1898 on the enormous size of Russian firms, considered that in the place of each such firm there would have been in the United Kingdom at least eight separate ones. He thought that it was the 'poverty of Russia's economic environment' which was the root cause of the large and integrated plant. He envisaged a splitting up of these conglomerates as and when the Russian economy became more advanced. Schultze-Gaevernitz was not very specific about what he meant by the poverty of the environment; he seemed to have had in mind the underdevelopment of the infrastructure and the need to provide the missing social capital by the firm itself, which resulted in high fixed costs.[119]

The tendency to create plants in which all processes were combined was also prompted by the desire to cut down costs of raw materials and intermediate goods due to tariffs which did not affect all products of a given industry equally. Schultze-Gaevernitz always maintained that where Russia was concerned the customary choice as between capital and labour intensive techniques was not at the centre of business calculations; the weight of raw materials in the total costs was always a priority concern. Partly this was due to the as yet unsophisticated nature of the final output in which raw material costs loomed large. Not only tariffs but also transportation costs and of services in general seriously affected unit costs because of the low value of the final product.

Among the factors which made for integration of processes within one concern, in addition to those already mentioned, was undoubtedly the desire, given high costs, to secure as large a slice of the market as possible, in order to influence the price and even more importantly credit terms to customers. This tendency was most pronounced in the textile industry. Large textile firms in Moscow and Vladimir province were more often than not the product of absorption of medium and small firms. These firms, while very flexible and able to work day and night to meet demand, tended to go for panic selling at cut prices when the market turned out worse than expected. Thereby they ruined the market for large firms which with their high fixed costs could not afford to switch in and out of the market as the small firms could. Therefore the large firms aimed at controlling the smaller firms, which in the long run led to absorption. Often these small units, though part of the larger in terms of accountancy, were spatially separated and often even scattered over large areas. In such instances concentration did not mean large production units.

Despite this tendency for smaller units to be absorbed, new small units were constantly surfacing and were effectively competitive even in well established industries in terms of unit costs. If they succumbed it was usually due to their vulnerability as regards reserves and access to credit, which put them at the mercy of larger firms. Moreover the large integrated firm, certainly in fibre processing, was showing signs of breaking up. The so-called 'full manufactory' integrating all processes was giving way to firms combining two processes only : say, spinning and weaving or weaving and dyeing. The Soviet historian of the industry thought that the market no longer favoured such organisation of production in the 1900s.[120] This change may have indicated an improvement in the 'economic environment' which Schultze-Gaevernitz had forecast.

Our information so far does not support the view that capital was being substituted for labour on a large scale.[121] Where this was the case, it was due to preferential access to capital on the part of foreign entrepreneurs and of the largest firms which had established credit connections with international banks before 1900 (and with St Petersburg banks after 1900). The aim to gain better access to capital and credit was in itself a reason for the tendency to enlarge business.

Though the ability to borrow technology and capital was undoubtedly an asset in Russia's industrialisation process, the disadvantages of backwardness were no less great. The high cost of capital made for slow replacement of equipment; market imperfections disallowed specialisation and made for slow commodity turnover; low labour productivity and high costs of raw materials and semi-manufactured goods made for high costs of the final product and reduced effective demand. The weakness of the commercial organisation and the inadequacies of the transport system weighed heavily on Russia's business life. The over 40 thousand miles of line which Russia had by 1914 were far from adequate for a country of her size. Moreover there were not enough branch and spur lines, and roads continued to be primitive tracks full of pitfalls and ruts in the spring and autumn and choking with dust in the summer. Only the winter months offered a fairly rapid sleigh road but frequent usage, as in factory areas, soon made it rutted and impassable. Climatic conditions still could impose a seasonal rhythm on factory activities with a consequent rise in costs. An English traveller had noted how separate layers of technological progress coexisted in Russia: '. . . and on that journey one came in contact with the different stages of progressive civilisation . . . the slow train on the main line; the slower train on the branch line; the *troika* to the noble country mansion; the sleigh and bullock to the peasant's home'.[122] Though much change has taken place since another Englishman wrote in 1877, his description was still applicable by 1914. There were still in Russia, he wrote, regions larger than the United Kingdom 'where the ancient solitudes have never been disturbed by the shrill whistle of the locomotive and roads have remained in their pristine condition. Even in the central region one may still travel hundreds of miles without ever encountering anything that recalls the name of Macadam'.[123]

In Germany too the tendency of industrial firms to expand, integrate and diversify seemed to have been induced by relative backwardness. Juergen Kocka of the University of Bielefeld in West Germany has argued recently that such industries as engineering and extraction which, unlike in Britain or only partly in France, 'did not grow out of pre-industrial structures' with ready trading facilities, had to assume commercial functions themselves. Another reason was the deep distrust of the middleman felt by the producer which inhibited the development of 'interdependent market relationships with functional specialisation of individuals and institutions'. Early trends towards product diversification were also often a consequence of the relative backwardness of German development. Engineering firms for example tried to produce as many things as possible, because the market was not developed sufficiently to allow the narrowly specialised plant to survive. Insufficient transport facilities, limited effective demand, unpredictable markets 'made it wise to stand on more than one leg'. The similarities with Russia as late as 1914 are almost uncanny and justify further quotation from Kocka.

Kocka maintains that the tendency to diversify on account of market imperfections was particularly true of those early entrepreneurs who founded their firms in a 'green field', with a technology and a size which was in excess of demand; capacities were often created which could only be utilised through resolute diversification, a development here clearly reminiscent of the steel–coke complex in South Russia after 1900. Kocka admits that some of these incentives to expand, integrate and diversify became weaker the more mature the German economy became, but early patterns often continued even though the conditions which brought them about had gone.[124]

Rural location of factories

In 1902 more than half of all industrial plant and 58 per cent of the factory labour force were outside cities. Rural location was most pronounced in the largest units employing over a 1000 workers each. Pogozhev found that rural location applied to 90 per cent of the labour force in mining and metallurgy and to about 66 per cent in manufacturing. Only paper manufacture and printing, of all main industries, had a distinctly urban location, with less than 40 per cent of their labour force outside cities.

Within European Russia, St Petersburg, Riga and Kherson provinces had between 83 and 89 per cent of their labour force employed in the cities themselves or in other towns of the respective provinces. Similarly Poland and the Caucasus had urban location of plants. Industry in Moscow province on the other hand was, to the extent of 60 per cent of its labour force, outside Moscow city itself and outside towns of the province.[125]

Elsewhere in Europe modern industry also tended to develop outside old established urban centres, but the particular feature of Russia was that with few exceptions the factory settlement did not acquire urban character by function, structure of its population, or its external appearance.

The obvious explanation which suggests itself, and which was advanced by Lenin,[126] was the lack of mobility of the peasant due to institutional constrains :

They [the authorities] do not let the peasant go to the factory – the factory goes to the peasant. The peasant lacks full freedom (on account of collective responsibility and the compulsory nature of communal membership) to seek for himself the most profitable employer, the employer is perfectly capable of searching out the cheapest worker.

However, the tendency towards rural location of industry has been observed after 1906, when the constraint ascribed to communal ownership no longer applied.

In part, rural location was a legacy of pre-modern industrialisation. Many factories under serfdom were set up in rural areas either by landowners or serf-entrepreneurs. Many continued to exist. Even those which went into liquidation left behind them a labour force with skills and habits of factory discipline which kept on surfacing after decades of dormancy. The less pronounced urban character of Moscow may owe something to 1849 legislation which attempted to restrict factory building in the city itself for partly sanitary reasons, but mainly on account of fears of the effect of large concentrations of workers upon order and stability of the city. However despite the fact that the law remained on the statute book, there was much new urban industry in Moscow right up to the emancipation, and a great deal of it in St Petersburg.

Lenin was right that employers were reaching for the lowest level of wages, but not because the peasant could not come to the employer but because he usually became more expensive when he moved to urban location. A survey of Kostroma province in 1911 in which about 83 per cent of the factory labour force of over 61,000 were employed outside towns, stressed the widespread tendency of factory owners of the province to transfer their enterprises to rural location.

The Vychugda factory owners, realising how all-important it was to acquire cheap and resident labour, have begun already in the 'sixties to transfer branches of their factories to non-factory areas, where it was possible to find cheaper labour by spreading oneself all along the railway; and the more provident ones, wishing to obtain along with cheap labour also cheap fuel, began to transfer their factories or only some branches directly to location on the Volga river. The firm I. Konovalov and Son was the first to set up a bleaching–dyeing and finishing branch of its Vychugda plant in Kamenka on the Volga. Others followed . . .[127]

The same report went on to say that the spread of large industry in rural areas was accompanied by a general tendency to plant businesses in those parts of the province in which there were cadres of workers, reared as *kustars* or workers of small manufactories. This led to the emergence of factory settlements with large populations but of non-urban appearance and a semi-rural life and customs.

An observer of the Vladimir province noted a great deal of factory construction in the province after 1906, i.e. after the abolition of the communal ownership that was allegedly acting as a determinant of rural location.

> Factory construction – we are being told in 1911 – is particularly strong not in large, already settled industrial centres like Ivanovo– Voznessensk but in new places, in the countryside, in the hitherto dark villages and hamlets . . . Near half-forgotten outposts and stations, among tiny hamlets and villages are mushrooming all kinds of workshops and factories, and sometimes whole manufacturing establishments with leviathan-size complexes. And where hitherto not more than a field track was ambling along, on which here and there a single creaking peasant cart might make its rare appearance, [the air] is filled with the din and whistle of manystoreyed factory buildings, towards which lines of carts are converging from all sides . . .[128]

Factory inspectors also reported on this tendency of factory industry to penetrate into the depth of rural areas after 1906, and especially in the years immediately before the outbreak of the First World War. They stressed not only cheaper labour as the reason, but also less formality involved in setting up enterprises in rural areas, lower installation and running costs; lower costs of land and of rents; availability of timber for building, of wood for fuel, and of water. Water power still played a large part in industry, especially in the central industrial region, though oil from the Caucasus had begun to be used on an increasing scale. The cost of various services was found to be much cheaper in undeveloped rural areas.

Nevertheless factory inspectors reported that the expectations of employers were often unfulfilled. Those who were penetrating more deeply into the countryside in Vladimir province in order to secure a cheaper labour force away from the competition of established factories in the region had come across unwillingness of the local peasantry to undertake factory work; consequently labour costs turned out higher than in the old established localities. They also reported that *kustars* of long standing were returning to agriculture, which was becoming more remunerative. However these were short-term considerations, which did not affect the long-term availability of labour from the countryside, a situation not unlike that in the early 1880s.[129]

An important reason for rural location of large-scale industry was the fact that many large conglomerates had started off by relying on the putting out system or by being in effect dispersed manufactories with distributing offices. Many of the factory complexes were grafted onto settlements of *kustars* who gradually became factory hands. Moreover as many of the large conglomerates were the product of absorption of a variety of workshops or small factories and of forward and backward integration of processes, an enterprise which had started off as a city factory could end up by having the bulk of its operations in rural location. This was still happening in 1914 in the linen industry in Vladimir province, where large yarn producers from Ivanovo–Voznessensk would make contracts for linen fabrics for two to three years with small rural weaving sheds, to whom they supplied the warp and weft. They even encouraged the workshops to increase their number of looms and provided them with credit. Given the higher labour and general costs of the large factories, the unit costs of the rural workshops were some 20 to 25 per cent lower. As long as they found it advantageous, the larger producers paid a commission which allowed them to benefit from the lower costs of the small workshops, but sooner or later by withdrawing credit for yarn they either squeezed them out of the market or forced them to work on their terms, often as an external part of the larger unit.[130]

The different location pattern in St Petersburg was due to a number of reasons. Much industry had developed there already in the eighteenth century, most of it connected either with the state or foreigners. Both types of industry enjoyed special advantages in the recruitment and maintenance of their labour force. Foreign specialists, skilled labour from other areas of Russia, bonded child labour, and orphans from the state orphanage were attracted or directed to St Petersburg. The factories there were leaders in technology and consequently had acquired earlier than the others a better trained and more stable labour force.

St Petersburg industries relied to a lesser extent than elsewhere on local raw materials and fuel. As a large commercial port the city was more closely connected with foreign sources of supply than with internal, especially in view of the distances from domestic supply sources such as South Russia (coal) or Central Asia (cotton). The cotton industry in St Petersburg grew up directly as a factory industry and was not grafted onto *kustar* settlements as in Moscow or Vladimir. Peasant immigrants into St Petersburg industry tended to come from more distant provinces rather than from the neighbouring localities. Population studies have shown that there was a positive correlation between urban factory labour and inter-provincial migration and negative correlation with intra-provincial migration.[131] Finally as a seat of government, a great commercial port, a naval and military base, the administrative seat of most joint stock companies and banks, the place of residence of foreign businessmen and engineers, a cultural centre and the largest city, it created demand for labour and offered wage levels which compared favourably with those in other parts of the country.

The rural location of industry, especially in the central industrial region but not including Moscow, was reflected in the pattern of urbanisation. Thus the weight of the urban population in the central industrial region was consistently below the average for the fifty provinces of European Russia : 7·3 per cent in 1863 (average 9·9 per cent), 8·8 per cent in 1897 (12·9) and 9·4 per cent in 1914 (14·4). The rate of increase of the urban population was also lower than the average for the country, i.e. 114·9 per cent against 202·2 per cent. On the other hand this region held in 1900 several hundred factory-type and *kustar*-type settlements.[132]

In New Russia and generally in the Ukraine some of the factory settlements were assuming visual and other aspects of towns and furthermore cities were expanding as a result of service industries connected with the population increase and industrial growth. In southern Russia industrialisation was accompanied by urbanisation because industry in this region did not depend on forests for fuel and water for power. Also the seasonal character of agriculture was less pronounced, and *kustar* industry developed here on an insignificant scale. Artisan industry took the form of *remeslo* in towns.

Kustar *industries*

Kustars to whom reference has been made several times, were small *rural* industrial producers usually working mainly in the winter and usually employing hand tools only, though a variety of mechanical tools began to be used after 1906. Estimates as to numbers involved differ widely. Official sources list some 3½ million *kustars* and urban artisans in 1917, which allows for a figure of just under 2 million for *kustars* alone. A figure double this would be nearer the truth. For 1900 a figure of 7–8 million was cited in a semi-official publication, and figures around 10 million were given as late as 1911.[133]

Estimates of the value of their output have been attempted but are unreliable, and the best that can be said is that the value of production of small industry was about one-third of total industrial production (a little over one-quarter according to Soviet calculation or nearly a third of factory industry).[134] There is however no doubt as to the

important social rôle of *kustar* production relative to the broad consumer market and especially the rural market and as a source of cash
and entrepreneurship.

Here we can only very briefly indicate the factors in their growth
and tenacity in the face of modern factory industry. These were : the
already discussed highly seasonal character of Russian agriculture; the
isolation of individual regions due to size, geography and transport
inadequacy making for price differentials between regions and seasons;
low overheads due to the availability of a primary source of susten-
ance and the high degree of self exploitation and family exploitation,
low or no taxation, the versatility and responsiveness to economic
opportunity, and finally the value the *kustar* attached to his independence. In most cases there was no competition between him and
factory industry, because they concentrated usually on different
products or worked for different markets. Indeed often there was
complementarity, or – given the versatility of the *kustar* who, except
for a few trades where specialisation obtained, was very quick and
ready to learn new skills and to adapt to changed circumstances – a
tendency to move to new lines of activity created by factory industry.

It would appear that the cost of raw material and fuel was a much
more frequent reason for discomfiture than was competition of factory
production, as was the fall in agricultural prices which affected the
rural market towards which he was orientated. In particular the rise in
cost of timber, a raw material which before the emancipation he simply
took from the estate forest, as well as that of wood for fuel affected
his margin of profit.[135] Factory competition where it existed (a factory
of rubber boots in distant Riga could ruin a *kustar* tanner in the Volga
region if he was not quick enough to switch to making felt boots,
residues from the Baku oil production for lubrication could kill production of tar in Northern Russia) or other difficulties led to tendencies : for the size of the *kustar* enterprise to diminish; to rely more or
entirely on family labour, to use the family home or shed as workshop
instead of a special building, and on the whole to work much longer
hours and a willingness to accept a much smaller margin of profit; to
undertake arduous journeys often on foot 'to earn' the raw material or
sell in a better market; to work off credit and interest in a variety of
ways, etc. Only when all failed would he seek work 'on the side' or
'going away work', eventually in a factory but not directly; he would
first try a variety of trades and occupations hoping to restore his
independence. There was always of course the possibility of concentrating on agriculture. However 'going away work' according to most
observers was the most frequent route ultimately to the factory,
usually for seasonal work at first. The 'going away work' especially to

the city was a channel through which the 'demonstration effect' was beginning to operate; umbrellas, ink and paper and other status symbols, as well as the prestige of the man who has been to Petersburg, were beginning to act as inducements.[136]

The evidence for the actual rise from *kustar* to factory entrepreneurship is very obscure for the latter part of the nineteenth and the early twentieth century. Tugan-Baranovsky gives some instances among the Bogorodsk metal workmen, but on the whole those dealing with the subject were either concerned to show that *kustar* industry was being rapidly squeezed out by the factory, or if they were *Narodniki* they tended to show that the opposite was happening.[137] Soviet historians, as Portal has observed, tend to look for commercial antecedents of the *bourgeoisie* in accordance with the theory that commercial capitalism preceded industrial; similarly in dealing with the later period they concentrate on aspects pointing to so-called monopolistic-financial capitalism which supersedes industrial capitalism in the Leninist conception of imperialism. It may nevertheless be true that given the high cost of setting up industry and high running costs and the obvious advantage of size, the scope for medium-size firms might have been limited, hence the dualism already referred to. However regional studies would undoubtedly disclose many fields in which the entrepreneurship of the *kustar* assumed larger dimensions. For the smaller units the developments after 1906 augured, if not better chances of survival, at least less hardship. There was the cheapening of credit and the special policy of the State Bank designed to provide credit to sectors and areas where the big commercial banks were less active, the growth of co-operative rural banks, and the activity of the *zemstva* which were providing small installations, brick ovens, kilns, etc. for common use by rural industries.[138]

The above discussion of the *kustar* sector is not romanticism but rather an attempt to search for possible lines of development along which the Russian economy and society could have developed had the holocaust of war and revolution not intervened. In so far as government inducing policies of the 1890s were mainly orientated towards industries not connected with the consumer market, they left the consummer goods industries well alone, which distinguishes, among other things, the Witte era from that of Stalin. Given the immense size of the agrarian sector and the likelihood of agriculture becoming ultimately 100 per cent peasant (already 88 per cent of production came from peasants), the fact that only a gradual shift of labour from the villages could take place in proportion to productivity increase in agriculture, as well as undoubtedly large capital requirements for factory industry and the extreme seasonality of agriculture some form of assisted complementarity, a conscious combination of capital intensive with labour intensive industrialisation was likely to be both economically possible and politically desirable. However such musings about the 'would have beens' of history are a dangerous self-indulgence. What is certain is that the *kustar* road, whether successful or not, and the 'going away' occupations were channels for education by the market, which was the most reliable basis for the induced and autonomous development streams alike.

There is no doubt in our mind that the public sector's rôle in the industrialisation process or in the economy in general was likely to remain a very vital if more subtle one, and entailing greater involvement of the municipalities and the *zemstva* rather than the state directly, as was actually happening during 1906–17.[139] The task of strengthening social overhead capital was still formidable. Until this was done private entrepreneurs would not readily undertake business entailing internalising social costs, unless offered powerful inducements. Individual firms apart, excepting the cotton and food industries, the net profits on capital invested were relatively low 'in Russia considering the risk involved. Our calculations suggest not more than an average 6 per cent of the basic capital during 1891– 1914.[140] The textile industry did better; its financial position was very strong, its amortisation funds amounted to nearly half its basic capital on the average during 1911–13, and it also had substantial undisclosed or under-valued assets.[141] The mining industry, especially coal, and the twenty, later seventeen, members of the *Prodameta* syndicate worked on a shoestring, and there is every indication, despite common assumptions to the contrary, that capital (e.g. for the deepening of coal mines, etc.) was not coming forward readily.[142] Neither was there much likelihood of a really open economy to emerge. Russia was unlikely to become competitive in international terms in the forseeable future where manufactures were concerned, though there was much scope for using her comparative advantage in various fields, eminently in timber and mineral resources and for import substitution given a market of some 170 million people.

It may be a useful corrective to a story in which the state figured so prominently that in terms of direct ownership, the public-co-operative sector accounted on 1 January 1914 for only 25·5 per cent of the total estimated wealth, and the state alone for only 8·3 per cent, according to A. L. Vaynshtayn. Though Vaynshtayn under-valued the property of the state by excluding land, forests and unexploited mineral resources from the concept of wealth (the value of land had been estimated by Strumilin at 90,400 million roubles against a figure of 55,600 million for the total estimated wealth by Vaynshtayn), it nevertheless remains true that in industry direct ownership by the state was low, in Vaynshtayn's estimate only slightly over 10 per cent. Only in railway transport was direct ownership by the state significant.[143]

GENERAL SUMMARY AND TENTATIVE CONCLUSIONS

The differential elements in the Russian environment, considered historically, had made for a strong position of the state in the economy and society. This in turn perpetuated the weakness of the autonomous forces so that the state, moved largely by military and prestige considerations, had to undertake the task of modernisation at incalculable cost in every sense. This gave rise to what we call 'the induced growth stream'.

Nevertheless from the eighteenth century onwards there was a steady if not spectacular growth of what we call the 'autonomous stream', which was in a variety of ways related to the 'induced' and which continued to grow, positively if indirectly affected by the renewed spurt of inducing policies of the 1880s and 1890s. These policies differed in kind from Petrine policies in that they operated by way of the market and were gradually eroding the economic and mental self-sufficiency of the rural sector. After 1900, and in particular after 1906, there is evidence for a tendency for the two 'streams' to coalesce, but there was still not only scope but actual necessity for an active rôle of the public sector.

By 1914 Russia had a significant industrial sector which was not an 'enclave' as modern sectors in contemporary underdeveloped countries tend to be, but closely connected with the rest of the economy through the market and the fiscal system. The boundary between the modern and 'traditional' sector was constantly moving forward mainly in consequence of transport development, the fiscal system, and as a result of growing responsiveness of the traditional sector to economic opportunity. There were on the whole few sociological 'rigidities' in the rural sector impeding economic development about which economists of contemporary underdevelopment are so despondent.[144] The reaction of the peasantry in Soviet Russia to price policies during War Communism and NEP is an excellent measure of the degree of their pre-1914 education by the market. Nevertheless the vast majority of the Russian population was not yet absorbed into an organised wage economy; neither however were they a pure subsistence sector. The bulk of the people were in the 'vast intermediate zone of economic activity with a very low degree of economic specialisation, devoting varying parts of time and resources to subsistence activities and cash earning activities.'[145]

The employment creating capacity of the modern sector had not been impressive. This was partly due to the fact that the expansion of the 'induced' sector has been obtained more from differential access to capital funds, mainly foreign, and not so much or as yet from a self-generating process of increase in productivity resulting in new resources for reinvestment. Where this was not the case, the profits available for reinvestment were often obtained only in part from a genuine increase in productivity arising out of modern technology, the profits having been artificially inflated by the existence of a 'closed' economy.

While the 'induced' sector has since Peter's time been acting as disseminator of skills and stimulator of small-scale rural industries, the latter had an equally 'educative' effect in providing a training ground for potential entrepreneurs. Though in relation to the size of the economy the modern industrial sector was small, it had succeeded in creating by 1914 a substantial pool of managerial and technical skill, so that despite the tumultous events of the revolution and its after-math, War Communism, with all the loss in personnel they entailed, the modern factory sector could be restored within a relatively short time, notwithstanding the bizarre notions about running the economy some Communist leaders entertained. This was partly due to vastly increased general education since the 1870s, and even more to the expansion of specialised technical and commercial education, especially secondary education. The social change which has taken place was reflected in the high proportion of non-gentry students in vocational higher education in 1910. Nearly 70 per cent of the total were of non-gentry origin and 13·5 per cent were of peasant parent-age. In secondary education 72 per cent were non-gentry by origin and 25·2 per cent were peasants. In the teachers' training colleges 70 per cent of the students were of peasant parentage in 1902.[146]

On the basis of the 1897 census, Erman calculated that just under 100,000 men and women were what he terms a 'technical-productive intelligentsia'. For a modern factory sector which in 1900 employed 2·4 million workers, 100,000 was a fairly impressive proportion, which to judge by the rise in numbers of students in higher and secondary technical education by 1914 must have increased substantially. These figures do not include the technical personnel in the military establish-ments nor those who learned skills in factory schools.[147] On the other hand factory industry, even the branches of long standing, still had need to employ foreign foremen and technicians on a fairly large scale.[148]

The structure of industry remained characteristic of an immature economy. In terms of employment and output value, textiles and food processing were still leading by 1914, except in St Petersburg. Though there was a tendency for business units in corporate industry to be large, small units still accounted for a very high proportion of the labour force, and they exhibited great resilience and versatility. So-called 'industrial concentration', commonly taken as an index of maturity of the capitalist system, was to a great extent a function of underdevelopment and of statistical distortion.

Government policies whether in intent or in effect were rarely consistent. As market forces became stronger, the effectiveness of government policies depended in the last resort on these forces. It has been argued ably if not quite convincingly that an alternative set of policies in the monetary, commercial and fiscal fields would have produced faster and higher industrial growth rates without the distortions and the tensions which accompanied the industrialisation policies of the 1880s and 1890s.[149] However, individual ministers apart, the specific policies pursued by the Russian government were not devised consciously with industrialisation in view. They emerged in response to general financial, political and military needs and not with a view to a macroeconomic optimum.

2 The Russian economy under serfdom*

Considering the commitment to the primacy of economics in Soviet ideology, there is a relative paucity of quality studies in the pre-1917 Russian economy by Soviet writers. The studies available tend to fall into two basic categories. Either they are works of a general nature dealing with large issues reflecting current ideological preoccupations of Soviet historians and only marginally of interest to the Western student with a specific piece of research in hand; or they are very detailed monographs, eschewing synthesis, concentrating on minutiae of a technical rather than an economic nature, descriptive rather than analytical in approach. Studies with just the right blend of detail and generalisation are not frequent, which makes the task of both researcher and teacher very difficult.

Nevertheless the works of Soviet historians are often the most essential source materials for the students of Russia in the West, and by and large there is now a considerable body of material of a sufficiently high calibre covering the seventeenth, eighteenth and early nineteenth centuries to enable the student to build up a fairly comprehensive picture of the Russian economy during the two and one-half centuries before the emancipation of the serfs. For the second half of the nineteenth and for the early twentieth century the field is less well served, though there has been marked improvement in the last decade. In general certain aspects, such as trade, are almost entirely neglected, others such as industry or banking are rarely treated from the viewpoint of the individual plant or institution, and despite many studies on the agrarian problem the economics of farming, whether estate or peasant, are insufficiently explored. As in the West until recently those with training in economics rarely venture into the study of the past. Moreover the Marxian framework, unless used by the most able, tends

* Pp. 56–60 and 70–2 of this chapter orginally published as a composite review in *The Slavonic and East European Review*, vol. LI, October, 1973 under the title 'the economic history of pre-Reform Russia', here expanded.

to impose a certain rigidity and uniformity upon the nature of the enquiry and its findings.

BUSINESS RELATIONS BETWEEN RUSSIA AND EUROPE

Only one of the works discussed below deals with the most neglected aspect of Russia's economy, her foreign trading relations.[1] It is a collection of essays, each dealing with fairly narrow aspects of business relations between Russia and Europe. Nevertheless the overall result is a comprehensive view of the nature of the relationship over the centuries. Though Russian authorities always insisted in their trade treaties on reciprocity, in practice such reciprocity was 'theoretical' rather than effective. Russia's trade remained essentially passive, in the sense that the trading initiative usually came from foreigners, that Russians rarely ventured to the West to seek out trading opportunities. Nevertheless the trade which European merchants plied in Russia was not 'colonial' in nature, which was probably due to the high degree of control exercised from an early stage by the government, of which insistence on reciprocity even if theoretical was undoubtedly a part.

Russia's failure to acquire a commercial fleet, the underdevelopment of banking services and of modern accountancy systems, her unreliable currency, lack of legal provision for the protection of financial claims and the arbitrariness of the authorities were all reasons why Russia's foreign trade failed to evolve fully and become a significant part of the national economy. The pronounced and continued *étatisme* of economic policy, the subordination of commerce to the state's fiscal interests at a time when Western governments were moving away from rigid regimentation of economic life in general and of foreign trade in particular negatively affected the opportunities for meaningful and comprehensive exchange of goods and services between Russia and Europe.

Kirchner's book is much more than a study of commercial relations. It is an intelligent introduction to an understanding of the nature of the Russian business community, of the rôle of the Russian state in business matters and of specific problems facing foreign businessmen in the Russian environment. The author believes that, as a rule, the Western entrepreneur was 'induced to engage in business with Russia by expectation of profit rather than by records of profit'.[2] Few Western firms dealing exclusively with or in Russia stayed in operation for more than one generation. This challenges the widespread belief that foreign businessmen made fabulous profits out of their association with Russia. Moreover as original capital outlays on business were high, and the attendant risks very great, Russian business tended to attract men, who if not outright gamblers, looked for profits on speculative deals rather than for serious business opportunities.[3]

The difficulties which a foreign businessman had to face in Russia were compounded by the fact that in view of the rapid advances made in Western Europe, especially in the eighteenth century, he no longer had any terms of reference or even a memory for dealing with particular socioeconomic and cultural problems. The foreigner was faced in Russia with situations and problems which in the country of his origin belonged to the distant past. No wonder that Russia appeared to him as a 'strange land'.[4]

Valuable though it is as an introduction to business relations between Russia and Europe, Kirchner's view of the Russian business community is essentially that of an outsider, seeing through the not unprejudiced eyes of foreign businessmen. Though usually justified, their jaundiced reactions were often attempts at self-exculpation for failure and ultimately for poor entrepreneurship by foreigners who had anticipated high profits but had failed to take into account the cost inherent in the 'strangeness' of the environment.

THE SEVENTEENTH-CENTURY MANUFACTORY

The seventeenth century was undoubtedly a period during which Russia's economic life began to display features commonly associated with a business economy. It is also a better documented century in so far as foreign accounts are concerned than the previous ones, hence there is more emphasis on business elements. Whether these features can be described as capitalistic or whether one can view the seventeenth century as a 'period of transition from feudalism to capitalism', an even larger claim made till recently by Soviet historians and implicitly by Fuhrmann,[5] is rather problematic and relies heavily on definitions. A recent symposium of Soviet historians[6] gives much support to the view that the 'transition to capitalism' can be more appropriately placed around 1762. Those favouring the seventeenth century as capitalistic are accused of economic determinism, narrow concentration on the growth of manufacturing – especially the technical features of manufacturing – as denoting capitalism, of ignoring the agrarian sector and social and institutional developments where 'feudalism' was in fact in the ascendant. The debate continues and the exponents of seventeenth-century capitalism have by no means renounced their stand.

Fuhrmann places the origins of capitalism in Russia in the seventeenth century, but rejects the Soviet view which sees the origin of capitalism in terms of the internal dynamics of Russia's economy and society. Like Soviet historians he also connects capitalism with the manufactory which, in his view, 'represented the real emergence of the tremendous productive forces of capitalism . . . the manufactory *was* capitalism'. But manufacturing as it evolved in Russia was, according to Fuhrmann, an 'external force' the bearers of which were individual foreign entrepreneurs in search of profit. The manufactories they set up were using the most advanced contemporary technology mainly based on water power. Most of them were staffed, especially at the beginning, by foreign workers. Fuhrmann identifies fifty such manufactories built in the seventeenth century, most after 1630, and seven in the sixteenth century. He argues that these enterprises were 'individual constituents of a unified and coherent process which propelled the Russian economy in a new and definite direction' and that 'appearing as they did in the context of a still rather backward feudal economy, [they] represented a significant first step in the development of Russian capitalism'.[7]

However Fuhrmann has not proved satisfactorily that the manufactory had in fact 'propelled the Russian economy in a new and definite direction'. The manufacturing sector, especially the large-scale manufactory, remained unrepresentative of the economy at large and barely nibbled at the vast agrarian sector. Individual manufactories seemed to have been extremely fragile and artisan production was definitely in the ascendant. The evidence with regard to the motivation of individual manufacturers is very vague and circumstantial. It is assumed that their profit expectations were high but it is not really clear whether they expected *entrepreneurial* profits or profits from their association with the government or from speculative deals. In this connection Fuhrmann might have gained by drawing more fully upon Kirchner's views on the subject of the profit expectations of foreign businessmen in Russia. There is indirect evidence of large amounts of capital sunk by foreigners but also much direct evidence of large subsidies and privileges actually received or anticipated from the government. It seems that manufacturing as such, at least in the short run, was not profitable from the investor's point of view, though it might have met the ends desired by the Russian government. However, even in this respect, the balance is uncertain to say the least. Domestic production undertaken as import substitution was very inadequate and vast imports continued to be indispensable. There are some doubts concerning the quality of the output of Russia's manufactories. If the price was on occasion lower this may have been due to the uneconomic price set by the Tsar which, if true, would account for the unprofitability of the manufactories to the investors.

Fuhrmann attributes the failure of incipient capitalism to evolve into full capitalism to the dichotomy between the new technology and industrial organisation and Russia's social and institutional system, in other words to serfdom. Serfdom is, for the economic historian of Russia, the residual element to which he resorts whenever he has difficulty in explaining a particular phenomenon. However, though one cannot deny that in the long run serfdom is incompatible with capitalism as we understand it, it still needs explaining why economic progress, of which capitalism was a manifestation, not only failed in Russia to sweep away serfdom but indeed strengthened and adapted it to manufacturing. One can legitimately argue, and developments in eighteenth-century Russia bear this out, that, in view of the under-development of the market in Russia, large-scale factory production occasioned by the needs of the state was possible only *because of serfdom* or some other form of compulsory labour. This is by and large the view of O. Ohlobyn, and of Peter Struve.

Though inconclusive as a study of the origins of capitalism, Fuhrmann's work provides much evidence of continuity in Russia's economic development, not in terms of the survival of individual businesses out of which the later capitalistic firms were to grow (the mortality of seventeenth- and eighteenth-century business firms was very high indeed) but of the survival, transmission and diffusion of skills acquired in the early manufactories, either to other factories in new regions, e.g. from Tula to Olonets and later to the Urals, or in a roundabout way through the application of skills acquired in factories by peasant–artisans working for a market. This latter form of transfer and diffusion of skills via the factory to the *kustar* workshop, so brilliantly expounded by Tugan-Baranovsky for the nineteenth century, was a characteristic feature of Russia's industrial evolution right up to 1917, bound up with the high seasonality of agriculture, the imperfections of the consumer market and the rôle of the state in the creation of factory industry and the mobilisation of its labour force.[8]

It can be inferred from Fuhrmann's study that, in the seventeenth century, there was already a certain dualism in industrial activity between the factory which produced the hardware needed by the state under some form of monopoly and the artisan workshop which produced a multiplicity of consumer goods for an open market. Foreigners tended to be prominent in the kind of activity which was favoured by the state and which in the short run was not directly remunerative. However native entrepreneurship and know-how do not seem to have lagged far behind whenever the profit expectations were high, which may indicate that foreign entrepreneurs were releasing native business enterprise, a feature noted by McKay for the late nineteenth century.[9]

It may be appropriate to draw attention here to a work by the

Soviet scholar E. I. Zaozerskaya,[10] which considers the same problem as Fuhrmann but from the angle of individual industries. It is a serious work of scholarship and contains some interesting observations based on extensive archive material. In particular Zaozerskaya shows the subtle interrelationship between local business initiative and government policy of fostering industry. The pattern, as interpreted by Zaozerskaya, seems to have been as follows : local skills and initiative arising from specific favourable circumstances, such as the availability of raw materials or the existence of convenient water routes, were encouraged to expand by the government, for its own needs, by the provision of privileges, subsidies and markets. Such encouragement was at first welcomed by local interests, but was soon found to be restrictive and the tendency was to try to reduce commitment to the government, especially in view of the growth of a consumer market.

Zaozerskaya identifies three spheres of manufacturing activity in which elements of large scale industry made their appearance. In the salt industry only the unit of management was large, that of production and technology was small and static. In metallurgy only some processes took the form of large-scale industry, organised mainly by the state, a few landowners and foreigners. In textiles most production was small-scale and, if some centralisation occurred, this was achieved by the Court administration (*dvorets*), did not substantially affect techniques, and was generally insignificant. Zaozerskaya looks for the inner springs of capitalist evolution in Russia to native craftsmen and merchants, as incipient proletarians and capitalists – the two main classes of an emerging social system. Like other Soviet historians she has little to say about the contribution of foreigners to large-scale industry.

THE IRON INDUSTRY IN THE URALS

Though R. Portal's study on the Ural iron industries in the eighteenth century was published twenty-five years ago, it has a place in this study as an illustration of the manner in which large-scale manufacturing could develop and thrive within the framework of a serf dominated economy.[11] Indeed the Ural industries, because of the large scale of their production and because of the growing foreign demand for iron, were not in a position to rely on the supply of labour by way of the market, but had to base themselves on labour direction and attachment to the works. The large-scale manufactory, far from being *capitalism* as claimed by Fuhrmann, meant in fact strengthening of serfdom.

Three main periods can be distinguished in the evolution of Ural industries in the eighteenth century. The first, the 'era of pioneers' ran from 1716 to 1745. It was connected with the names and activities of the first Demidovs who represented private initiative and with those of Tatishchev and Von Hennin who represented government initiative as delegates of the *Gornaya Kollegiya* (the mining board). The second period, the high-water mark of growth, extended from 1745 to 1762. It witnessed the expansion of industry in the central Urals and the opening of the southern Urals, the national home of the Bashkirs. Towards the closing years of this period social disturbances began to loom large, but it was only in the third period, which ran from 1762 to 1807, that the peasant *jaquerie* led by the Cossack Emelyan Pugachov swept along the southern and part of the central Urals, bringing devastation to some of the works in its wake. The years which followed the *Pugachovshchina* were years of reconstruction, involving little if any advance in techniques.

The Ural industries meant in the eighteenth century the production of copper and iron in the main. When in the seventeenth century metallurgy began to develop in Russia, attention was drawn towards the potential wealth of the Urals. However attempts to open the Urals failed. The Urals were too far, there was the danger of nomadic raids, and most importantly the demand for iron was not as yet very pressing and it could be satisfied from other sources. Therefore, in so far as some development was taking place, it was mainly tied to the search for precious metals.

The very same factors which delayed the development of the Urals accounted also for the predominant rôle of the state in the opening up of the central Urals when the cutting off of iron imports from Sweden and the pressing need for more war materials made it imperative that new supplies of iron be found within the country. It would appear that state initiative was not a matter of principle but of necessity, especially as foreign businessmen, who played a significant part in planting industries in central Russia, were not too eager to face the extremely harsh conditions of life and the severity of climate in the Urals. There was finally the question of speed in view of the pressures of the military situation. The first rapid development occurred between 1698 and 1710 under the direct pressure of military events and was due entirely to government initiative. However as early as 1702 the government handed over the Nevyansk works it had built to Nikita Demidov, a clear sign that the original initiative taken by the government was *étatisme de nécessité*. Very soon, Nikita Demidov, owner of the Tula works in central Russia, began to look upon the Urals as his main centre of activity, and he became the founder of a family of the most powerful entrepreneurs of the time in Russia. The government opened the way and private initiative followed. However government continued to be active, though its enterprise was intermittent, short periods of advance being followed by sudden often prolonged troughs. Private entrepreneurship, on the contrary, followed a regular upward curve. During the administration of von Hennin (1722–34) a kind of balance between the two types of enterprise was established, but it did not last long. On the whole the rôle of the state owned works was to take and give a lead in innovation, to provide training for foremen and workers, while privately owned works were usually better managed, their owners had better concepts of accountancy and economy.

Peter's aim was to set up industries and expand production whatever the cost. Consecutive governments however became rather apprehensive of the mounting costs of state owned enterprises. They began to consider handing them over to private enterprises in the hope not only of cutting state expenditure but also of raising fiscal revenue from private industry. The negotiations were protracted so that it was only in the 1750s that most of the plants in the central Urals became privately owned. As the opening up of the southern Urals, which occurred at the same time (from 1745 onwards), was affected by private interest too, the state's rôle became fairly limited. By the end of the century the government owned some fifteen plants, most of which were acquired after 1760 from bankrupt owners. While initially government policy was motivated by the desire to cut costs and to derive revenue, the actual manner of transfer may indicate that political considerations were involved. Nearly all new owners were members of the nobility; the purchase price was very low; in the majority of cases the transfer of works was more in the nature of a grant than a commercial transaction. Nevertheless by and large it was merchant capital and initiative which in addition to government action were responsible for the development of the Urals. Even in the southern Urals where the nobles had a vast field of activity, and though many merchants became ennobled, very few were successful and the field was left open to commercial interests. The main reason was the distance of the Urals from the majority of landed estates and the lack of operating capital which could not be easily raised from estate farming, while long-term capital was immobilised in land and serfs.

'L'Oural doît aux étrangers et particulièrement aux Allemands les bases de son developpement industriel,' writes Portal. There was not a single enterprise set up before 1730 which did not have a technician, worker, miner or even carpenter of Scandinavian or German origin. The techniques of the West were also transmitted by way of the metallurgical works of central Russia. By the end of the 1730s Russian technical personnel was more or less assured. Only towards the end of the century was there some influx of British specialists, largely due to the closer political relations between Britain and Russia, and certain minor changes were effected under their influence.

By 1762 Ural industries had a practical monopoly in copper output. Though they accounted only for half of the metallurgical works in Russia, their share in total output was over 60 per cent. The Urals had superior technology and higher output per plant. Growth of output was export led, which was also reflected in the nature of the final products. Most of the demand came from Britain which absorbed imports from the two main suppliers of iron, Sweden and Russia, the latter leading. The internal market, though of some importance, could not and did not account for the rapid growth of metallurgy in the Urals by mid-century. The repeal of internal customs duties in December 1753, which facilitated commerce in metals and raised profit margins somewhat, was of some significance. The favourable natural conditions undoubtedly contributed to growth. These were rich beds of excellent quality iron ore and copper in relative proximity to abundant forest, affording fuel and building material. The many streams and rivers were used as power and transport.

The transport factor was of strategic importance because the market for Ural industries lay either outside Russia or in the north-central provinces where the plants used Ural iron for processing and fashioning into various articles. The transport factor was rather unfavourable. The Nevyansk works were situated at a distance of some 150 *versts* (100 miles) from the Chusovaya river connecting the works with Moscow; many works were even further away. In order to shorten the distances to markets, smaller works for the smelting of the ore were set up closer to the rivers leading to markets, but at a distance from the ore. The consequence was decentralisation, dispersal of production units and fragmentation, which occurred on a considerable scale in the course of the nineteenth century.

The French *chargé de mission* in St Petersburg, Maurice Verstraete, left us an excellent description of the Urals in the nineteenth century.[12] He stressed the formidable transport difficulties faced by producers, not only in shipping goods to markets in central Russia, but within the Urals itself. Transport costs were very high relative to the cost of the product at the plant, and the remedy of decentralisation meant that economies of scale could not be applied. In the 1750s transport difficulties could be overcome by vast resort to the labour, carts and horses of the local population. This was possible and practicable as long as labour was cheap and the demand for iron growing.

The problem of labour was solved by resort to the use of *adscribed peasants* from among the local population, who were mainly state peasants. The duty of work in the mines and iron works, most often as auxiliary workers for felling trees, burning charcoal and carting, was imposed upon these peasants as a form of state service. At any given time only a fraction of the total population, between one-fifth and one-quarter, were engaged in this work. Another category of workers were *possessional peasants*, who were serfs attached to the plant and not to the person of the owner. Some of them worked inside the plant, but the majority performed subsidiary duties requiring less skill, but involving large numbers and consuming much time. The core of the industrial labour force in the Urals consisted of a motley of people – craftsmen, convicts, soldiers, serfs from landed estates, fugitives serfs from other parts of Russia, prisoners of war, pupils of mining schools, etc. In the course of time and as a result of a number of legislative acts attaching them to factories, they merged into one group of industrial serfs, *forever* part of the factories, the *vechno-otdannyye*. As late as 1807, when elsewhere in Russia labour began to be recruited on an increasing scale from among rent paying serfs by the way of the market, in the Urals a proportion of the *adscribed peasants* were *for ever* attached to the works as industrial serfs *par excellence*. Different conditions in this region remote from populated estates dictated different policies with regard to labour provision.

Can our knowledge of the development of Ural industries in the eighteenth century help us to explain why growth could not be sustained in the nineteenth century, why indeed the Urals stagnated? Conventional wisdom has it that while in the eighteenth century resort to serf labour was still productive of growth, in the nineteenth century serfdom acted as a brake and led to stagnation. This answer does not explain why the Urals were left behind in the second half of the nineteenth century when serfdom was abolished and a metallurgical complex was growing rapidly in South Russia from the 1880s onwards. Neither does this interpretation explain the success of the sugar industry equally based on serf labour.

The question can best be answered by attempting to assess whether the factors which made for the success of the Ural iron industry in the eighteenth century were still operative, and what if any were the changes which had reversed the position. Undoubtedly the changes in techniques of iron smelting, associated with the industrial revolution in Britain, were among the most important factors in the falling off in demand for Russian iron in Britain. With it went the most important stimulus for production expansion in Russia. The wars at the turn of the century could only postpone the debacle; they could not halt it. The favourable resource endowment, in particular the proximity of abundant forests to excellent ore deposits, the second factor in the story of eighteenth-century success, became also less favourable

as time went on. Forests became depleted, especially those closest to
the works, which entailed higher costs in long hauls in a situation
where transport was in any case a problem. Though real costs of
adscribed labour are not easy to assess, it seems that the cost of transportation of ore or timber by road was very expensive indeed by the
end of the nineteenth century, for which we have contemporary
accounts from M. Verstraete. Indeed it would appear that costs of
production *loco* works in the Urals compared favourably with those
obtaining in the technologically advanced South Russia metallurgical
plants. Given high costs of road transport, Ural entrepreneurs tended
to keep stocks till spring in order to use the cheaper mode of transport
by river. This entailed loss of interest and added to costs. Neither were
the rivers an ideal form of transport : shallowness frequently held up
cargoes, which unless bailed out by a few centimetres of water from
the reservoir of a neighbouring plant, which had to be dearly paid for,
would have to stay on the river till the following spring. In the meantime the market, especially that of the Nizhny Novorod fair which was
in the autumn, would be lost.

Rivers were mainly used for the shipment of the final product, while
carts and sleighs were used for shifting fuel and raw materials. The
cost of conveying raw materials, not counting loss of interest on the
stocks accumulated during the summer, accounted for a third of
production costs of a *pood* of iron. Transport difficulties led, as already
mentioned, to decentralisation of production and to the necessity of
limiting the field of activity of an enterprise to a maximum radius of
100 *versts*, and most frequently to that of 40 *versts* only. Within this
limited area everything necessary for production had to be found. It
is not surprising therefore that the Urals found it more and more
difficult to compete with regions more favoured by natural conditions.
Transport by rail played as yet a very insignificant part, as the
enormous region was served by two lines only, placed in the main too
far from the works to be of much use.

Of course these were not the only reasons for the failure of the
Urals to modernise in the nineteenth century. The use of wood fuel
acted as a constraint on the size of blast furnaces, conservatism of
established markets militated against shifting production to more lucrative products, the availability of a settled labour force which looked
upon employment in the works as a right inhibited adoption of modern
technology, the persistence of *possessional* rights of the state prevented
owners from selling part of their estates of forests to procure capital
for innovation.

This discussion of an industry which was on the whole successful
under serfdom and failed to modernise subsequently shows how danger-

ous it is to make facile generalisations about the inhibiting effects of legal and institutional factors upon economic reality.

MANAGEMENT OF ESTATES IN EIGHTEENTH-CENTURY RUSSIA*

It is refreshing to have a work on agrarian relations in Russia which has as its point of departure not the peasant but the noble landowner. True, the peasant does in the final analysis emerge as the hero. Professor Confino, of the University of Jerusalem, shows that it was the peasant who imposed his outlook, his habits of thinking, and his ways of doing things upon the noble landowner, who in the latter part of the eighteenth century, imbued with the scientific notions of the age of enlightenment, set out with optimism and enthusiasm to organise his estate on new lines.

Confino describes how the Russian gentry, freed from obligatory service to the state in 1762, given an assured position in local government by the reform of 1775, and new corporate rights by the Charter of 1785, began to feel that running an estate was dignified and on a par with holding administrative or military office and that by successful management of their estates they were in fact performing a service for their country. Moreover rising agricultural prices, government concern for increasing sales of agricultural produce both in the country and abroad, and currency depreciation seemed to enhance the attractions of agricultural activity.

However from the start the gentry seemed to be preoccupied with the administrative rather than the strictly economic or technological aspects of estate activity, or rather they hoped to attain economic ends by administrative measures. Elaborate manorial chancelleries were established, especially on the larger estates; sets of minute instructions were drawn up designed to foresee every possible contingency and involving a system of offices controlling one another, checking and counterchecking. Blueprints of the desired qualities in a bailiff and the duties and responsibilities devolving on him were such that it was unlikely that any such person could be found, least of all in Russia. To forestall the bailiff's abuse of his powers to the detriment of either the *pomeshchik* himself or the peasants, elected officers of the village commune were called upon to assist in the administration of the estate, while the whole peasant community was made responsible for the conduct of their chosen officers.

In this way, Confino argues, did the Russian landowner cynically

* This section from *Slavic Review*, vol. XXV, December, 1966. Review of M. Confino, *Domaines et seigneurs en Russie vers la fin du XVIIIe siècle . . .* (Paris, 1963). Reprinted by permission.

utilise institutions developed by the peasantry for the purpose of self-government and mutual defence to further his own interests and those of the local government and the treasury. However, though he had thereby achieved the submission of the peasant community to the administration, in the long run he himself submitted to the slow influence of the peasant environment; peasant traditions, habits, and agricultural practices gradually affected the running of his estates.

In devising the elaborate estate organisation the owners' main aim, stressed over and over again, was to increase the profit of their estates. However in their loose use of this term the landowners had no concept of costs of production and confused gross cash revenue with profit. Because they lacked any concept of costs, Confino argues, they considered demesne farming based on labour services of the serfs more profitable than income from money rents though the latter required practically no outlay on the part of the landowner.

Where agricultural techniques were concerned, the technological level of the demesne was no different from that of the peasant farm. Nor could it be different for it was the peasant's plough, his harrow, and his horse that were used on the estate – the landowner rarely owned any. Furthermore the estate was rarely consolidated or enclosed, and while it represented a large unit of ownership, from the point of view of production it was a conglomeration of small units, usually in intermingled strips, frequently among strips of peasant land and hence of necessity subject to the agricultural routine established by the village commune. 'Grands domaines, petites exploitations', says the author. Even where marketability was concerned, the estate had all the features of a peasant economy in that only the residue was sold, the main aim of production being to ensure continuity of production and to meet the consumption needs of the nobleman's family and of his town residence, if any.

Given the growing needs of the gentry, the estate owner tried to raise the cash income of his estate through enlarged production by buying or ploughing up more land, by increasing the pressure on serf labour, by introducing mixed forms of peasant services, and by miserly attention to petty detail and economy. Distilling, letting of forest land, mortgaging the estates – such sources of cash were eagerly sought.

Confino shows how false was the image of the *grand seigneur* type of landowner that has been drawn for us by Russian writers. Confino's *pomeshchik* was petty, parsimonious, closely following everything on the estate, certainly not an absentee landowner, either physically or in mentality. He was concerned about the welfare of the peasants because he knew that his profits were dependent upon it.

Gone is the myth of 'conspicuous consumption' of the Russian landed nobility, at least for the eighteenth century. If the noble landowner had large sums at his disposal the source was usually the treasury, not the estates. Confino's nobleman lived in constant fear of ruin not because he spent too much but because he was not entrepreneur enough to earn more. He had no concept of roundabout ways of making an income through investment. He could not hold such a concept because of the incompatibility of production for a market with the structure of an estate economy based on serf labour.

In his introduction to the book Professor Portal suggests that Confino may be over-pessimistic in his conclusions. The Russian nobleman was not unique in eighteenth-century Europe in not being guided by rational economic calculation in making production decisions. One might add that, though the Russian nobleman often invoked the 'merchant-like' approach as the model to be followed, one could hardly consider the Muscovite *kupets* as very advanced in business methods. He was mainly concerned about buying cheap and selling dear, not about building up a clientele by fair dealings through small profits and a large turnover. The noble envied the merchant his ability to lay hands on cash and tended on occasion to undertake commercial functions himself, for they seemed to be a much easier road to profit than agriculture.

Though his accounting principles were faulty, the Russian agricultural producer knew well that the price he obtained was not simply a function of supply and demand but more often depended on the proximity of roads and navigable rivers. The subscribers to the *Trudy Vol'nogo Ekonomicheskogo Obshchestva* obviously knew that agricultural prices were rising – but what was the real meaning of such a rise to the individual landowner? Even by the middle of the nineteenth century the difference in price between, say, St Petersburg and Orenburg could be in the range of 14 : 1

Moreover how great really was the opportunity which the Russian estate owner had supposedly missed at the turn of the eighteenth century? How large really was the challenge of expanded markets? The urban population rose from an estimated 3 per cent of the total in 1724 to 4·1 per cent in 1796, but a fairly large proportion of the 1·3 million people classed as urban in 1796 were either inhabitants of the annexed Western provinces or inhabitants of Catherine's new urban 'foundations', of which only a few were towns in the real sense of the word. As late as 1852 there was in Russia only one town to every 130·5 square miles of territory, and most towns still had an outer ring inhabited by peasants cultivating vegetables and crops in open fields.

Undoubtedly the northern central provinces were becoming industrialised and relatively densely populated and offered a market for grain from the central agricultural area. But by 1800 these provinces still provided a large proportion of their own food grains despite the low fertility of their soil, while the fertile south and south-east were still areas of extensive cattle breeding with few areas under crops. Thus, the internal market for grain, while growing, was still very limited. The foreign market was expanding, but grain accounted for a very small proportion of total exports, and only around 1 per cent of the harvest was exported by the beginning of the nineteenth century. Flax and hemp were important agricultural export staples, but these cash crops were mainly confined to the north-western provinces and were in the main peasant crops requiring labour-intensive methods of cultivation. This may explain why Confino's nobleman did not switch over to crops which gave a better return.

Then there was the question of capital shortage, not only of capital for investment – though this was serious enough – but of short-term working capital. The noble landlord, like the peasant, could not afford to wait; he was often forced to sell in the glutted autumn market because he was pressed for cash, because he had incurred unavoidable debts arising from the fact that his needs had to be satisfied all year round while his income was seasonal, and there were no commercial banks to finance him.

In the circumstances it seems quite reasonable that he was conservative in his habits, avoided risks, and, if he expanded at all, preferred to buy more land, usually more fertile land beyond the Volga or in the south which he could buy cheaply, as did Aksakov's father. It made good economic sense to transfer agricultural labour from land with poor yields to new areas where it yielded more abundantly. That Russian landowners succeeded in substantially increasing the grain supply became evident at the end of the Napoleonic Wars, more precisely from the 1820s, when they found themselves producing more grain than they could dispose of, despite increased export *via* the new Black Sea ports and improved canal facilities under Alexander I.

The preference for labour services as against money rents, except where special circumstances favoured the latter, also made good economic sense. Though the serf worker was not very willing, under supervision he had willy-nilly to carry out the tasks assigned to him. Income from *obrok* paying serfs was much less certain. A peasant had a million reasons for not paying his rent or for not paying it promptly; he certainly did not pay if his harvest failed, or if he suffered from fire or cattle disease – he would even ask the landlord for a subsidy. The landlord's costs on an estate on *obrok* could be substantial too; he might have to give the peasants seeds, provide them with cattle, forgo rents, and wipe out arrears.

The most important factor which militated against money rents was the difficulty which the peasant encountered in trying to obtain cash for the payment of rents if agriculture was his sole source of income. It was rarely possible for a peasant to command a high price for his surplus, for he was in the power of the local merchant, who could dictate the price. Though often with difficulty, the estate owner could nevertheless obtain a better price not only because he was selling larger quantities but also because, having at his disposal the cartage services of his serfs, he could by-pass the local peddler and sell to a larger merchant in the city. Haxthausen had this in mind when he said that the plight of Russian landowners would have been worse still if it had not been for 'serfage'.

Finally, if the structure of demesne farming had the effect of stifling entrepreneurial initiative, how is one to explain the industrial activity of the nobles? Haxthausen tells us that they were quick enough to note that it was more profitable to pay their serf workers a wage rather than treat factory work as a form of labour services. They showed considerable enterprise in developing the sugar beet industry at first in Kursk province and then in the Ukraine, where it became entre-preneurship *par excellence* though based entirely on serf labour.

Confino's excellent study, scholarly and thought provoking, has provided one set of factors which shaped the economic decisions of the Russian landowning class; another set might be provided by analysing the overall economic situation which faced the Russian agricultural producer during the period under consideration.

THE SPECTRE OF SERFDOM

Soviet historians tend to look upon the reign of Nicholas I as a period of crisis, a period during which the development of 'productive forces' came into conflict with the dominant system of sociopolitical and legal relationships. On the whole there seems to be a consensus of opinion on this point, and the difference between individual historians is not one of principle but of diagnosis of symptoms. The juxtaposition of the evidence adduced by individual historians, and occasionally by one and the same historian, discloses much confusion and much loose thinking. N. S. Kinyapina sees government promotion of industry as a way out of the dilemma facing the government of Nicholas in that it did not entail tampering with serf ownership and created opportunities for strengthening the national economy which was stagnating under serfdom.[18] The very evidence of progress which

Strumilin classifies as an industrial revolution is quoted by other historians as symptoms of the dissolution of the dominant 'feudal system', because of the incompatibility of these changes with the system. Strumilin himself, while amassing data showing the unprecedented and, according to him, unsurpassed rates of technological change, of the value of output and of effective purchasing power of the population, still talks of the constraints imposed by serfdom on the consumer market and on the productivity of labour.

As in Fuhrmann's book serfdom is the spectre which haunts the economic historian of Russia. Even such brilliant scholars as Tugan-Baranovsky and Professor A. Gerschenkron see in it, in the last instance, the basic constraint upon Russia's economic development. This view seems to go logically hand in hand with a tendency to ascribe the relatively slow pace of economic change in the first two and one-half decades after emancipation to the inadequate provisions of the Act of 1861.

This preoccupation with serfdom as the cause of economic retardation has its origin in the common cultural heritage of past and present historians and, as Alfred A. Skerpan shows in an essay 'National Economy and Emancipation', goes back to the basic teachings of the father of political economy on the concept of labour.[14] Skerpan discusses the evolution of Adam Smith's concept in Russian thought under the influence of the teachings of other Western European political economists and of specifically Russian conditions. On the eve of the emancipation, Russian concepts of the economic effect of serf labour had crystallised into three basic propositions. It was held that serfdom inhibited economic growth by restricting the supply of labour, by impeding the expansion of a consumer market, and by the low productivity of compulsory labour.

Skerpan discusses each proposition in turn, dismissing them all as fallacious. But as the intelligentsia and, in part also, the government believed them to be true, these propositions affected the general expectations of the benefits to be derived from the abolition of serfdom. However, as the emancipation was taking shape and as finally enacted, a basic contradiction emerged between the concept of the desirability of free labour and the concern for peasant security of tenure, between the supply of labour to landlords and the fear of a proletariat. Not only the government but liberals and reformers like Chicherin, Vernadsky and Kavelin shared some of this concern. In the actual provisions of the Emancipation Act Skerpan says it also seemed as if a 'free' cheap labour force was precisely what the government sought to avoid. Skerpan concludes that, among the motives of emancipation, the economic one of furthering economic power by freeing labour was not consistently followed. However, he argues that the economic aim was frustrated not because of the inadequacy of the final provisions of the Act 'but because serfdom as constituted was not a drag on the national economy'.[15]

3 The state peasants under Nicholas I*

It is customary to look on mid-nineteenth-century Russia as a serf-owning country *par excellence*. About 40 per cent of the rural population, which still formed over 90 per cent of the total population in 1858, were the serfs of private landowners, and it cannot be denied that the persistence of serfdom, particularly in the harsh form which it took, had left an indelible imprint on every aspect of Russian life. Nor can it be denied that serfdom was bound to some extent to affect agriculture, which remained the most important sector of the country's economy, and with it in the last resort Russia's ability to maintain her status as a great power.[1] But it is very often overlooked that the state or Crown peasants were practically as numerous as the serfs of private landowners and that like the serfs they constituted approximately 40 per cent of the rural population and 37·5 per cent of the total population.[2] Novelists and story writers have immortalised the master–serf relationship in the countryside under Nicholas I. But the state peasants by contrast received relatively little attention, and in so far as the history books have considered them, it has only been in the sense of recognising the formal distinction between serfs of private landowners and serfs of the state.

The state peasants attracted considerable official interest in Nicholas I's reign and became a focus of the government's legislative activity. In 1836 the Tsar entrusted N. D. Kiselyov with the task of reforming their position, and in the process of preparing his reform, Kiselyov accumulated a wealth of material which throws light on every aspect of their life. This provides the basis for examining the rights, duties and conditions of the state peasants before and after Kiselyov's reform and for assessing their place and influence upon the so-called 'serf economy' of mid-nineteenth-century Russia.

By introducing the poll tax Peter the Great combined various sections of the Russian peasantry into a juridically fairly uniform group. By

* From the *Slavonic and East European Review*, vol. XXXVII June, 1959. Reprinted by permission.

another fiscal measure imposing an additional tax of 40 kopeks on specified groups of peasants whose common characteristic was that they had no other master but the state, he drew a distinction between these 'state peasants' and peasants belonging to private landlords, monasteries, and the imperial family.[3] In 1724 when Peter introduced his new legislation these state peasants numbered over a million males and accounted for 19 per cent of all male peasants.[4] As the Tsar enumerated them, they can be divided into four main groups.

The most important were the 'black ploughing peasants of Northern Pomor'ye'. These were heirs of the formerly free peasants of mediaeval Russia whose land, in the course of time and with the growing power of the princes, had begun to be looked upon as 'black', i.e. as belonging to the prince in his capacity as the bearer of state power.[5] Closely connected with and descending from them were the *polovniki* who rented land on the basis of written contracts either from fellow peasants or from townsmen in return for a share of the harvest.[6] A second group consisted of 'the *odnodvortsy* of the southern provinces'. These were the descendants of petty service men who had been granted a fief (*sluzhiloye pomest'ye*) on what had once been Muscovy's southern frontier which they had to defend against the inroads of the Astrakhan and Crimean Tartars. When the army was reorganised on a regular basis, all service men whose sphere of activity and mode of life resembled those of the peasants rather than of the gentry were ordered to pay the poll tax and subsequently an additional 40 kopek tax known as *obrok*. But their original quasi-gentry status was reflected in their right to own a few serfs and to effect transactions in land which subsequent legislation limited to sales of land to other *odnodvortsy*. Their numbers greatly increased in the course of the eighteenth and at the beginning of the nineteenth century with the dissolution of the land militia and the regiments of the 'ploughing soldiers of the Trans-Volga and southern Ural districts and of the South', and with the gradual withdrawal of the privileges of the 'Little Russian Cossacks'.[7] A third group comprised 'the *yasak* paying Tartars' who included the various nationalities of the middle Volga area such as Tartars, Chuvashes, Komis, and Mordvians, whom Muscovy had conquered in the fifteenth and sixteenth centuries. The majority of them made a living as hunters and paid a tax in furs known as *yasak*. They also owed minor labour services to the state. The fourth group covered the 'agricultural people of Siberia'. These were peasants cultivating a specified portion of their land directly on behalf of the state for the maintenance of the Siberian garrisons which could not be maintained from the centre owing to the distances involved. They were under the supervision of bailiffs acquainted with agriculture.[8]

At the time of Catherine II's accession the state peasants numbered nearly 3 million and accounted for 40 per cent of all male peasants.[9] In 1764, following on the secularisation of ecclesiastical estates, their numbers were further increased by the addition of a very substantial group of peasants who lived on these estates and were known as 'economic' peasants. Later the proportion of state peasants showed some decline mainly as a result of the grants of state land which Catherine and Paul both made to their favourites.[10] But their absolute numbers continued to increase chiefly in connection with Russia's territorial expansion. The tenants on the Crown domains in Estonia, Livonia, and Courland, and on the territories acquired in the three partitions of Poland, and the peasants on the estates of the former Georgian rulers and Tartar Khans of Trans-Caucasia all came to be labelled and administered as state peasants. In 1822 the former Jesuit estates in Poland and the confiscated estates of Polish nobles and Catholic monasteries also began to be administered as state land. Finally, after the Polish rising of 1831 Nicholas I tried to make the patriotic petty *szlachta* ineffective by ordering that unless they could produce written documentary evidence of their noble origin they should be degraded to the status of the '*odnodvortsy* of the western provinces'. Soon afterwards, he ordered such *odnodvortsy* to be transferred to the northern Caucasus where they were settled on state land and ordered to pay *obrok* like the other state peasants.[11] During the first half of the nineteenth century the number of state peasants also increased through the entry into their ranks of freed serfs who either chose or were ordered to become state peasants when given their freedom. When the eighth census was taken in 1835 the proportion of state peasants to the total number of peasants was 34 per cent. At the tenth census in 1858 it had again risen to 40 per cent.[12]

The common characteristic of all the various groups of 'state peasants' many of which retained peculiarities indicative of their origin, was the fact that they 'had no other master but the state', as Peter had stated in his legislation. It was not till the 1830s however that official documents began to use the term 'state peasants' exclusively in this broad sense. Previously they had interpreted the term to apply either in the narrowest sense to the black ploughing peasants of Pomor'ye only or to tenants of state domains administered by a special department of the treasury.[13] By 1836 the black ploughing peasants of Pomor'ye, the former economic peasants, and the *yasak* paying peoples accounted for roughly 64 per cent of all state peasants. The descendants of petty service men and Cossacks made up another 25 per cent, while the Crown peasants of the Polish and Baltic provinces accounted for over 8 per cent.

Geographically the largest numbers of state peasants were to be found in areas where gentry landownership either never developed as in the north or developed very late as in the Ural region and the Ukraine; where the multinational *yasak* paying peoples had been concentrated as in the Urals and the middle Volga area; and where the southern frontier of the Muscovite state had once run and the descendants of the *odnodvortsy* and the Ukrainian Cossacks had settled in large groups. In the outlying northern, eastern, and south-eastern provinces, they constituted the predominant proportion of the peasant population. But they also existed in fairly large numbers in practically every *guberniya* of European Russia. In 1835 they represented an absolute majority (i.e. over 50 per cent of the total population in fourteen out of fifty-three *guberniyas*, covering substantial parts of the black earth region of the central provinces, the middle Volga area, and the southern Ukraine. In relation to the rest of the peasants they were in an absolute majority in twenty-one out of fifty *guberniyas*, many of which were in the black earth region of the centre.[14]

Thus the sheer numbers and wide distribution of the state peasants over extensive areas of the Russian empire would suggest their importance in the country's economic life.

What was the legal status of the state peasants and what justification was there for regarding them as 'serfs of the state'?

When M. M. Speransky was serving as governor-general of the province of Perm and later of Siberia, he noted that every *pomeshchik* serf wished to become a state peasant. The Code of Laws of 1832 defined the state peasants as 'free rural dwellers'. Unlike serfs, they had civil and political rights. In common with other free classes they took the oath at the accession of a new Tsar. They were represented at consultative assemblies on the rare occasion when these assemblies met. Thus they took part in the *Sobor* of 1613 and in the abortive legislative commission of Catherine II. They had personal and property rights and could undertake all manner of financial commitments. They could buy land, though not estates with serfs. Their children could enter universities. They could change their place of residence, become townspeople, and renounce their peasant status. Since 1802 they had even enjoyed the politically very significant right of inheriting the property of a convicted person, a right granted to the gentry in the *Zhalovannaya Gramota Dvoryanstvu* of 1785.[15] Yet state peasants were known to say of themselves: 'we are not free, we belong to the state.'

There are a number of reasons for this contrast between the status of the state peasants as reflected in the Code of Laws and the common view that they were serfs of the state. In the second half of the 18th century the peasants laboured under very real legal disabilities, and Semevsky's account of their condition at this time in his *Krest'yane v tsarstvovaniye Imperatritsy Yekateriny II*, published between 1901 and 1903, has influenced all subsequent writing and thinking about their status even in later periods. Most of the legal disabilities from which they suffered were removed during the first quarter of the nineteenth century, and the legislation improving their status was later incorporated in the Code of Laws. But the freedom which they enjoyed was very precarious in the sense that the Code of Laws contained not a single clause which guaranteed it. Both Catherine II and Alexander I entertained the idea of issuing a *Zhalovannaya Gramota* to the state peasants on the model of those issued to the gentry and the towns; but nothing came of it. In practice Catherine and Paul I by their lavish grants of state lands to court favourites turned 'free rural dwellers' into *pomeshchik* serfs overnight. Though Alexander I made a solemn promise to discontinue this practice, 'free' state peasants were summarily turned into members of military colonies or, to suit administrative convenience, into *udel* peasants, i.e. into serfs of the Imperial family. During Nicholas I's reign, in the course of implementing a reform of *udel* estates which involved transfers of state peasants under the *udel* administration, the minister of the interior overheard a state peasant say that he was not free and belonged to the state. In view of what was happening at the time such a remark was hardly surprising. But it is well known that the state peasants resisted these transfers tooth and nail, and as the *udel* peasants were often better provided for economically than the state peasants, this resistance by the state peasants suggests that they must have been fully aware of a difference in principle between themselves and the *pomeshchik* and *udel* serfs.[10]

Another reason for the contradictory interpretations of the status of the state peasants was the dual relationship which existed between them and the state. On the one hand the state peasant faced the state in common with other sections of the peasantry and townsmen as a taxpayer and recruit to the army. On the other hand he also faced the state as a tenant paying a rent known as *obrok* for the use of state land. In the first capacity the state peasants like other rural and urban taxpayers were collectively responsible through their communes for the prompt payment of taxes and the provision of recruits; and this collective responsibility effectively limited the freedom of the individual state peasant by making the commune subject him to various restrictions designed to ensure that it could meet the collective liability towards the state. Even in their other capacity as rent paying tenants the state peasants were subject in practice to conditions which caused

confusion about their status. Though the additional tax which Peter
the Great had imposed on the state peasants as distinct from other
sections of the peasantry was conceived as a rent, no attempt was made
until the end of the eighteenth century to connect it even approximately
with the value of the land held. Moreover it was levied per soul like the
poll tax; and neither the peasants nor most of the treasury officials
who prepared the taxation lists can have been very conscious of a
difference in principle between what the peasants had to pay the state
as taxpayers and what they paid it as tenants. The collective responsibility which applied to the payment of taxes also applied to the payment of rent and could entail similar legal disabilities, and so an
impression could be gathered that the state peasant had his freedom
restricted not only in his capacity as a taxpayer to the state but equally
as a tenant of the state. N. M. Druzhinin had this in mind when he
wrote that 'the gentry [governed] state regarded them [i.e. state
peasants] as feudally dependent rent-payers approximating to the
pomeshchik serfs.'[17]

Difficulties also arose from the confusion between ownership of
land and possession of land. The state peasants were aware of their
status as tenants. But ample evidence exists to show that they acknow-
ledged their tenant status in a very special way. While they vaguely
recognised the state's ultimate right to all the land in their possession,
as in the phrase *zemlya gosudaryeva no nashego vladeniya*, they often
treated the land as their own by selling, bequeathing, dividing and
exchanging it. This was particularly widespread among the black
ploughing peasants of Pomor'ye and among the *odnodvortsy*. The
government tried to check these practices by a series of laws, while
the local authorities tried to instil into the peasants the idea that the
land which they lived on was the state's and that they must not call
state land their own. But the very fact that the laws had to be repeated
at intervals suggests that they were not respected. In practice the
government was often led to recognise the *de facto* changes in land
holding which resulted from private transactions among state peasants,
particularly those among the black ploughing peasants. It even came to
recognise the right of *odnodvortsy* to sell land, though only to other
odnodvortsy. The traditions of earlier days when colonists could take
unimpeded possession of vast tracts of frontier land still held in the
eighteenth century; and in the last resort the government nearly always
recognised the rights of illegal emigrants who set up farms on state land
even in the nineteenth century. The instructions which Kiselyov gave
to his inspectors in the 1830s urging them to respect ancient rights to
holdings of state land and to clearings in state forests would indicate
that at that time the Russian government still recognised the *pravo*

truda, i.e. the right to the land by virtue of the accumulated labour put into it over a long period of time.[18] Among Russian statesmen there was no clear conception even in principle of what state ownership involved. Men like Speransky and Kankrin were inclined to limit the rights of the state to those of ultimate ownership of the properties administered by a state department and to admit the right of peasant communes to direct ownership of arable land, pastures, meadows, etc., by virtue of the labour which they expended on their cultivation.

This vagueness of interpretation on both sides was workable in practice because most state peasants held and cultivated their land in communes. As Prince Kurakin expressed it in another connection, while land was in communal ownership the individual peasant was only a *khozyain*; as soon however as the holding became the individual property of a peasant it turned him into a *gospodin*. Kurakin was concerned about the political implications of a change of this kind mainly on account of the repurcussions which it was likely to have on *pomeshchik* serfs; but the economic consequences could have been equally important. This explains why transactions in land were more developed among the peasants of Pomor'ye and the *odnodvortsy* where landholding was by family. Finally, the abundance of land, particularly in the outlying provinces, coupled with the relative sparseness of the population had always meant that on the whole the state was never sufficiently hard pressed for land to assert its claims to the land settled by state peasants.[19]

Consequently the power of the landlord state over its tenants was never exercised in either the economic or the legal sphere with as much force as that of the *pomeshchik* over his tenants. Even at worst the state peasants never sank to the condition of chattels like *pomeshchik* serfs. Moreover, most of them paid a money rent which by its nature gave them much greater freedom from indirect pressure. By contrast *pomeshchik* serfs to the extent of 70 per cent on the eve of the emancipation owed labour services to their masters.[20]

All state peasants throughout the empire paid a rent in money except about 8 per cent living in the former Polish and Swedish districts where rents in labour and kind had been maintained. The labour services of the ploughing peasants of Siberia were abolished in 1769 and their rents in kind towards the end of the century. When first imposed by Peter the money rent amounted to 40 kopeks. It was increased to 1 rouble in 1760, was doubled in 1768, and was raised to 3 roubles in 1783. By the end of the eighteenth century, with the development of industry in certain areas and the emergence of areas of agricultural deficiency, four different grades of *obrok* existed; and the rate of the tax was raised in all grades and ranged from 5 roubles in the highest grade to 3½ roubles in the lowest grade. Three further increases in the *obrok* were made in the first quarter of the nineteenth century, and the last in 1823 was accompanied by an upgrading of *guberniyas*. The rates fixed in 1823, which varied from 5½ roubles in the lowest grade to 10 roubles in the highest, were maintained till Kiselyov's reform in 1838.[21]

The poll tax increased concurrently. But while the *obrok* was only about half as much as the poll tax in Peter's day, the position was reversed later on, and the *obrok* became about two and one-half to three times as high as the poll tax. Though the depreciation of the currency made the effective rise much less significant than the figures themselves would suggest, the absolute increase was still substantial. But the rents which the serfs were obliged to pay to their masters increased at a much higher rate than the rents of the state peasants, especially in industrial areas.[22]

In addition to paying poll tax, the state peasants were under the obligation to supply recruits. For this purpose special recruiting districts were formed, each comprising 1000 male peasants and cutting across the natural and administrative units. All males between the ages of twenty and thirty-five were liable and performed the obligation in turn. A great deal of insecurity attached to the system because no one knew exactly when he might be called up. The larger families contributed first, and this led to the subdivision of families, which was disastrous from the economic point of view. In theory five recruits a year were due from each district; but in fact seven a year were provided during the first half of the century. The communes also had to pay a tax for the outfitting of recruits. Speransky put the expense incurred on each recruit at over 50 roubles, and as no fewer than 94 levies took place between 1725 and 1830, it is clear how heavy the obligation to supply recruits must have been.[23]

These obligations towards the state were supplemented by a variety of local taxes and dues for the maintenance of roads and bridges, and the building, heating and lighting of barracks. They were collected every three years from the taxpaying population of the *guberniya*. Finally there were the *mir* (i.e. communal) taxes.

The collection of taxes was facilitated by a system of collective responsibility (*krugovaya poruka*) covering the village as a whole. It became obligatory under a law of 1769 and was a convenient administrative device for helping the treasury to collect taxes promptly. It made the elected officers of the communes responsible for collecting taxes from the individual peasant and so relieved the treasury of the need to maintain direct contact with him. If the officers of the commune failed to collect the taxes they were liable to arrest. But by 1838 this liability was no longer strictly enforced. Among other things, collective responsibility for taxes helped to moderate the injustice and inequality of taxation per head which made poor and rich pay exactly the same amount. The commune as a whole provided the total sum due in taxes from its individual members and reapportioned and collected it not according to heads but according to means.

A review of the duties of the state peasants must take into account not only the letter of the law where it existed but the practice and methods actually in use; not only the institutions but the people who worked them. When Kiselyov ordered a general survey and examination of the conditions of the state peasants in 1836, the resulting picture was very grim indeed. The communal taxes offered most scope for unlawful action. Officially the amounts payable were determined by the communal assembly and ratified by the local treasury office (*kazyonnaya palata*). But in practice assembly decisions and official sanction were very often missing, and the money was used to enrich the provincial and district officials and the elected head and officers of the *volost'* and the *mir*. The inspector of the Yaroslav *guberniya* collected evidence of an infinite number of petty dues totalling more than the whole poll tax. In so far as expenditure sheets were kept at all, some of those which have been preserved show that much money went to procure vodka for various official meetings and for the entertainment of *guberniya* officials visiting the *mir*.

In principle taxes were distributed among the various households according to their means, and account was taken not only of the size of the allotment but also of the quality of arable and other land and its distance from the village. But in practice the matter was arbitrarily decided more often than not by a small group of influential householders, and nothing was set down in writing. At the end of the year a district official signed the decision on tax allocation in the name of the peasantry as a whole. Unintentional mistakes arising from the very low educational standards of officials were accompanied by deliberate exploitation of the ignorance of most of the peasants and the lack of proper supervision by the central government. A great many abuses have been recorded in connection with military recruitings. Baron Haxthausen, who travelled all over Russia in the 1840s, says that the few influential householders and lower officials, collectively known as *miroyedy* ('devourers of the commune'), were guilty of the most corrupt proceedings on these occasions; to control them was almost impossible. In his report to Nicholas I in 1850 Kiselyov wrote as follows : 'Two terms which have become rooted in our official terminology . . . best explain conditions . . . : "devourers of the commune" and "faked expenditure". The "devourers of the commune" sapped all the resources of the peasants for their personal benefit, while "faked expenditure" concealed all the illegal activities of the villagers'.[24]

The evidence of Kiselyov's inspectors shows that the so-called self-government of the state peasants was very different from the ideal picture drawn by the Slavophils, though all reports seem agreed that in the north and among the dissenters justice, honesty and equality were maintained. The _mir_ assemblies were held outside public houses; vodka flowed freely, and votes were bought for spirits or small sums of money. As a rule the wealthy peasants rarely stood for election themselves; they were too busy in their farms or businesses and on the whole avoided direct responsibility towards the authorities. What they did was to put up as candidates impoverished peasants likely to be pliable instruments in their hands. As the position of an elected _mir_ officer carried considerable advantages and scope for exercising power, it often happened that men of rather low moral and intellectual standards filled these positions. The scribe was often the only literate person in the state village and one of its most important members in consequence. But this did not mean that his moral standards were any the higher.

This state of affairs was one of the most important reasons for the frequently wretched condition of the state peasant and explains why he was commonly looked upon as a serf. Though a free man in law, he was at the same time a victim of administrative oppression and abuse which often made it impossible for him to use his freedom in the way he desired. In this respect he was often even worse off than the _pomeshchik_ serf, especially the serf of a big landowner. Haxthausen noted that 'serfs or peasants belonging to landowners have more protection and security against the oppression, impositions, and maltreatment of officials than the peasants of the Crown'.[25]

At all levels of the administration the overriding and almost exclusive concern of the authorities, whether appointed or elected, was to meet the fiscal demands of the treasury. Whatever may have been the intentions of Paul I, who sanctioned peasant self-government by law in 1797, the elected heads of _mir_ or _volost'_ were little more than fiscal agents and the peasants were mainly taxpayers. It was this stress on fiscal needs in the government's policy towards the state peasants which accounted for their desperate condition in the first quarter of the nineteenth century. What was needed were institutions which would really be concerned with the welfare of the peasants and which would be strong enough to protect them against oppression and exploitation and authoritative enough to make and keep the central government alive to their needs.[26]

In the *volost'* which was an administrative unit established by Paul I comprising 3000 heads, the state peasants were under dual subordination, and for both sets of authorities concerned the administration of the peasants was only a side issue. In economic matters the *volost'* came under the economic department of the *kazyonnaya palata*, which had been set up in 1775. Not only was it very remote, but it consisted of only one councillor who dealt with a variety of problems in addition to the state peasants. In police and judicial matters the *volost'* was subordinated to a 'lower court', which may have been less remote geographically but was no closer in interest. It was run by the gentry and the *ispravnik*, who headed it, was elected by and from among the gentry. In the event of clashes between state and *pomeshchik* peasants he naturally tended to take the side of those to whom he owed his office. In so far as the more educated members of the nobility resided in the provinces at all, they tended to keep out of local politics, and their aloofness put the election of *ispravniki* in the hands of the most uncultivated and corrupt elements among them. This meant that elections went in favour of the worst kind of people. The election of the *ispravnik* was just a mockery: he literally 'bought his office' either by bribes or by flattery and used it to obtain money and other advantages. The state peasant was his easiest prey because he had no one to turn to. Speransky felt that the state peasants were sometimes no better off than serfs under a master: the *ispravnik* was the same person as the *pomeshchik* except that he was appointed for three years only and that a petition could be filed against him.[27]

At the highest administrative level, the state peasants were the responsibility of a department of the finance ministry. Its sole aim was the collection of revenue, and it was interested in the state peasants only as taxpayers. It did not even know the amount of land and the number of peasants under its administration. It had no control over or knowledge of peasant movements to new areas; and thousands of peasant families who had long since resettled continued to be taxed in their old place of residence and were unknown in their new homes. In 1837 in the Kursk *guberniya* alone over 400,000 roubles were counted as tax arrears due from people who had long left the area.[28]

This lack of proper care and control had its repercussions not only on the peasants, who became impoverished, but eventually on the treasury's revenue from state domains as well. It was a principle of government policy that a state peasant should have an allotment of a minimum of fifteen *desyatinas*, which was subsequently reduced to eight *desyatinas*, and even to five *desyatinas* in the most densely populated regions. But although there were ample reserves of land and certain peasants held over twenty *desyatinas*, some in practice held no more than two *desyatinas*, or even one or less. Some peasants had no land at all and had to rent it from private owners. In view of this it is not surprising that tax arrears accumulated almost as fast as they were remitted. The authorities entrusted with the administration of state peasants who concentrated so zealously on the one function of collecting taxes thus found themselves failing in precisely this respect.[29]

Private landowners took advantage of the careless attitude of the authorities to seize large portions of state property, which also deprived the state of a source of income. In 1837, which was the first year for which Kiselyov's inspectors reported, over 500 *desyatinas* of land which private individuals had seized were under dispute. Peasants were short of timber while unauthorised persons were able to deplete state forests owing to lack of supervision. When draining their fields landowners in the west conducted the water into state forests and turned large tracts of them into morasses. In 1837 income from state forests was only about 604,000 roubles, while the estimated loss on them was over 4 million roubles.[30] Rentable assets such as state owned distilleries, etc. had no proper inventories and consequently yielded little income. The rent producing assets of the communes were similarly unknown, and the income which reached the state was only about 10 per cent of actual income.

As no fire insurance existed, whole villages might be turned into homeless beggars overnight. Grain reserves were also badly organised, and the government was forced to go to the help of state villages stricken by famine. One of the main scourges was drunkenness. As the gentry refused licences to sell spirits in privately owned villages, the farmers of the spirit monopoly centred their activity in the state villages. The result was that in fifteen *guberniyas* of Russia there was one public house to every 701 souls in the state village and one to every 2691 souls in privately owned villages.[31]

It is no wonder that in face of these facts about life among the state peasants Kiselyov began to feel very strongly that all reform must start with the establishment of a new administration. Without it even the noblest and best conceived measures for improving the general welfare of the peasant were bound to remain worthless.

Though Nicholas I was convinced of the evil of serfdom, he lacked the courage to force the emancipation of the serfs upon a gentry which still clung to its privileges. But he felt more free to tackle the reform of the state peasants as one facet of the peasant question in general and hoped in this way to give the gentry a lead. While desiring the abolition of serfdom, the Tsar and his advisers were somewhat apprehensive about the inevitable void which would be created if the *pomeshchiki* renounced the administrative functions over their serfs which they had been performing for good or evil for two centuries. If the government could prove to itself and the gentry that it was capable of establishing efficient administration and with it real prosperity for some twenty million peasants, it could look forward with more confidence to the day when the serf owner was no longer present to act as the state's agent in relation to the twenty million or so privately owned peasants.[32]

The significance of Kiselyov's reform of the state peasants can be understood only if it is looked on as the starting point for an eventual reorganisation of the conditions and status of the peasants in general. This explains why Kankrin, the finance minister, who tried to isolate the reform from the general peasant problem and treat it purely and simply as an administrative measure, had to make way for Kiselyov who served as chief of the fifth department of the Tsar's personal chancery and spent twenty years collecting information and discussing and studying all aspects of peasant problems. Using the military language to which he had grown accustomed, Nicholas I made Kiselyov 'the chief of staff of the peasant unit'.[33]

Kiselyov's original plan was to concentrate first on the economic side of the life of the state peasants and give priority to such problems as the provision of economically sufficient allotments, the transfer of taxation from souls to land, and the separation and protection of village forests. Problems associated with administration were put second, while problems concerned with raising revenue from the rent producing assets of the state were to come last. But Kiselyov's own travels through the country, his conversations with peasants, and the reports of his inspectors, all of whom he picked himself for their zeal and integrity, convinced him that although the question of economic change was urgent, the problem of administrative reform was more urgent still.

A novel idea underlay Kiselyov's new administration. The main duty of the new institutions was to improve the welfare of the state peasant and look after his interests independently of his relations with the treasury. At the top, the state peasants became the concern of a special ministry called the ministry of state domains (*gosudarstvennykh imushchestv*) with Kiselyov himself in charge of it. By this means the administration of state lands was separated from the finance ministry, which in itself was a clear indication that the fiscal interest was no longer to be the guiding principle in the administration's attitude to the state peasants. The new ministry implemented its policy locally through its *guberniya* offices (*palata gosudarstvennykh imushchestv*) and through captains and their assistants appointed to newly created units called *okrugi*. These coincided with one or more districts (*uyezdy*), which formed the general administrative subdivisions of the *guberniya*.

While the administrative organs between the ministry and the communes were bureaucratic in composition, the elective principle was retained in villages and *volosti*. The self-government of the village and *volost'* communes was preserved, but the field of their activity was more clearly defined and the composition and prerogatives of their assemblies were set out in detail and without equivocation. Subdivision of the village or *volost'* into sections for particular administrative purposes such as recruiting, etc. was forbidden. The number of souls comprising a *volost'* was doubled and in some cases even raised to 8000 provided it did not entail the incorporation of villages more than forty *versts* from the *volost'* centre. By enlarging the *volost'* in this way Kiselyov hoped to make the maintenance of the elected *volost'* organs less burdensome to the peasants. The village court, which was closer to the peasants and well acquainted with their laws and way of life, became obligatory and was no longer optional as before.[34]

Kiselyov's reform of the administration of the state peasants, like Paul I's reform of 1797, contained a strong element of paternalism springing from the conviction that the peasant needed guidance. The difference was that under Paul the administrative apparatus was not prepared for the task, and that the fiscal interests of the treasury still outweighed all other considerations in the official attitude towards the state peasants. The tasks which Kiselyov set for himself and his subordinates were also simple, specific, and realistic and very unlike the instructions which accompanied Paul's *ukaz* of 1797. In addition Kiselyov applied himself to his task with sincerity, enthusiasm, and energy and succeeded in imparting his attitude of mind to his various associates who were as far as possible chosen from men of the same mind as himself. Given the corruption and lack of integrity among Russian officialdom, this was not easy to achieve, and the human material on the spot as distinct from the centre was not always above reproach. But Kiselyov never hesitated to remove a man from his post, whatever his standing might be, if he found him guilty of abusing his authority. As he knew that low salaries were often the cause of dishonesty, he induced the Tsar to let him raise those paid to his subordinates.[35]

The new administrative organisation had its weaknesses. The most obvious was the great power of the purely administrative organs as distinct from the elected organs at the bottom. Another weakness was the possibility of conflict between the organs of the administration of state lands and those of the general state administration. The 'general supervision' over the functions of the *palaty* exercised by the governor-general was too imprecise not to be dangerous, especially in areas far removed from the centre of government. Herzen wrote that the 'power of the governor-general grows in direct proportion to the distance from St. Petersburg'. Whilst men like Tyufyayev as portrayed by Herzen could exercise 'general supervision' over the *guberniya* administration of state peasants, the auguries for their well being were not good.[36]

But for all its imperfections and inherent weaknesses the reform of the administration had something dynamic about it. The dynamism lay not only in the new principles underlying the reform but in the wholeheartedness with which the Tsar and Kiselyov and his associates set about implementing it. The strength of the new system lay in its precise definition. The duties of each office and official were defined as fully and as positively as possible. The peasant's personal and property rights as well as his duties were also clearly defined, and with them the measure of his responsibilities. Kiselyov emphasised most strongly that the state peasants were *not* serfs of the state, but a 'free rural estate' living on land belonging to the state. Though he was unable to get their rights confirmed by a special manifesto for fear that it might create a false impression among *pomeshchik* serfs, he achieved his aim in practice by putting a final end to transfers of state peasants under the *udel* administration. He also made the state peasant's freedom of movement and right to change his status much more of a reality than before. Moreover he established successful relations on this matter with the general administration.[37]

In the economic sphere, his reform aimed first of all at providing the peasant in the purely agricultural areas with an allotment whose produce would be sufficient to maintain him and cover his taxes. Where industry was the main source of income, the produce of the allotment should maintain the peasant while his taxes should come out of industrial earnings. If the land reserve in a given region was insufficient to meet these minimum requirements, industrial villages were to be transformed into towns, or if the region in question was an agricultural area the peasants were to be resettled.

All this involved detailed surveys of state land and the delimitation of boundaries, which meant in turn a very substantial increase in the number of surveyors. The task was enormous, and it presented Kiselyov and his assistants with very complicated issues. Large numbers of peasants officially entitled to allotments were in fact urban citizens. Great confusion also existed over the arrangement of holdings. More than eighty years had passed since the last general delimitation of boundaries, and the documents still in use to settle boundary disputes were hopelessly out of date. The intermingling of strips of *pomeshchik* land and of land held by state peasants was widespread. The same was true of joint fields. What Kiselyov did was to appoint special representatives for 'peaceful land delimitation'. They had to contend not only with *pomeshchik* opposition but also with the procrastination and indifference of the peasants themselves, especially of peasants who let their land instead of cultivating it and who engaged in industry or trade. Not surprisingly they found it impossible to eliminate intermingled strips entirely. But they achieved a great deal.[38]

The delimitation of boundaries disclosed many illegal seizures of state land by the gentry. Kiselyov and his officials gave the peasants effective help in claiming this land back and protecting themselves against similar seizures in the future. This was very significant for the subsequent success of Kiselyov's reform. For the first time the state peasants felt that 'it was possible to obtain relief from injustice' and that they could 'receive protection not only from the officers chosen by themselves but also from the minister and even from the emperor'.[39]

By 1856 more than 53 million *desyatinas* of land had been surveyed. Nearly two and one-half million *desyatinas* had been allocated from the government reserve to communes with insufficient land and half a million *desyatinas* to peasants who had previously been landless. About 170,000 male peasants had been transferred from areas where the allotment per soul was under five *desyatinas* to areas where they each received eight to fifteen *desyatinas*. In addition some 2 million *desyatinas* of state forests were made available in order to allow one *desyatina* of forest per head. Though Kiselyov very soon found out that the size of the allotment often bore little relation to the prosperity of the peasant since agriculture alone was rarely an adequate source of income, his policy left the state peasants better supplied with land than other sections of the peasantry. When the government extended the Emancipation Act to the state peasants in 1866, their allotments proved to be much larger than those of the former *pomeshchik* serfs and even than those of the former *udel* serfs. In some provinces their allotments were over three times as large. Even in the central agricultural region, where land shortages were notorious, the holdings of state peasants were about twice the size of those of *pomeshchik* serfs.[40]

The reform of the tax system was even more complicated than that of the land allotments. Kiselyov set himself the task of bringing taxes

as far as possible into balance with income from land and other pursuits. This could be achieved by transferring taxes from persons to
land and extending taxation to industrial incomes. Details of these
changes were worked out later after a survey had been started to
evaluate incomes received from agriculture and industry. The new
system was first tried out in two *guberniyas* only : St Petersburg, which
was a typically industrial *guberniya*, and Voronezh, which
was a typically agricultural one. By 1845 the tax per soul had been
converted into a land tax in six provinces and by 1851 in fourteen
provinces. By 1858 the process of conversion was nearly complete. The
documentary evidence available for the Moscow *guberniya* indicates
what a gigantic and involved undertaking it was; and the special commission for the evaluation of incomes must have shown considerable
resolution to be able to deal with so complex a problem in the face
of opposition from peasants and *guberniya* officials.[41]

Another feature of Kiselyov's tax reform was the substitution of a
general communal tax for the various *mir* and special taxes. It also
covered the new dues for delimitation of land, the maintenance of
schools, and the building up of a reserve of agricultural capital. In
this way Kiselyov aimed at ending the scope for exploitation of the
peasants by lower officials and unscrupulous officers of the *mir*. The
new taxes were fixed for fourteen years when a new assessment was
to be made. This was an obvious weakness, particularly as regards
incomes from industry which were subject to much fluctuation.[42] Haxthausen found that some peasants grumbled at first because their taxes
were somewhat increased; but 'when they found that the extortions of
the *ispravniks*, which far exceeded the direct taxes, ceased . . ., they
acquiesced.' Ivanov, who studied the Moscow *guberniya* where industrial incomes were fairly high and some opposition might have been
expected, found no opposition from the peasants on the substance of
the reform.[43]

Though the fiscal aspect of the reform took second place with
Kiselyov's administration, taxes from the state peasants flowed into
the treasury in larger amounts and more punctually than previously.
The administration had fairly wide powers to enforce prompt payment of taxes, including even the right to send insolvent taxpayers to
factories and use their earnings to meet tax arrears. But on the whole
Kiselyov's ministry relied mainly on a policy of improving the productivity of state properties and adjusting taxation to actual capacity to
pay. A comparison between the rents and dues of state peasants and
those of privately owned serfs in the Moscow *guberniya* shows very
clearly how infinitely lighter was the burden of the state peasants as
a result of Kiselyov's reform. In the 1850s state peasants paid 2·24

roubles per *desyatina* of land while serfs paid on an average 9·23 roubles per *desyatina*. In addition the serfs performed cartage duties and other services. Ivanov also noted that in the Moscow *guberniya* the tax reform, with its fairer distribution of taxes, not only lightened the disproportionate burden previously borne by the poorest elements but also assisted the accumulation of capital resources in the villages.[44]

Kiselyov also reformed recruiting practices. First he laid down that the call-up could take place only on the twentieth birthday, and that those not drafted were henceforth free from liability. Secondly recruitment by lot replaced the selection of recruits by the commune.[45]

Other measures of Kiselyov's new administration soon began to bear fruit. Some of them were designed to assure economic security in state villages by the rational organisation of the central and communal food reserves and seed reserves, the introduction of a mutual fire insurance scheme, the provision of help and advice of government architects in building and rebuilding villages, the supply of bricks from government kilns, and the setting up of kilns in state villages, etc.[46] Others tried to improve productivity and profitability by extending the cultivation of potatoes, tobacco and vines, introducing new breeds of cattle, creating model farms and studs, encouraging crafts and industries by means of exhibitions, setting up savings banks and mutual credit banks, and opening schools.[47]

The general lack of doctors and nurses made it hard to achieve much in the way of medical services. But in practice more was done than might have been expected. Attention was first of all given to the prevention of epidemics and particularly to mass inoculation against smallpox. Training in midwifery and a school for the training of medical auxiliaries were also established. At Kiselyov's prompting, clerical seminaries introduced the study of elementary medical science in order that future village priests would be able to spread it among their parishioners.[48]

Kiselyov further tried to raise the moral standards of the peasants. This aspect of peasant life was the least amenable of all to administrative intervention. But with his good practical sense he concentrated on practical problems. He encouraged the construction of churches, saw to the repair of old ones, and attended to the satisfaction of the clergy's material needs. At the same time he instructed his local officials to protect the peasants against the clergy's extortions. He asked officials and clergy to join in curbing drunkenness : the officials by restricting the issue of licences and the clergy by moral exhortation. He believed that the spread of general education would be the best means of all of improving the peasants. But he had to overcome a great deal of opposition because official circles mistrusted the whole principle of educating the common people. This meant that his achievements in this field implied official recognition of popular education and so represented the victory of a new principle.[49]

Kiselyov's reform was hardly two decades old when Alexander II emancipated the serfs and embarked on a series of administrative and other reforms. Not unnaturally these new developments overshadowed those in the state villages and explain why until recently historians have shown little interest in them. But in view of the tendency of Russian historians to discount the rôle of individuals in history, they have paid a perhaps unconscious tribute to the man responsible for the reform of the state peasants by passing it on to posterity as 'Kiselyov's Reform'. The pattern of administration which Kiselyov introduced may have owed much to Speransky. But it would have been totally inffective without Kiselyov's drive, energy, administrative talent, and above all his practical sense and capacity to strike a compromise. Without Kiselyov himself the reform would have remained one of those cleverly formulated abstractions of which Speransky was a master and which filled the files of the score or more committees which discussed the peasant question under Nicholas I. But in one vital point Kiselyov carried his realism too far. Originally he had planned to substitute family landholding for communal landholding in the belief that it would make for greater agricultural efficiency. But he subsequently thought that it would be too dangerous to interfere with a system which had become ingrained in the peasantry's whole mentality and manner of life through the practice of centuries. He was also afraid that the change he contemplated would lead to the appearance of a class of landless peasants which industry was not sufficiently developed to employ and which would consequently be dangerous. Finally he was apprehensive about its effect on the serfs. This was the greatest weakness of his reform, and it was a weakness which was reproduced in the Emancipation Act of 1861 and was always considered a major factor in the low productivity of Russian agriculture.[50]

It is doubtful whether Kiselyov's reform had the intended effect of inducing recalcitrant nobles to free their serfs, though ample evidence exists to show they feared and opposed the reform. On the other hand many links can be found between the reform and the Emancipation Act of 1861. Many members of the editing commissions of the act had been trained in Kiselyov's ministry and were imbued with his ideas. N. A. Milyutin was Kiselyov's nephew and owed his interest in the peasant problem to Kiselyov's influence. The idea of liberating the serfs *with* land also owed much to Kiselyov who was always very much to the fore in supporting legislation favouring the right of serfs to purchase land and other real estate, since 'to live, work and acquire without right of ownership is an unnatural condition'. Though Kiselyov himself did not directly participate in the preparation of the Emancipation Act, he was rightly considered one of its forerunners. 'All Russia is convinced', wrote Samarin, 'that the name of Count Kiselyov is connected with the idea which we serve.'[51]

On the eve of emancipation there thus existed in Russia a big group of smallholders who were almost as numerous as the serfs and who constituted a 'free estate' not only *de jure* but since Kiselyov's reform *de facto* as well.[52] Though they tended to be concentrated in the northern and eastern provinces of Russia, they could be found in fair proportions in nearly every Russian province. What still has to be considered is their importance in the country's economy.

All the evidence indicates that the state peasants played a relatively important part in industrial and commercial activities even in the eighteenth century when they had to contend with a multitude of restrictions. They were known to engage in non-agricultural activities over whole provinces of the non-black earth regions, and particularly in the provinces of Moscow, St Petersburg and Tver. Their commercial and industrial activities developed on a much larger scale during the first half of the nineteenth century, as is evident from eyewitness accounts and the number of passports and certificates issued. Even in *guberniyas* which had been the first to be drawn into industrial activities, privately owned serfs tended to engage in these activities on a much smaller scale than state peasants. The reason for this undoubtedly lay in the difference in the social and legal status of the two groups. Industrial activity required prolonged absence, and a privately-owned serf would need his master's sanction for this.[53] Where serfs and state peasants both engaged in activities not connected with the cultivation of their holdings, the state peasants were free to choose the occupations which were both more remunerative and less exacting. Haxthausen says that this also had its negative aspect. While landlords trained their young serfs for 'productive' occupations, state peasants, being their own masters, would in their thousands 'follow callings which held out the prospect of large earnings with the smallest trouble and labour . . . The strongest state peasants became *kalatchi*-carriers, pedlars, etc., whereas with the private serfs these are only the occupations of the weak and infirm.' Serfs also tended to seek earnings in the large centres only, partly because they paid much higher rents and needed a bigger margin of profit and partly because of the anonymity which a large centre afforded them. State peasants on the contrary often went to the smaller district towns, which was an advantage from the general economic point of view in that it helped to relieve the stagnation of these towns and promoted their growth. This was particularly noticeable in black earth *guberniyas* such as Kharkov which were unfavourably placed for outlets for their agricultural produce.[54]

The kind of activity in which the state peasants engaged differed from province to province according to geographical location and the opportunities available. They also varied with the seasons of the year : in winter when sledge tracks formed, many state peasants engaged in carrying trades. On the basis of official data Ivanov has established for the *guberniya* of Moscow that in 1848–50 about 67,000 state peasants engaged in 'industrial activities', about 37 per cent of them as factory workers, and 26 per cent as craftsmen. A further 11 per cent were engaged in the carrying trades; about 8 per cent owned industrial and commercial establishments; 8 per cent were in service; 7·21 per cent were manual labourers; and about 2 per cent were employed in local government. On the whole the 1840s and 1850s saw much greater mobility among the state peasants and longer periods of absence.[55]

Many state peasants were peasants in name only and had lived for long periods in the towns. But they continued to be classed as members of the rural communities partly through inertia, partly because the title of 'free rural dweller' was more attractive, and partly because the commune insisted on it. Haxthausen met a rich merchant living permanently at Ustyug with his wife and family who retained his membership in the commune and paid a rent for land which he did not cultivate because otherwise 'he had no secure position in life'. He also visited a village near Arzamas where :

> about 500 members of the commune are always absent with passports . . . some remain away ten or fifteen years, others establish themselves permanently in various towns never returning to their homes; they do not however cease to belong to the Commune, but pay their taxes here, and retain their houses, gardens and communal rights which they let out or deliver over to some other persons.[56]

Thus the number of state peasants who in reality became members of other classes was much larger than the recorded figures would indicate. According to official data for the years 1838–45, about 17,000 peasants joined the citizen class (*meshchane*) and the guilds; 6345 took out certificates as 'trading peasants'; and 441 joined the learned professions, 785 the clergy, and 2868 the various services. After 1845, when Kiselyov's new ministry was established, this social and geographical mobility increased.[57]

The better opportunities for earning and the relatively low rents of the state peasants gave them greater possibilities of accumulating capital. This was reflected in the land purchases which they made after the coming into force of a law of 1801 sanctioning such purchases. Most of the capital required came from industrial earnings.[58] The relatively large proportion of state peasants who took part in exhibitions organised by the ministry of state domains and the number of their exhibits and of the prizes awarded to them would also indicate their greater productivity and interest in agricultural improvements.[59]

But even when allowance is made for a somewhat higher degree of prosperity among the state peasants and for their greater role in industrial and commercial activity, the impression still remains that their contribution to the economy as a whole was singularly ineffective in relation to their numbers. In agriculture, except for a few insignificant improvements, their techniques remained primitive and their yields low. Even in areas where they were in an overwhelming majority, they achieved on the whole no major economic advances. From a purely economic point of view their activities were not essentially different from those of the serfs paying money rents, who represented about 28 per cent of all privately owned serfs. Though these serfs were sometimes victimised, as for example the wealthy trading serfs from Arzamas, and until 1835 could be recalled from their urban employment by their masters, it happened rarely on the whole because the *pomeshchiki* were unlikely to kill the goose which laid the golden eggs. Moreover, in areas where non-agricultural activities developed on a large scale, the serfs enjoyed a freedom which was very real and could show very successful opposition to masters who tried to interfere with their trade.[60]

On the whole all the evidence points to a very low level of agricultural incomes in Russia in the 1840s. Kiselyov noted that income from agriculture was nowhere sufficient to maintain the peasant and pay his taxes except in the immediate vicinity of large towns. He also noted that state peasants with very large holdings in the black earth region were often poorer than peasants who had very small holdings and poor soil but who were closer to large urban centres and important river routes. Haxthausen observed that income from agriculture was so low that 'no one will invest capital in improved methods of cultivation.' This applied also to estate farming. 'The consequence is', he went on, 'that agriculture in all its branches is prosecuted without energy and retrogrades instead of advancing. This would be still more the case if in many districts serfage did not come to its aid.'[61] It is not surprising therefore that the gentry nowhere showed any inclination to dispense with serfdom. Even the peasants really devoted their energies to the land only in areas which offered no other outlets for their labour. Elsewhere they resorted on a large scale to every available opportunity for other kinds of earnings.

But the crux of the matter was that opportunities for non-agricultural earnings were limited. Russia was not backward because serf relations dominated her economy; it was her backwardness which made serf relations persist. Serfdom was a symptom not the cause of the slowness of Russia's economic growth until the 1850s. This is not the place to enter into the very complex reasons for Russia's backwardness. Haxthausen put his finger on one of them when he wrote :

> Russia – an immense plain, whose best districts in the interior are at a great distance from the sea, whose navigable rivers are shut up three-fourths of the year, whose high-roads are impassable during the rains, which possesses no paved roads, and in which railways are hardly contemplated – requires improved means of communication more than any other country. Without it she is a colossal, unwieldy giant, whose hands and feet are tied . . . The greatest requirement of Russia is improved and suitable means of communication.[62]

The serf problem had bedevilled political and social thought in Russia for nearly three-quarters of a century. It created unbearable tensions in all spheres of life and endangered the very safety of the state. From these standpoints the abolition of serfdom was long overdue. But the commonly accepted view that it was the panacea for the economic ills of the country would appear to need basic revision.

4 Russian financial policy and the gold standard at the end of the nineteenth century*

Ever since Russia had attained the status of a great power in the eighteenth century the military requirements for the maintenance of that position imposed on the Russian treasury a task of a magnitude disproportionate to the largely natural economy of the country and the poverty of its people. This imbalance led to chronic budgetary deficits, despite increased taxation, and recourse to the printing press and foreign loans. It was no accident that both Russia's foreign indebtedness and the regime of paper money had their beginnings under Catherine II, whose reign marked Russia's advent as a great power.[1] As foreign borrowing was not always possible, the financial strain imposed by an active foreign policy was frequently reflected in inflation and the squeezing out of circulation of metallic currency. Since the first issue of roubles-assignats in 1768 in connection with the first Turkish war, the volume of assignats issued had been swollen by the second Turkish war, the wars with Sweden, Poland and Persia under Catherine II, the Italian campaign under Paul, and the Napoleonic wars under Alexander I to over 800 million roubles. By 1815 the value of the rouble-assignat in terms of silver had shrunk by nearly four-fifths.[2] Only the relatively long period of peace under Nicholas I after 1830 made possible the currency reform of 1839–43 associated with the name of Count G. F. Kankrin, whereby the 'credit rouble', freely convertible into silver, replaced the rouble-assignat in the ratio of $1:3\frac{1}{2}$.[3] The Crimean war, as a consequence of which the volume of paper roubles more than doubled, forced Russia back on to an inconvertible currency. The downward tendency continued in the 1860s, and only during the period 1868–75 did M. K. Reutern succeed in strengthening the rouble and in arresting the violent

* From the Economic History Review, 2nd ser., vol. vi (1953). Reprinted by permission.

fluctuations in the rates. The Turkish war of 1877–8, involving an expenditure of more than 1000 million paper roubles, inflation and indebtedness, undid all Reutern's achievements.[4]

In the long run an active foreign policy not only affected Russia's finances but tended indirectly to perpetuate the backwardness of her economy, as all potential savings were skimmed off by taxation and absorbed by the budget for military and other mainly unproductive expenditure. When defeat brought home the realisation that to maintain her international status she must increase the productivity of her economy, the process of modernisation was conditioned by the legacy of the past. Among the outstanding features of this legacy was the depreciated, unstable and inconvertible paper currency.

In itself the depreciation, though averaging about 38 per cent during the decade 1879–88, had been a lesser evil, for in the course of time prices did adjust themselves to the changed value of the currency. More damaging to the economic life of the country were the frequent and violent fluctuations with a range of over 30 per cent in some years.[5]

The instability of the currency was prejudicial to Russia's credit and commercial relations with the West. That long-term foreign investment was discouraged by currency fluctuations is borne out by the unprecedented influx of foreign capital which immediately followed the stabilisation of the rouble in 1894.[6] Similarly short-term credits from abroad tended to be influenced by the general economic condition of the country rather than by the soundness or otherwise of the individual enterprise. This probably explains why prior to 1894 only a few firms could obtain short-term credits from foreign banks.[7] Witte also saw in the higher rate of interest some sort of insurance premium for the exchange risk.[8] Russia's state finance likewise suffered, as most of her foreign loans were floated either in gold or silver or currencies based on them, whilst the state revenue was collected in paper currency.[9] An unstable currency also affected foreign trade. Depreciation stimulated exports and restricted imports as well as softened the impact of falling agricultural prices resulting from overseas competition. On the other hand good harvests which gave a favourable turn to the exchange rate of the rouble tended to keep down the exporter's paper rouble income from agricultural exports. Thus in 1890, following an appreciation of the paper rouble, grain producers who had expanded production in anticipation of a fall in rates faced ruin when this development failed to materialise.[10]

Currency fluctuations likewise played havoc with Russia's commercial policy. From 1877 onwards customs duties were collected in gold, so that any rise in the exchange rate of the paper rouble tended to reduce the yield of import duties in paper roubles and to reduce the protective action of Russia's customs policy. Thus in 1890 to offset these consequences the duty on most imports was raised by 20 per cent, and in 1891 Vyshnegradsky even proposed to peg the customs duties to the exchange rate of the rouble.[11] Moreover the most serious argument advanced abroad against commercial treaties with Russia was that the unstable currency rendered her tariff concessions illusory.

All these considerations had made currency reform a priority issue in the last two decades of the nineteenth century. Political considerations were also of some importance in making currency reform a major issue. Schultze-Gaevernitz even saw in the reform 'die finanz-politische Seite von Russlands Weltpolitik'.[12] An unstable currency constituted an element of weakness in Russia's international position, as in 1877 and 1887, especially since Germany could, and on occasion did, utilise her position as the main market for Russia's currency for purposes of intimidation.[13] The political aspect of currency reform had been frequently referred to at various stages of discussions preceding reform.[14]

The monetary reform as finally completed by Witte in 1897–9 consisted of the introduction of the gold standard and the devaluation of the currency. It introduced the gold rouble equivalent to one-fifteenth of an Imperial with a fineness of 17·424 doli (0·7774234 gr.) as the basic monetary unit.[15] The choice of gold had been determined by the importance which gold had gained in international transactions since the 1870s. By then Russia had become an integral part of the world economic system. In foreign trade she occupied by 1895–6 the sixth place in the world with a turnover of 853·2 million gold roubles out of a world turnover of 22,318 million.[16] More than 50 per cent of her state and state guaranteed debt consisted by 1893 of bonds payable in gold or foreign currency based on gold, almost all of which had been placed abroad.[17] Moreover Russia had no special interest in the maintenance of silver as she had no silver production or reserves of any importance in face of a gold output by 1895 of about 15 per cent of world production.[18]

Historically the beginnings of the monetary reform can be traced back to M. K. Reutern, who introduced payment of customs duties in gold[19] and also proposed to admit business transactions in gold at the rate of the day. The latter proposal was tantamount to official recognition of the premium on gold, but did not become law until 1895 because of the opposition of the state council to any measure savouring of devaluation.[20]

N. K. Bunge, formerly professor of economics at Kiev University, who initially shared the state council's view and thought to raise the value of the currency by withdrawing the notes issued during the 1877–8 war, soon realised that, as his predecessor in office A. A. Abaza so aptly expressed it, 'notes once in circulation are as difficult to withdraw as it is to separate wine from water'.[21] Growth in population and in commercial and industrial activity had increased demand for money in circulation without any corresponding expansion of transport and banking facilities to counteract the need for an increased circulation.[22] This fact and the desire to avoid currency fluctuation induced Bunge to take up Reutern's project to permit transactions in gold at the rate of the day. This project however was again vetoed by the state council.[23]

These initial setbacks did not seriously affect Bunge's general financial policy, as he saw the solution of the monetary problem in a general growth and strengthening of the economy which would create favourable conditions out of which a sound currency would emerge as a natural consequence. By means of a more liberal taxation policy towards the peasantry and of agricultural credit for both the landowners and the peasants, Bunge sought to promote the increased productivity of agriculture, and by a protective customs policy he endeavoured to further industrial development.[24] This however was a long-term policy, and in the meantime the support afforded to agriculture reduced revenue and increased the difficulty of balancing the budget.[25] In search of revenue he introduced a number of new duties, mainly indirect, which did not however make good the reduced revenue from peasant taxes.[26] Bunge's experience throws an interesting light on the dilemma which any government, however well disposed towards the peasantry, had to face in a country where over 80 per cent of the population was in one way or another connected with rural occupations. What Bunge ultimately achieved was to replace direct by indirect taxation whilst the taxpayers remained largely the same. Bunge maintained that the cause of the country's budgetary difficulties lay in the cost of the war and naval ministries (over 32 per cent of average annual expenditure during 1881–6) and of the service of the public debt which had increased by 50 per cent since the Turkish war of 1877–8 (nearly 30 per cent of average annual expenditure).[27] To meet the budget deficit recourse to new foreign borrowing was necessary, which made the improvement of Russia's balance of trade all the more imperative. However export surpluses, achieved mainly by import cuts, were not sufficient to balance Russia's external accounts, especially as agricultural prices in the 1880s were falling. At the same time agricultural production did not increase sufficiently to make up for falling prices. As import of foreign capital declined consequent upon the Turkish war,[28] no new regions were being opened up. Moreover the period of Bunge's administration was not favoured by good harvests. The political situation, with the Afghan crisis involving sales of Russian securities in London in 1885 and the Bulgarian crisis of 1886, was unfavourable to Bunge.[29] The fall in the rate of the paper rouble to a level never before reached in its whole history, and Russia's financial weakness and helplessness in face of a critical situation, brought home the realisation that 'pour se guérir il fallait avoir recours à des remèdes sérieux et décisifs et peut-être même changer de médecin en trouvant un homme à poigne . . .'[30] Such a man had been found in the person of I. A. Vyshnegradsky.

Like Reutern and Bunge, Vyshnegradsky understood the necessity for a thoroughgoing reform of the country's economic system, but unlike the latter considered such a reform unthinkable given the existing monetary system.[31] Nor had he any illusions as to the possibility or the desirability of restoring the paper rouble to par.[32] His aim was to stabilise the paper rouble at the existing level or near it, and as the best means to this end he considered the admission of transactions in metallic currency and the accumulation of a gold reserve. Faced like his predecessors with the state council's opposition to the first project,[33] he concentrated on the latter. To create a favourable balance of payments, to expand exports and keep down imports and other expenditure abroad, to attract gold into the country and to direct this gold into the treasury became the guiding, all-pervading objective of his policy.

Unlike Bunge, Vyshnegradsky had been greatly favoured by 'His Majesty the Harvest'. Two consecutive excellent harvests in 1887 and 1888 enabled Russian exports to reach the peak of the century, at a time when the fall in American wheat exports increased European demand for Russian wheat. Moreover he employed a series of artificial measures to stimulate Russian exports, such as differential railway tariffs to encourage exports from distant areas and a campaign against arrears in taxation to force the peasantry to market their grain.[34]

The increase in exports was accompanied by a fall in imports. Vyshnegradsky's commercial policy culminated in the Unified Tariff of 1891, which was dominated by fiscal and monetary considerations although the protectionist aims also had their importance.[35] The result was considerable surpluses on the balance of trade, averaging 311·2 million paper roubles annually during 1887–91 as against 68 million during 1882–6.[36] In addition he endeavoured to prevent an increase in expenditure abroad, the main item of which was the service of the public debt. The replacement of the '5 per cent Mendelsohn Bonds' of 1877 by a 4 per cent loan of 500 million francs issued on the Paris market at the end of 1888 marked the beginning of the vast conversion operations on the French market and opened a new era in the history of Russia's foreign credit.[37] By 1891 a debt of over 1000 million gold roubles had been converted into a debt the nominal value of which was some 102 million gold roubles higher but the annual service of which represented a saving of 12½ million gold roubles.[38] At the same time Vyshnegradsky refrained as far as possible from new loans abroad, confining himself for indispensable loans to the home market which by then, thanks to Bunge's policy of encouraging the development of savings banks, was beginning to take up state securities on an increasing scale. The prices at which the issuing banks took up Russian loans, the prices of issue, the number of subscribers, and the extent of over-subscription and bourse quotations all indicated the progressive improvement in Russia's credit abroad.[39]

Although the obvious improvement in Russia's financial administration and the general abundance of capital on the European money markets in the 1880s[40] partly explain the success of Vyshnegradsky's foreign loan policy, political factors probably played an even greater role. In the 1880s and the opening years of the following decade France tried to end her isolation in Europe by winning Russian friendship,[41] and Vyshnegradsky could not but welcome the opportunity of profiting financially from the political situation. He did not contemplate a total abandonment of the German market which during the years 1876–86 had acquired a virtual monopoly of Russia's credit, but he realised the dangers of dependence thereby created.[42] He agreed with N. K. Giers that 'a system which would permit Russia to choose between the Berlin and Paris bourses would be the wisest, most expedient and desirable for Russia.'[43] If a break with the Berlin market actually took place, and if the French market gained a larger degree of influence over Russia's credit to the detriment of the German market, this had been largely due to Bismarck himself who, by encouraging a press campaign against Russia's credit and by the *Lombardverbot*, caused a panic among German holders of Russian bonds.[44] It was then that the French purchased considerable numbers of Russian securities 'expelled' from the Berlin bourse and the great conversion operations contemplated by Vyshnegradsky were carried out with great success on the French market. 'Les Français ont prouvé non en parole, mais en action, toute leur sympathie pour la Russie',[45] wrote a contemporary writer on financial matters, although the French capitalists who purchased Russian bonds were handsomely rewarded. The rise in the price of Russian securities which followed brought them by the middle of the 1890s a profit of some 540 million francs, not to mention the considerable profits on issues, whilst the Germans who had substituted Italian rentes for Russian securities lost heavily on the deal.[46] French readiness to absorb Russian securities had also been assisted by the commercial conflict with Italy which had cut off the Italian market from French capital.[47]

Although Vyshnegradsky had been less successful in restricting the expenditure abroad of Russian travellers 'qui s'y distraient de la mélancholie monotone de leur climat et y dépensent en quelques mois les revenus de quelques années',[48] the export surplus running at some 300 million paper roubles annually was sufficient to balance the country's external accounts and to ensure an influx of gold into the bargain.[49]

In order to take advantage of the new situation and to strengthen the gold reserve for monetary purposes the government still had to find funds for the purchase of gold bills abroad from Russian exporters. This Vyshnegradsky in part did by increasing revenue from indirect taxation, state owned railways, Crown lands and forests, and by reducing expenditure on the service of the external debt already described above.[50] But although he had put an end to budgetary deficits, and even produced surpluses, these were not sufficient to make possible the purchase of gold bills abroad on the scale he contemplated. He therefore employed a portion of the resources of the State Bank and of the reserves of the treasury for this purpose. As the gold thus acquired could not be circulated the resulting immobilisation of funds of the State Bank may explain the shrinkage in its commercial activities during the period 1888–92, not otherwise warranted by the state of the market, and the need for special paper rouble issues in 1891–2 for relief to regions hit by harvest failures.[51] In purchasing gold bills Vyshnegradsky exercised considerable caution to avoid undue depreciation of the paper rouble. There was even some export of gold from Russia, the increase in the gold reserve inside the country being due to domestic output.[52] The realisation of bills and the withdrawal of gold from abroad called for even greater prudence in order to avoid disturbing the money markets, as in 1891 when the critical position of the London money market, where the greater part of Russia's credit balances was at that time maintained, had to be considered.[53] By the end of 1892 the withdrawal operations from abroad were almost complete; and by January 1893 the gold reserve amounted to 581 million gold roubles representing an increase of 281·5 million roubles during Vyshnegradsky's administration.[54]

At the same time Vyshnegradsky's attempts to stabilise the currency met with complete failure, nothwithstanding the increased gold reserve and the general improvement in the country's finances. Fluctuations in the rate of the paper rouble were even more violent than before, for which political factors were largely responsible.[55] However the minister himself had some share of responsibility for the failure, for while concentrating on the accumulation of a gold reserve he lost sight of his other objective and frequently encouraged a fall in the rate to stimulate exports.[56] The most important factor in the instability of the currency however was the speculation in paper roubles which developed on the Berlin bourse, an important centre for transactions in Russian currency since the 1870s. Originally the forward transactions in paper roubles which had developed on the Berlin bourse had been a positive factor in promoting commercial relations between the two countries, widening the market for the paper rouble and facilitating the flotation of 'credit loans'.[57] In the 1880s however these transactions, though in some cases still genuine, had on the whole taken on the character of purely speculative deals, and the paper rouble became the favourite object of bourse speculation which also involved Russian securities and her external credit in general and furthermore furnished Germany with a political weapon, as in 1887.[58] Unfortunately also, Russian banks, exporting firms who had an interest in low exchange rates, and the minister of finance himself participated in this speculation.

The famine which affected some twenty provinces of Russia in 1891, the harvest failure in some localities, and a cholera epidemic in 1892 threatened to thwart Vyshnegradsky's plans,[59] and his insistence on the continuation of the export drive in face of the plight of the population was considered as characteristic of his whole policy based on the exploitation of the agricultural population by ruthless taxation and 'starvation exports'.[60] But although he was responsible for an increase in certain indirect taxes, a study of his budgets does not quite confirm the customary opinion that he pursued a policy of 'sucking dry' the agricultural population to find the resources required by the treasury. The relative promptness with which direct taxes were paid may indicate harsh methods of collection, but the obvious connexion between harvest results and taxation revenue does not quite confirm this assumption. It seems feasible that the policy of his predecessor, Bunge, slow in showing improvements in the country's public finance, contributed to an increase in well-being of the agricultural population and indirectly to a higher state revenue under Vyshnegradsky, a conclusion suggested by the increase in small savings in state savings banks.[61] Furthermore an examination of harvest and grain export figures indicates a close correlation between these two phenomena.[62]

On the other hand, his attitude to the project of establishing a ministry of agriculture would seem to illustrate his general lack of interest in that most vital branch of the economy which provided a livelihood to the overwhelming majority of the population and on which, in the last resort, depended the success of the schemes of the minister of finance.[63] Furthermore by concentrating with such zeal on his financial operations and on the husbanding of state resources, he did little to develop the productive forces of the country. Based as his policy was on harnessing, and not on extending, the existing forces, its success depended in the last resort on the strength and resistance of these forces. The famine of 1891–2 seemed to indicate that the limit of endurance had been reached. Also Vyshnegradsky's almost prohibitive customs policy caused retaliation on the part of the Germans which eventually developed into open tariff war,[64] whilst the 3 per cent Gold Loan of 1891 met with very incomplete success owing to the hostility of the Rothschilds consequent upon the anti-Jewish policy of the Imperial government.[65] Nevertheless, whatever the weaknesses of the system built up by Vyshnegradsky, the six years of his administration marked an enormous advance in Russia's finances, and he went a long way towards bringing the monetary reform near completion.

About Vyshnegradsky's successor, S. Y. Witte, one could say without qualification, more than about any other Russian finance minister, that he had a long-term policy, or rather a theory of economic policy, which, in spite of several deviations in practice, underlay all his activities as minister of finance.[66] He saw the roots of the country's economic backwardness in the one-sided character of its economy, which had put Russia's very existence at the mercy of the annual harvest and which turned even a partial harvest failure into a national calamity. The way out of this predicament was to promote rapid industrialisation of the country or, as Witte called it, 'widening the application of national labour'; and the means to this end was the protection of the young Russian industries and, even more important, the intensive application of foreign capital.[67] His belief that only foreign capital could enable Russia to speed up her economic growth made him attach great importance to the country's credit abroad. An unstable currency, in his opinion, obscured the real progress made by Russia in the financial and economic spheres, and prevented foreign financial circles from fully appreciating the promptness with which Russia had always met her commitments abroad, whatever the circumstances.[68]

With the immediate object therefore of stabilising the currency he took energetic measures to combat speculation in paper roubles. Having first of all ascertained the extent of the movements of paper roubles in and out of the country, by making speculative currency transactions illegal and by imposing a strict control over the activities of the Russian bourses, he succeeded in overcoming internal speculation in the rouble.[69] Foreign speculation he eliminated by a carefully staged campaign of counter-speculation against the Berlin bourse.[70] The *coup de force* of October 1894, though met by an outburst of indignation from German official and financial circles, proved effective,[71] as demonstrated by the movement of the rates of exchange of the paper rouble from 1894 onwards.[72] To reduce to a minimum the fluctuations still taking place he ordered the State Bank to continue purchasing and selling gold bills to maintain fluctuations within the gold points.

Having *de facto* stabilised the currency Witte began to contemplate introducing gold into circulation which was of immediate importance in connexion with the paradoxical situation in which the State Bank and treasury found themselves as a result of Vyshnegradsky's policy of purchasing gold with their resources. The situation was aptly described by Maurice Verstraete as follows: 'la situation de la Russie thésaurisant de l'or improductif ressemblait à celle d'une armée dont l'armement va être renouvelé; elle conserve ses anciens fusils pendant que des fusils nouveaux s'entassent momentanément à rien et constituent un luxe qu'il faut payer.'[73] Being aware of the conservative attitude of the state council to currency reform Witte tried to introduce partial gold circulation in the form of gold transactions at the rate of the day; and, unlike his predecessors, he succeeded in winning the consent of the council to such a measure.[74] When this measure however failed to act as a substitute for gold circulation because of lack of confidence among the public, Witte had to resort to the 'unconstitutional' procedure of introducing full gold circulation by a series of separate imperial decrees.[75] Not until 7 July 1899 was the new Monetary Statute consolidating the Imperial Decrees promulgated with the legislative sanction of the state council. This procedure was necessary because the council would have agreed to the convertibility of the paper rouble only on the basis of parity with gold, while Witte realised that the raising of the paper rouble rate to par was hardly practicable, as it could be achieved only in one of three ways: by gradually strengthening the paper rouble; by substantially increasing the gold reserve; or by reducing the volume of paper roubles in circulation – all of them impossible or dangerous.[76] Even assuming that raising of the paper rouble to par with gold was possible the cumulative effect of such a measure would have been to worsen Russia's balance of payments position. Russian agricultural producers in particular would have been severely hit, as grain prices would have immediately fallen, while costs of production, with the exception of imported machinery, would have adjusted themselves only slowly to the changed conditions. This would have been the case, particularly in the eastern and southern regions, the centres of export grain, where wages were paid in money and where, especially as labour in the south was migratory, agricultural producers had to compete for labour with the mine and mill owners.[77] As debtors whose debt consisted almost entirely of 'credit loans', agricultural producers would have been faced with an increase of the real burden of interest payments of one-third. Likewise the Russian state would have found its liabilities on account of that part of its public debt which was expressed in paper roubles increased by a third.[78]

Thus only on the basis of devaluation could the convertibility of the paper rouble against gold be established without adversely affecting the economic relations of the country. As to the precise rate at which the paper rouble was to be exchanged against gold, that of $1\frac{1}{2}:1$ or $66\frac{2}{3}$ gold copecks to one paper rouble had been considered the most advisable. This rate had been the nearest to the arithmetical average of the average rates of the paper rouble in gold copecks since 1877, and also to the rouble rates as determined by the country's balance of trade which according to official calculation averaged 63·94 gold copecks during 1878–94 and $66\frac{2}{3}$ copecks during 1888–94.[79]

By the reform of 1897–9 the parity between the paper and gold rouble was restored by reducing the value of the gold rouble in proportion to the depreciation of the paper rouble through a lowering of the gold content of the gold rouble, so that the imperial and the demi-imperial equalled 15 and $7\frac{1}{2}$ roubles respectively. The State Bank had the right to issue notes up to 600 million with a 50 per cent gold backing and over and above that amount each note required 100 per cent backing. This stringent regulation deprived the monetary system of the necessary elasticity in times of crisis when more cash might be required. Russia however was not yet ripe for the adoption of the system current in Germany for example, where in addition to gold, first-class securities were used as cover for the note issue.[80] In order to secure the necessary elasticity of the monetary system the government maintained gold reserves far in excess of legal requirements and refrained from fully exercising their right to issue uncovered notes. The maintenance of this large gold reserve was a luxury, especially in view of Russia's position as a debtor state, but was felt to be neces-sary for purposes of elasticity and to sustain foreign confidence. On the other hand the State Bank on which devolved the task of controlling the currency had not been adequately reorganised for the purpose, as old Statutes of the Bank contained many clauses incompatible with its new position as a bank of issue and also clauses which gave the minister of finance scope for abusing the right of issue for fiscal purposes.[81]

In spite of its defects the monetary system justified the hopes placed in it. Internally it solved the problem of the immobilised funds of the State Bank and treasury, and externally it stimulated the import of foreign capital into Russian industry to such an extent that during the single year 1898 the amount of foreign capital invested exceeded that of the whole period 1851–92.[82] This method of acquiring foreign capital, besides promoting Witte's plans of industrialisation, was more acceptable to him than formal flotations of loans abroad by the Russian government, which tended to raise doubts as to the true state of Russia's finances. His preference for unobtrusive procedures is also seen in his practice of raising capital by selling Russian securities through the medium of foreign banks and by short-term credit operations.[83] All these transactions were rendered possible by the prevailing confidence in the stability and convertibility of the currency.

A vital question remains to be answered, namely, how Witte managed to accumulate the imposing gold balances which by the end of 1897 amounted to 1548·45 million roubles of the new coinage representing an increase of 676·95 million during his administration.[84] A part of this increase can be accounted for by the domestic gold output which during the period 1893–7 amounted to over 239·5 million.[85] An examination of Russia's bullion and specie balance indicates an excess of gold imports of 436·9 million[86] not accounted for by Russia's balance of trade; on the contrary there had been a definite deterioration in this respect as compared with the export surpluses obtained under Vyshnegradsky. There had been an increase in imports, especially of machinery and metal goods in connection with the new minister's programme of industrialisation.[87] Witte considered this increase a temporary phenomenon only, and believed that within a short space of time Russian industries, provided with the essential materials and equipment from abroad, would be able to satisfy internal demand. He even dreamed of capturing Far Eastern markets for the products of Russian industry. Witte's attitude was certainly more far sighted and constructive than the rigid and restrictive mercantilism of his predecessor, but, though Witte did score substantial successes with regard to domestic industrial output, demand grew at a faster pace, and it was not until the turn of the century that an industrial crisis stemmed the tide of fast growing imports.[88] Other factors contributing to increases in imports were the tariff reductions consequent upon the Commercial Treaty of 1894 with Germany and the stabilisation of the currency which freed importers from fears of loss from the constantly depreciating currency.

At the same time the value of Russian exports fell, although the minister did all in his power to stimulate grain exports by what has been described as a 'railway Drang nach Osten' and by a railway tariff policy encouraging exports of grain from the newly opened eastern regions.[89] Although Witte succeeded in increasing the volume of grain exports both in absolute figures and as a percentage of the annual harvest,[90] the fall in international grain prices depressed the value of Russian exports, so that the balance of trade deteriorated,[91] and the surplus balances achieved by Vyshnegradsky were from 1892 onwards replaced by a deficit.[92]

How then did Witte succeed in bringing the accounts into equilibrium? Above all, how was he able to ensure an appreciable surplus on the bullion and specie balance? An examination of the credit operations of the Russian State abroad explains this. During the period 1893–8 the various credit operations of the Russian government abroad yielded 1100 million roubles.[93] Thus Witte could form large credit balances in the name of the State Bank and the treasury abroad, and by drawing bills on its foreign correspondents the government could balance the external accounts and even use part of the credit balances for the purpose of strengthening the gold reserve for monetary purposes.

Likewise the influx of foreign capital into industrial enterprises, which was among the basic factors in the industrial expansion of the 1890s, affected the monetary position in the same way as did the flotation of new loans or the sale of old bonds abroad. During 1893–8 approximately 700 million francs of foreign capital were invested in Russian joint stock companies.[94] Not all this capital entered the country effectively; large amounts remained in the hands of foreign bankers and brokers; also Russians who sold their mines, mills or land to foreigners were often paid in part at least in shares. There is no doubt however that a large amount of this capital crossed the frontier effectively. The well informed Maurice Verstraete believed that the effective capital stood very near its nominal amount.[95] The fact that a portion of this capital entered Russia in the form of machines, tools, raw materials, etc., does not diminish the importance of this capital influx from the monetary point of view as such items were accounted for on the debit side of the balance of trade.

All this foreign capital, attracted in one form or another, only indirectly contributed to the solution of the monetary problem. Directly this foreign capital served to increase the productivity of the economy and to develop the dormant natural resources of the country. This applied not only to the credits directly devoted to industrial purposes, but also Russia's state and state guaranteed debt had been with few exceptions used to increase the country's economic potential, mainly in the construction of railways.[96] Railways stimulated industrial and commercial activity, as did the influx of capital into industrial enterprises; and both contributed to the growth of state revenue. The credits from abroad rendered Russia a double service : they had first been used to strengthen the economy and secondly they contributed to the formation of large, easily realisable funds in gold at the disposal of the government. Furthermore, although Russia's debt increased substantially, there was little increase in the amounts due for the service of this debt as the improvement in Russia's credit abroad made possible the conversion of the public debt, which resulted in the reduction of the average rate of interest from 4·9 per cent in 1891 to 3·86 per cent in 1902.[97]

Despite the substantial increase in the public debt, Russian state credit abroad reached a level never attained before; her 4 per cent gold rente which in 1880 stood below par approached par by 1895 and exceeded it by 1898; the 3 per cent and 3½ per cent gold bonds stood almost as high as the equivalent German bonds.[98] Russian loans lost the speculative character which they had in the main possessed when held by Germans and became 'placements du père de famille'[99] enjoying in the heart and 'portefeuille' of the French *rentier*, a place almost equal to that of the French state *rente*. This spectacular success of Russia's credit policy abroad was due on the one hand to the relative abundance of capital on the international money markets and on the other hand to the financial advantages derived by Russia from the alliance with France, where the bulk of Russian loans had been placed[100] and whence also came a large part of the capital invested in private enterprise in Russia.[101] The stabilisation of the currency and the obvious determination of the minister to introduce metallic circulation and the productive application of the foreign credits were factors in strengthening state credit abroad the importance of which cannot be over-emphasised.

Two more factors should be mentioned. The first is the use of publicity through official channels and through the French press, the *abominable vénalité* of which proved very useful.[102] The second factor was the skill, bordering on genius, of the finance minister. He knew how to avail himself in time of the opportunities offered by the contemporary situation, and accomplished the reform just before the deterioration in the international money market which set in in 1899. By a skilful use of the treasury balances abroad, those 'principaux pivots de sa politique financière', he could create relative abundance on European money markets when about to float a loan so that 'en dernière analyse l'emprunt russe est couvert au moyen de l'or russe lui-même'.[103]

If all this skill, creative energy and practical sense were essential factors in bringing the monetary reform to a successful conclusion, perhaps even greater skill and a more sustained effort was required in the years to come for the purpose of maintaining a sound and stable currency. Before the new productive forces set in motion could enable Russia not only to balance her international accounts without resort to borrowing but also to assure a reasonable standard of living for her population, many years of 'starvation exports' and of heavy taxation lay ahead of her. However a *sine qua non* of her ability to steer her course through difficult times and emerge as a country with a modern, efficient economic organisation, capable of paying her way, was the maintenance of peace.

That Witte himself was fully aware of this is brought out in his report to the Emperor in January 1898 where he stresses the connexion between foreign policy and state finance and issues a warning against 'dangerous fancies' and advises the pursuit of a peaceful foreign policy 'alien to aggressive aspirations'.[104] Furthermore on the short-term view he was conscious of the dangers to his monetary policy inherent in heavy military expenditure which not only added to the budgetary burden but also represented a drain on reserves of foreign exchange, as much of this military expenditure involved the purchase of military and naval equipment from abroad. Maurice Verstraete's apt comment on Witte in his much quoted report to Delcassé of 31 March 1898 was that 'En dépit de son tempérament combatif il serait peut-être à l'heure actuelle l'homme le plus pacifique de l'Europe.[105]

5 Banking in the industrialisation of Tsarist Russia, 1860–1914[*]

Between 1856 and 1914 Russia made substantial progress in overcoming its backwardness. This was reflected in the rapid growth of a modern transport system, the emergence and expansion of mining, metallurgical, and textile industries equipped with modern technology,[1] the creation of a fairly advanced and flexible credit system, and a moderately wide money market.

After the 1880s the rate of growth in industry was sustained on a fairly high level on the average, the rates being quite impressive by any standards for the latter part of the 1890s and from 1910 to 1913, as indicated in Table 5·1. The weight of agricultural production relative to the total remained very high however. Agricultural production grew at a lower rate than industry, thereby reducing the growth rate of national income. Given a rapidly increasing population, income *per capita* remained low in comparison to that in the major European countries and the United States, as shown in Table 5.3.

Modern industry developed mainly under the aegis of large-scale

TABLE 5.1   Annual rate of industrial growth[2]

Year	Percentage
1885–9	6·10
1890–9	8·03 (nearer 9 1894–9)
1900–6	1·45
1907–13	6·25 (7·5 1910–13)
Total 1885–1913	5·72

* Originally published in *Banking in the Early Stages of Industrialization: A Study in Comparative Economic History*, by Rondo Cameron. Copyright © 1967 by Oxford University Press Inc. Reprinted by permission.

TABLE 5.2 Selected indicators of Russian economic development, 1860–1913

	1860	1870	1880	1890	1900	1910	1913
1 Population (in millions)	74·1	84·5	97·7	117·8	132·9	160·7	175·1 (1914)
2 Pig iron (m. poods)	20·5	21·9	27·4	59·6	179·1	185·8	283·0
3 Coal (m. poods)	18·3	42·3	200·8	367·2	986·3	1,526·3	2,200·1
4 Railways ('000 km. end year)	1·6	10·7	22·9	30·6	53·2	66·6	70·2
5 Consumption of cotton (m. poods)	2·8	2·8	5·7	8·3	16·0	22·1	25·7
6 Imports (m. roubles)	159·3	335·9	622·8	406·6	626·3	1,084·4	1,374·0
7 Exports (m. roubles)	181·3	359·9	498·6	692·2	716·2	1,449·0	1,520·0
8 Budget revenue (ordinary, m. roubles)	407·6 (1861)	480·5	651·0	943·7	1,704·1	2,780·9	3,417·3
9 Budget expenditure (ordinary, m. roubles)	413·7	481·7	694·5	877·8	1,599·1	2,473·1	3,094·2

Sources:
1 P. A. Khromov, *Ekonomicheskoye razvitiye Rossii v XIX–XX vekakh* (Moscow–Leningrad, 1950) Table 4, pp. 453–5.
2 *Narodnoye Khozyaystvo* (St Petersburg, 1914) p. 372. One pood = 36 lb.
3 Khromov, op. cit.
4 *Mirovyye ekonomicheskiye krizisy 1848–1935 gg* (Moscow–Leningrad, 1937) p. 517.
5 For 1860, 1870, 1880, M. Tugan-Baranovsky, *Russkaya fabrika, v proshlom i nastoyashchem* (Moscow, 1934) p. 244; for 1890–1913, P. I. Lyashchenko, *Istoriya narodnogo khozyaystva SSSR*, 2 vols, II (Moscow–Leningrad, 1952) pp. 414–15.
6–7 1860–1900, V. I. Pokrovsky (ed.), *Sbornik svedeniy po istorii i statistike vneshney torgovli*, I (St. Petersburg) 117, 141; Khromov, op. cit., p. 487.
8–9 *Ministerstvo Finansov*, 2 vols (St. Petersburg, 1902) I, pp. 623, II, 640–9; Khromov, op. cit., 269.

TABLE 5.3 Gross national product *per capita* (in roubles)

	1897[3]	1913
USA	346	682·2
Great Britain	273	460·6
France	233	–
Germany	184	300·4
Russia	63	101·4[4]

firms, either joint stock companies or so-called 'share associations'. According to Strumilin's 1926 estimate, corporate industry in Russia accounted for two-thirds of the total nominal capital in industry by 1900.[5] A more recent computation puts the proportion of corporate capital invested in industro-commercial companies at 74 per cent of the total in 1900 and at 86 per cent by 1914. However data for so-called 'small industry' have been understated in Russian industrial statistics.[6]

Little reliable information is available on non-corporate industry, which consisted of a variety of small concerns, workshops, associations known as *artyels*, and several million *kustars* or cottage workers. Though non-corporate industry was losing ground in so far as capital was concerned, it was still very significant socially and, except in the textile industry, it probably largely satisfied consumer demand, especially in the countryside.[7]

In the older industries, such as textiles and food processing, corporate industry mainly took the form of 'share associations', i.e. their shares were registered and could not be sold to third parties without the consent of the other partners, who had the right of prior purchase. The denominations of shares were very large, from 5000 to 10,000 roubles. The majority of firms, especially in Moscow, were family partnerships. Their legal position was similar to that of joint stock companies : both required sanction of the appropriate government department before incorporation.[8]

The newer industries, e.g. mining, metallurgy, and in part also machine construction, had in the majority of cases developed from the start in the form of joint stock companies. By 1914 the largest amount of capital was invested in the group of industries comprising heavy and light metallurgy, metal goods and machine construction (858·6 million roubles), mining (791 million), and textiles 713·0 million).[9]

Parallel with the increasing weight of corporate industry went the increase in the average capital per company, rising nearly three-fold from 1861 to 1917. By 1911, 309 concerns, with a capital of over 2 million roubles each, represented 22·3 per cent of all concerns and owned two-thirds of the total capital.[10]

THE FINANCIAL STRUCTURE AND ITS EVOLUTION

The history of Russian banking from the beginning of organised banking in the 1750s to the 1860s is an uninspiring recital of the vicissitudes of a small variety of government organised and government operated banking institutions which in the main confined their activity to granting long-term credit on mortgages of landed estates, or rather of their serf working force. The position was somewhat different in the Polish and Baltic regions, but in Russia proper the twenty-odd banking institutions classed as private by the Law Code of 1857 had a combined capital of only 500,000 roubles. The only bank with the specific purpose of granting commercial credit was the government owned State Commercial Bank, which was founded in 1817. Notwithstanding the bank's substantial resources, and its ability to attract large deposits, which showed the availability of savings, the structure of its assets reflected the stagnation of business life and the inertia of the business community.

There is no satisfactory analysis of the credit organisation before 1860, and this is not the place to attempt it.[11] It should be said however that banking functions were in evidence throughout. They took the form of commercial credit which in conditions of Russia's transport and commodity circulation meant at least medium-term credit. Credit operations applied to all stages of commodity circulation down to the final consumer. In foreign trade foreigners exporting goods from Russia made advances to Russian wholesale merchants, the latter advanced credit to other intermediaries or producers and so on all along the line. Even long-term credit for equipping industries was sometimes advanced in this way, foreigners acting as brokers and underwriters. The famous Knoop performed such functions for the Moscow cotton mill owners. The cost of such services was reflected in the price of the final product and in the profit expectations of the commercial sector.

As regards organised banking some causes of its inadequate development can be suggested. The most important reason was the as yet limited rôle of money in the life of the bulk of the population. Markets were largely regional or even local, and the few commodities for which there was a national market passed through the large annual fairs, the largest of which was in Nizhny Novgorod. Certainly on the local but to an overwhelming extent also on the regional and national level face to face relations or recommendations of persons of proven probity were the basis of credit. Commerce was as yet not specialised on a particular commodity but, given the generally limited and unpredictable demand, on a particular region or trade route, which again entailed face to face connections. On the whole resources were immobilised in land which, in so far as large owners were concerned, was a commodity only in a very special sense. The value of the land as a basis for the advance of credit was assessed with reference to the working potential of its serf population in fertile areas and its earning power in marginal areas.

The high seasonal nature of agriculture and, resulting from it, the low level of urbanisation; legal disabilities affecting Jews who elsewhere were among the most energetic promoters of credit institutions; the lack of adequate laws and judicial procedures for the enforcement of credit claims in the face of a very low level of commercial ethics and a prevailing anti-commercial mentality of the population; the tendency of the authorities to interpret any form of activity that implied compensation for risk-taking as usury – were among the causes for the failure of organised private banking to develop.

Government sponsored banking institutions which emerged in the middle of the eighteenth century failed to stimulate the economy for a number of reasons, the most important being the limited scale of the resources the government could put at the disposal of the banks prior to the 1880s. Furthermore there was no clear-cut view as to what the rôle of the banks should be; the inclination was to look upon them as weapons against 'usury' or as means of salvaging declining fortunes of eminent personages. Even when funds were provided for commercial and industrial purposes, as after 1817, they were often not taken up, partly out of ignorance, partly because borrowers had to comply with bureaucratic supervision and a multiplicity of annoying regulations, partly because given the nature of Russia's pre–1861 commerce a special type of banking would have to be devised for which neither the funds nor the expertise were available. The arbitrariness of the authorities or fear inspired by past arbitrariness and abuses tended to deter the public and firms from entrusting their resources to formal institutions and led to concealment of wealth.

Monetary chaos must have also acted as a deterrent to organised banking. In private arrangements compensation for risk arising from currency fluctuations could be taken care of. Fear of currency depreciation led to a disinclination to hold resources in liquid form. On the whole fortunes in Russia were very transitory and fragile. Only where industrial and commercial activities entailed ownership of landed property, forests or mineral resources, does one note fortunes surviving over several generations, e.g. the Stroganovs or Demidovs. Even in such cases inheritance laws and lack of entail led to parcelisation of wealth. It was not easy to get wealthy in Russia or to remain wealthy, and the failure of money to inspire confidence as a store of wealth and the cumulative memory of past abuses of administrative and tax authorities acted as constraints upon the monetisation of the economy even where and when conditions were favourable. The superstructure of organised credit could only be built on a base of a sound, confidence inspiring currency.

It was characteristic of the manner in which changes took place in

Russia that in undertaking to set up a new credit system the old one was almost completely dissolved. This was in part a necessity because of the critical situation of the State Commercial Bank after the Crimean War. In part however the dissolution of the existing network was prompted by the desire to start anew on a quite different basis. One Russian authority, Migulin, maintained that 'doctrinaire' considerations were the dominant ones and that the financial position was not beyond repair.[12] A special committee of enquiry set up to consider the nature of the credit system to be created expressed itself against

TABLE 5.4 Assets and liabilities of the Russian commercial credit system

Year	Main assets	Net worth	Main liabilities
	(*m. roubles*)		
1875	913·5	173·9	1,051·1
1881	971·9	182·6	1,077·1
1893	1,106·1	241·7	1,383·5
1900	1,989·6	431·9	2,364·5[a]
1908	2,823·7	510·7	2,458·3
1914	7,203·0	1,110·8	6,918·9
	(*% change*)		
1881–93	+14	+32	+29
1893–1900	+80	+79	+71[b]
1900–8	+42	+18	+43[c]
1908–14	+155	+117	+146[d]

[a] 1,747·5 without treasury deposits in the State Bank.
[b] 47% without treasury deposits in the State Bank.
[c] 19% without treasury deposits in the State Bank.
[d] 140% without treasury deposits in the State Bank.

Sources: Tables 5.4–5.8 are based on I. F. Gindin, *Russkiye Kommercheskiye Banki* (Moscow, 1948), pp. 66, 104, 142, 203, and *Yezhegodnik Ministerstva Finansov, 1869–1915* (for the appropriate years).

state banks and suggested that the central bank then under consideration should be a joint stock bank modelled on the Bank of England, but the system that emerged had a very large element of state participation and control in it.[13] It was necessity however rather than tradition or ideology which dictated this course.

The credit structure of Imperial Russia was still fairly simple even in 1914 and the variety of financial intermediaries as yet very restricted. At the apex stood the State Bank with a monopoly of issue. It was under the direct supervision of the state council and under the immediate jurisdiction of the finance ministry. Though its credits were increasingly reaching the economy through the medium of other financial institutions, the State Bank continued right up to 1914 to grant credits directly to several branches of the economy.

Directly connected with the State Bank were the state savings banks, the balances of which were on deposit with it. The Peasants' Land Bank and the Land Bank for the Nobility, founded in 1882 and 1885,

TABLE 5.5 Share of banks in main assets and liabilities of the commercial credit system, 1875–93 (%)

	State Bank	Joint stock banks	Mutual credit societies	Municipal banks
1 Jan 1875
Main assets	14·0	56·4	15·3	14·3
Net worth	13·2	62·3	13·5	11·0
Main liabilities	26·5	48·5	12·2	12·8
1 Jan 1881
Main assets	26·1	36·5	15·3	22·1
Net worth	15·5	53·1	12·6	18·8
Main liabilities	26·5	48·5	12·2	12·8
1 Jan 1893
Main assets	19·2	58·6	12·4	9·8
Net worth	12·0	63·0	11·0	14·0
Main liabilities	33·0	47·8	10·3	8·9
change 1881–93
Main assets	− 16·0	+82·0[a]	−8·0	−49·0
Net worth	+3	+56·0[b]	+14·0	−1·0
Main liabilities	+34·0	+84·0[c]	+5·0	−48·0

[a]St Petersburg banks alone +166 per cent.
[b]St Petersburg banks alone +112 per cent.
[c]St Petersburg banks alone.

respectively, were creations of the State Bank, as was the Zemstvo and Urban Bank, founded in 1912. The State Bank had also important interests in the Russo–Chinese Bank, founded in 1895, and in the Loan and Discount Bank of Persia, founded in 1894, which had the aim of furthering Russian interests in China and Persia, respectively.

The joint stock commercial banks were the most important channel through which credit flowed into the economy. On the lower rungs of the commercial credit ladder were the municipal banks and the mutual credit associations. After 1905 a variety of co-operative banks rapidly expanded in rural areas. They were grouped under the general heading of small credit institutions. Long-term mortgage credit was provided in 1914 by fifty-six institutions, of which two were state owned, one was a *zemstvo* [district council] bank, and ten were private joint stock banks. The remainder belonged chiefly to the co-operative banks of land and property owners.

Tables 5.4–5.9 present a summary quantitative view of the evolution of the commercial credit system from 1875 to 1914. The pages that follow supplement that summary with some of the more relevant institutional details.

TABLE 5.6   Share of banks in main assets and liabilities of the commercial credit system, 1900–8 (%)

	State Bank	Joint stock banks	Mutual credit societies	Municipal banks
1 Jan 1900				
Main assets	21·6	61·3	10·6	6·5
Net worth	12·3	70·0	8·7	9·0
Main liabilities[a]	36·6	48·9	8·8	5·7
change 1893–1900				
Main assets	+102·0	+89·0	+55·0	+16·0
Net worth	+81·0	+99·0	+40·0	+15·0
Main liabilities	+89·0[b]	+75·0	+45·0	+10·0
1 Jan 1908				
Main assets	22·6	61·8	10·2	5·4
Net worth	10·8	69·1	10·7	9·4
Main liabilities	24·5[c]	59·8	10·0	5·7
change 1900–8				
Main assets	+48·0	+43·0	+36·0	+20·0
Net worth	+3·0	+17·0	+44·0	+24·0
Main liabilities[d]	—20·0	+45·0	+38·0	+17·0

[a]If treasury balances are excluded the share of the State Bank was only 15·6 per cent, that of joint stock banks 65·1, mutual credit societies 11·6, and municipal banks 7·7.
[b]Without treasury balances the State Bank's share fell by 3 per cent.
[c]Without treasury balances the share of the State Bank was only 13·7 per cent and the share of others appropriately rose to 68·3, 11·5 and 6·5, respectively.
[d]Main liabilities without treasury balances increased by 36 per cent for the State Bank.

Banking in the industrialisation of Tsarist Russia

TABLE 5.7 Share of banks in main assets and liabilities of the commercial credit system, 1908–14 (%)

	State Bank	Joint stock banks	Mutual credit societies	Municipal
	1 Jan 1914			
Main assets	16·4	68·0	12·2	3·4
Net worth	5·0	76·1	13·5	5·4
Main liabilities	18·5	66·9	10·8	3·8
	change 1908–14			
Main assets	+85·0	+182·0	+199·0	+60·0
Net worth	+133·0	+147·0	+175·0	+24·0
Main liabilities	+84·0	+176·0	+163·0	+62·0

TABLE 5.8 The share of St Petersburg joint stock commercial banks[a] in the total assets and liabilities of the commercial credit system, 1875–1914 (%)

Year	Assets	Growth (+ −)	Liabilities	Growth (+ −)
1875	5·6	n.a.	9·9	n.a.
1881	3·8	n.a.	9·4	n.a.
1893	10·3	+166·0	15·3	+112·0
1900	13·7	+101·0	25·4	+109·0
1908	29·7	+109·0	41·0	+115·0
1914	30·2	+222·0	43·2	+208·0

[a] Volga–Kama Bank not included.

TABLE 5.9 The Russian credit network

Banking institutions	1875	1881	1893	1900 (1 Jan)	1908	1914
State Bank						
St Petersburg	1	1	1	1	1	1
Moscow	1	1	1	1	1	1
Provinces	47	55	89	112	114	135
Additional treasury offices performing simple banking operations	–	–	–	600	700	791
Savings banks	72	76	2,439	4,781	6,710	8,553
TOTAL excl. treasury offices and savings banks	49	57	91	114	116	137

TABLE 5.9—*continued*

Banking institutions	1875	1881	1893	1900 (1 Jan)	1908	1914
St Petersburg joint stock commercial banks						
St Petersburg head office	5	5	10	10	11	13
Local branches	–	–	–	3	7	22
Moscow	1	1	4	7	12	26
Provinces	19	19	24	84	225	495
Abroad	–	–	2	19	25	31
TOTAL St Petersburg banks	25	25	40	123	280	587
Moscow banks						
Moscow head offices	4	3	4	4	5	8
Local branches	–	–	–	–	2	3
St Petersburg	–	–	–	1	1	5
Provinces	2	1	7	25	42	134
Abroad	–	–	1	8	4	3
TOTAL Moscow banks	6	4	12	38	54	153
Provincial banks						
St Petersburg	1	1	2	2	1	1
Moscow	–	–	–	1	–	–
Provincial head offices	30	25	26	29	23	29
Provincial branches	26	13	34	124	74	58
TOTAL Provincial banks	57	39	62	156	98	88
Total joint stock commercial banks						
Head offices	39	33	40	43	39	50
Local and other branches	49	35	74	274	393	778
TOTAL	88	68	114	317	432	828
Mutual credit societies						
St Petersburg	2	3	2	3	7	29
Moscow	2	2	2	1	1	10
Provinces	80	97	97	113	296	1,069
TOTAL	84	102	101	117	304	1,108
Municipal banks	235	281	242	241	267	317
TOTAL all banks	456	508	548	789	1,119	2,390
of which:						
St Petersburg	9	10	15	20	28	71
Moscow	8	7	11	14	21	48
Provinces	439	491	519	728	1,041	2,237
Abroad	–	–	3	27	29	34

In addition, treasury offices and savings banks as above under State Bank.[a] One
banking office per 56,500 people in 1914 (excluding savings banks). If the savings
banks are included the proportion is 1:15,300.

[a]In 1911 the State Bank began a programme of building its own elevators and grain
stores. Those situated at a distance from branch offices had the right to grant loans
against grain. By 1914 it had nine such sections. It also had forty-five settlement
sections.

The State Bank

The State Bank, founded in 1860, had to assume the payment of interest and the refund of deposits of the prereform government owned banking institutions, a task which seriously deflected it from serving the economy until well into the 1880s.[14] Until 1897 the State Bank was not a bank of issue. Paper currency was issued on the basis of a law of 1843 by the State Printing Office, and was carried out solely on the demand of the government. However the notes issued and their redemption fund were entered in a special section of the balance sheet of the State Bank, and that part of it which was not secured by the fund was reckoned as the debt of the treasury.

Until the 1890s the State Bank held approximately 30 per cent of the current accounts and deposits of the whole commercial credit system, which it attracted by offering high interest rates. The Bank's own capital grew as well, from the initial 15 million roubles derived from the resources of the liquidated banks to 25 million in 1879 and to 50 million in 1892. Its reserve capital grew to 5 million in 1893. Its network of branches expanded from forty seven in 1875 to eighty nine in 1893, not counting the offices in the two capital cities, St Petersburg and Moscow.[15]

Though the State Bank was an integral part of the financial structure of the state, it was not, even at this early stage, simply an instrument of the treasury. The treasury had its current account with the Bank and employed the Bank for issuing and subscribing to state loans and short-term treasury bonds. The Bank also paid the interest and amortisation of the state debt. During the 1870s as a consequence of the Russo–Turkish War, the debt of the treasury to the Bank on account of note issues increased very substantially.[16] In the course of the 1880s the debt of the treasury began to decrease. The issue of notes almost ceased, and gold stocks, thanks to special buying and loans, grew appreciably. Until 1894, when the rouble finally became stabilised, the State Bank was effectively used for the purpose of counteracting the adverse effects of currency fluctuations. In addition to its purely financial and monetary rôle, it did play – though more effectively from the mid-1880s onward – an important part in directing and controlling all the credit and financial relations of the country.

The currency reform of 1897 converted the State Bank into a central bank by making it the only bank of issue in Russia. The introduction of the gold standard also required the Bank to redeem the government paper currency. At the beginning of this operation the value of notes in circulation had reached 1068·8 million roubles, while the entire stock of gold belonging to the Bank and the treasury, reckoned in terms of the new currency unit, amounted to 1131·7 million roubles. To carry out the exchange of notes the treasury transferred to the Bank 862·5 million roubles in gold, and the remaining debt of the Treasury was gradually redeemed. It was extinguished by April 1900.[17] From then until the outbreak of war in 1914 the notes of the Bank were convertible into gold on demand.

The liabilities of the State Bank (other than note issues, which, except during the autumn harvest, did not vary greatly) consisted mainly of treasury deposits both on current account and in special deposits. After 1893 the Bank also held the current accounts of the state and private railways. Private deposits and current accounts, which had run to large amounts, fell off after interest on them was first reduced and then eliminated in the 1890s. At the same time there was a noticeable development of conditional current accounts (*giro* accounts) introduced in 1895 and reformed in 1900. They were designed to form a basis for the clearing house operations of the Bank. The Bank did not charge any commission on such operations.

The discount rates of the State Bank were regulated by the 1894 statutes. A minimum was laid down for bills up to three months, which rose progressively for bills of longer duration. In 1910 a flat rate was introduced.

Throughout the period under consideration the State Bank continued to act as a large-scale commercial bank granting direct credit to the public. Even when intermediary banking institutions took over the bulk of transactions the State Bank continued to advance credits to areas or industries which the other credit institutions left unattended or insufficiently served : small and medium concerns, small towns in depressed areas, etc. It did so by carrying out banking operations of all kinds on a very large scale. This was possible because there were a large number of provincial branches and because several hundred local treasury offices were utilised for carrying out simple banking operations. In the earlier stages, the confidence of the public, still shy of private banks, enabled the Bank to attract more private deposits than all joint stock commercial banks together.

After 1897 the most important factor in the State Bank's operations was the availability of large treasury balances. The Bank still provided credit directly on a large scale, but increasingly it relied on intermediaries, mainly banking institutions. Direct credit fell from 45·5 per cent in 1909 to 23·5 per cent in 1913. In January 1914 42·5 per cent of the Bank's aggregate discount and loan operations were with private commercial banks, against only 7·8 per cent in 1893.[18] At the beginning of 1914 the balances of the treasury represented 70 per cent of the Bank's total resources, which had increased three-fold since

1893, when they already accounted for 44 per cent of the Bank's resources.[19]

Joint stock commercial banks

The first joint stock commercial bank ('commercial' being their official designation) was the St Petersburg Private Commercial Bank, founded in 1864. The state provided half of its initial capital, taking 40,000 shares for 1 million roubles. It renounced its right to dividend during the first ten years if the dividend did not exceed 5 per cent.[20] Until 1870 however the number of joint stock banks remained small.

In the meantime Russian contacts with foreign money markets and bankers were being established through the flotation of government and government guaranteed loans abroad and through foreign participation in Russian railway construction. This speeded up the development of the private banking system in Russia. The good dividends distributed by the first few banks gave a further impetus. Government encouragement – especially on the part of Finance Minister Reutern, who was convinced of the advantage to the economy of private business and credit, and of the ability of Russian industry to interest foreign banks – accounted for accelerated growth. A number of German and Austrian banks participated in the share capital of several banks in St Petersburg and in the Polish and Baltic regions.

On the whole however private initiative was not easily aroused. This was particularly so in Moscow. Encouraged by the director of the Moscow branch of the State Bank, V.A. Kokor'ev, a merchant who had made a fortune in tax farming, managed to get 113 Moscow merchants and cotton mill owners to subscribe 2·2 million roubles for the Moscow Joint Stock Commercial Bank. It took two years to agree on the statutes, during which time nearly half the merchants who had originally promised to subscribe withdrew. They feared that they might 'offend the authorities' and thereby prejudice their chances in any future transactions with government departments. Thus the initial capital of the bank upon opening in 1866 was only 1·2 million roubles. Nevertheless the finance minister was delighted, and sent a telegram announcing the opening by the State Bank of a credit up to 1 million roubles for rediscounting bills, and an open credit on securities.[21] By 1873 there were thirty-three joint stock banks and forty-nine branches in the provinces.

The slump of 1873 and difficulties connected with the Russo-Turkish War of 1877–8 led to the collapse of six of the newly created banks.[22] The State Council began to fear 'too much competition' among banks, as well as the effect of bank failure upon public opinion,

TABLE 5.10 Evolution of deposits of the Russian State Bank
(1 Jan, 1875–1914) (m. roubles)

Year	Treasury deposits	Current accounts of savings banks	Private deposits			
			Long-term	Current	Together	Total
1875	30·3	0·7	92·5	132·2	224·7	255·7
1876	48·2	1·0	94·6	166·9	261·5	310·7
1877	60·0	0·1	95·6	134·0	229·6	289·7
1878	38·8	0·5	106·1	159·5	265·6	304·9
1879	30·3	1·0	115·7	142·3	258·0	289·3
1880	42·1	0·8	124·5	100·3	224·8	267·7
1881	88·9	0·8	123·5	99·9	223·4	313·1
1882	69·5	0·4	124·1	105·0	229·1	299·0
1883	58·4	0·2	135·8	123·9	259·7	318·3
1884	78·8	0·5	145·4	119·3	264·7	344·0
1885	65·9	0·8	155·0	135·7	290·7	357·4
1886	71·8	0·5	174·8	144·9	319·7	392·0
1887	117·0	1·4	171·4	116·6	288·0	407·3
1888	167·1	1·5	166·6	97·0	263·6	432·2
1889	185·0	1·5	164·2	85·3	249·5	436·0
1890	162·0	2·7	161·1	63·5	224·6	389·3
1891	199·6	3·7	158·4	75·5	233·9	437·2
1892	204·1	17·9	148·4	83·4	231·8	453·8
1893	147·7	52·4	159·8	66·7	226·5	426·6
1894	172·0	74·3	135·3	72·0	207·3	453·6
1895	331·2	50·7	128·7	69·0	197·7	579·6
1896	323·6	46·7	117·6	68·2	185·8	556·1
1897	332·4	27·9	109·6	89·7	199·3	559·6
1898	419·1	73·0	91·8	114·0	205·8	697·9
1899	471·5	8·3	86·6	117·6	204·2	684·0
1900	594·0	23·0	83·3	112·3	195·6	812·6
1901	479·8	23·9	72·6	95·0	167·6	671·3
1902	499·3	54·4	68·3	115·6	183·9	737·6
1903	354·0	114·5	58·9	198·6	257·5	726·0
1904	553·6	69·7	52·7	178·3	231·0	854·3
1905	351·2	43·7	53·0	202·1	255·1	650·0
1906	289·8	–	59·5	204·3	263·8	553·6
1907	301·2	36·4	66·2	183·0	249·2	586·8
1908	357·4	51·3	64·1	167·0	231·1	639·8
1909	433·4	52·0	57·5	252·2	309·7	795·1
1910	427·2	37·7	55·9	217·8	273·7	738·6
1911	651·2	24·0	48·9	212·4	261·3	936·5
1912	857·0	18·3	38·6	219·7	258·3	1,133·6
1913	872·9	15·1	33·9	232·1	266·0	1,154·0
1914	951·2	13·9	28·5	234·6	263·1	1,228·2

and began to restrict new promotion. Only during the 1880s, when Finance Minister Bunge, concerned about the depressed state of business, intervened forcibly with the state council, did the council allow further bank promotion. Each individual case had to be considered on its own merits however and promotion was liable to prolonged bureaucratic delay. Laws regarding the minimum size of the capital, the stipulated ratio of liabilities to the bank's own resources, etc., also worked in this direction. Government policy was thus partly responsible for the small number of banks and early concentration of capital in a few banks.[23]

In 1900 there were forty-three joint stock commercial banks, of which six accounted for 46·6 per cent of the total liabilities.[24] Of these six, three had resources of 100–150 million roubles each, and the remaining three had between 60 and 75 million.[25] By 1908 the six largest accounted for 51·7 per cent of total liabilities. From 1909 to 1913 the aggregate liabilities of all joint stock commercial banks nearly trebled, the six largest increasing their share to 55·3 per cent of the total. Of the fifty banks that existed in 1914, banks with liabilities under 100 million roubles accounted for only 17 per cent of the total, against 71 per cent in 1900.[26] The greater concentration of banking during this period was connected with the increased promotional activity of the banks and the special relations that developed between the largest Russian banking houses and foreign banks.

Before 1890 the largest bank was the Volga–Kama, which, with its vast network of branches, reached into the most remote centres of European Russia. Although it was a St Petersburg bank, it differed in character from other banks there. It was connected with commercial credit in the strict sense of the word, and in that it resembled Moscow banks. (It was founded by a Muscovite.) Unlike the Moscow banks however, which gradually became banks of a regional rather than a national character, the Volga–Kama was much more comprehensive in geographical coverage. The second largest joint stock bank was the Moscow Merchant Bank, which was connected with the Moscow textile interests.

By 1900 the Volga–Kama still held first place, but the Moscow Merchant Bank had fallen to fifth. Between 1909 and 1914 the Volga–Kama dropped to sixth and the Moscow Merchant to eighth place. In 1914 the five largest banks in order of their importance were the Russo–Asiatic Bank, founded in 1910 through the amalgamation of the Northern Bank, which had been founded in 1902 by the French Société Générale, and the politically compromised Russo–Chinese Bank; the St Petersburg International, with strong German connections, run by the brilliant Rothstein who had assisted Witte in effecting cur-

TABLE 5.11   The activity of the twelve largest Russian joint stock banks, 1 January 1914 (m. roubles)

Bank	Bills and goods credits	Trans-actions in guar-anteed securities	Trans-actions in unguar-anteed securities	Other corre-spondents[a]	Main assets	No. branches	Total net worth	Deposits and current accounts	Liabil-ities to corre-spondents[b]	Main liabil-ities	Redis-count and redeposit
1 Russo-Asiatic	258	42	280	92	672	102	78	367	184	629	63
2 St Pet. Intntl	144	40	199	105	488	56	79	265	118	462	21
3 Azov-Don	173	28	168	29	398	73	92	206	90	388	8
4 Foreign Trade	187	33	108	103	431	76	67	227	107	401	9
5 Main Ind. & Comm.	178	25	83	90	376	111	44	193	127	364	41
6 Bank of Siberia	116	19	81	21	237	57	36	164	46	246	7
7 United of Moscow	143	12	52	17	224	80	35	117	52	204	54
8 St Pet. Loan & Disc.	42	13	93	18	166	6	30	63	70	163	4
9 St Pet. Priv. Comm.	65	6	82	21	174	1	44	52	74	170	7
10 Comm. Bank in Warsaw	49	8	31	73	161	12	32	55	69	156	7
TOTAL	1,355	226	1,177	569	3,327	574	537	1,709	937	3,183	221
In % of aggregate balance of all joint stock banks	62	60	73	78	68	74	64	66	77	69	66
11 Volga–Kama Bank	179	40	82	20	321	60	38	246	31	315	11
12 Moscow Merchant	147	25	55	4	231	20	30	164	21	215	14
TOTAL 12 banks	1,681	291	1,314	593	3,879	654	605	2,119	989	3,713	246
% of all commercial banks	77	76	81	81	79	84	72	82	82	80	73

[a] Mainly industrial concerns or banking syndicates.
[b] Mainly foreign banks.
Source: Gindin, *Kommercheskiye Banki*, p. 381.

rency reform; the Azov–Don, run by Kamenka, which was closely connected with the new industries in the Dnieper Basin; the Russian Bank for Foreign Trade, known for its British connections; and the Russian Commercial and Industrial Bank. Seventh was the Siberia Commercial Bank, run by the capable and spirited Soloveychik, who had refused to amalgamate his bank with the Russo–Chinese Bank; and ninth was the Moscow United Bank, founded in 1910 by the amalgamation of three small banks by the Union Parisienne.[27]

Municipal banks

The municipal banks were organs of the municipal administrations, which were given limited self-government in the 1870s.[28] They accepted both current account and time deposits. They granted short-term credit, made loans to municipalities and district councils, and also granted loans secured by real estate. They engaged in pawnbroking business as well. The minimum capital of a municipal bank was 10,000 roubles. The total liabilities could not exceed ten times the ordinary stock and reserve capital jointly. Liquid assets had to represent at least 10 per cent of total liabilities.[29]

In 1881 municipal banks accounted for 22 per cent of the assets and liabilities of the commercial credit system, but many failed during the depression of the 1880s. By 1893 the assets and liabilities of the municipal banks represented only 10 and 9 per cent, respectively. After 1908 they resumed growth, but they continued to decline in relative importance, so that by 1914 they accounted for not more than 3·4 per cent of the aggregate assets and 3·8 per cent of the aggregate liabilities of the commercial credit system.[30]

In general these banks were located in towns with poorly developed trade, where they were the sole credit institutions. It was to such towns, often situated in depressed agricultural areas – the *mestechka*, proverbial for the lethargy of their business – that the State Bank turned its attention shortly before the war. As much as 30 per cent of these banks' assets took the form of long-term loans secured by urban property.[31] Many of the credits were granted to government officials, who often borrowed on second and third mortgages on their houses; the banks frequently were unable to foreclose on bad debts because of the depressed state of the market.

The mutual credit societies

The mutual credit societies were institutions of a co-operative character. Their capital was composed of members' subscriptions and served as security for the societies' operations. Liability of a member for the society's business was ten times the amount of his contribution. As a rule no outside resources were attracted and credits were granted to members only. No individual member could receive a credit larger than ten times his entry fee.

The societies conducted all types of short-term credit operations. Several of them, especially in the two capitals, owned very large resources and closely resembled joint stock commercial banks. The majority however operated in the provinces. They granted credits of less than 100 roubles (about £11) to their members, for the most part small shopkeepers and artisans, who were unable to obtain credit from the joint stock banks.[32] They frequently operated in areas where the joint stock banks had no branches. They weathered the difficult years of crisis and depression much better than the municipal banks, and they developed with a spurt during the pre-1914 boom (1908–14), when they grew four-fold in number, mainly in the provinces but also in the two capitals. During the pre-war boom the assets of the societies increased by nearly 200 per cent and their liabilities by 163 per cent.[33]

By 1914 there were 1108 mutual credit societies. On 1 January 1914 they accounted for 12·2 per cent of the aggregate assets and for 10·8 per cent of the liabilities of the commercial credit system. They greatly benefited from increased credit from the State Bank.[34]

Other banks of private commercial credit

Not enough is known about the so-called banking houses or offices that are sometimes known as 'bourse banks'. Several of them emerged in the first half of the nineteenth century, mainly in the Baltic and Polish regions; they were merchant firms that had turned to banking activities. New ones gradually made their appearance throughout the period, especially during the promotional booms of the early 1870s, and from 1908 to 1914.[35]

It is difficult to assess the rôle of these offices in banking activities, as they were registered as commercial firms. It is known that they were very active in stock exchange speculation. The largest among them amalgamated with or were absorbed by joint stock banks, or turned themselves into joint stock banks. For the period 1903–14 several such cases are known. The Junker Banking Office became the Moscow Industrial Bank, Ryabushinsky and Brothers became the Moscow Bank, and Wavelberg became the St Petersburg Bank of Trade and Industry.[36] Several went into liquidation; a few turned into commission offices undertaking all manner of bourse and commercial transactions. Some of them specialised in currency exchange, but this line became much less profitable once the rouble became stabilised and the State Bank concentrated the bulk of foreign exchange transactions in its hands. On 7 July 1914 the assets of the banking offices amounted to 117 million roubles, about half the assets of municipal banks; their deposits amounted to 88 million roubles.[37]

Small credit institutions

The small credit institutions in Russia were comprised of a variety of popular co-operative banks which served rural districts. The majority of them fell roughly into two main types : loan and saving co-operatives and credit societies. The co-operatives served both peasants and rural cottage workers, and even urban craftsmen, while the credit societies served peasants only. There were also differences in the composition of their capital : in the societies it was made up from deductions from profits, while in the co-operatives it consisted of members' fees. In both types the members were mutually liable for their obligations. A portion of their working capital consisted of subsidies from the treasury.[38]

After 1905 the small rural banks grew very quickly; there was undoubtedly a connection between the expansion of the co-operative movement and the dissolution of the compulsory rural communal organisation after the Revolution of 1905. In that year, after fifty years of authorised existence, there were only 1629 credit societies and loan and savings co-operatives in the whole of Russia.[39] More important however was government policy : in 1910 a special department was organised in the State Bank for the provision of credit to them. In addition credits at a maximum interest of 2 per cent were granted from the deposits of the state savings banks through the medium of the State Bank for the formation and increase of the capital of small credit institutions. Operations of this type developed very rapidly.[40] Over 10 million participants by 1914 entailed 10 per cent of the peasant population, man, woman and child. If only heads of households are considered ten out of twelve households would be involved.

The societies and co-operatives advanced money to peasants, as individuals or in groups, for periods up to twelve months against personal or material security or against sureties of third parties. If the bank had long-term deposits, they could loan for periods up to five years against material or personal security. In addition to credit for the purchase of land, cattle, agricultural equipment and fertilisers, for renting land and the erection of buildings, loans were also granted for the purchase of goods for sale.[41]

Many co-operatives not only undertook sales of agricultural produce for their members, they also traded on behalf of non-members on a commission basis, and on their own account. Some of the societies had their own grain stores to which members could deliver their grain, the societies seeing to it that it was dispatched either to more distant markets in the grain-deficit areas or to the ports, and sold when the market was good. Some societies succeeded in by-passing all intermediaries and even formed county and district committees for the purpose of joint sales of peasant produce, thereby freeing the peasant from the necessity of selling in the glutted autumn market or to local merchants who could dictate the price.[42] The trading activities of the co-operatives were especially well developed in the southern and eastern districts of Russia, and they dealt in other agricultural products as well as in grain.[43]

The transactions of small credit banks are shown in Table 5.12.[44]

TABLE 5.12 Activity of small Russian credit banks, 1 January 1910–14

Year	No. institutions	No. Participants (thousands)	Operations (million roubles)			
			Advances	Own Resources	Deposits	Borrowings
1910	9,978	4,644	213·0	75·0	144·2	24·9
1911	11,567	5,578	279·2	87·0	198·8	37·7
1912	13,627	7,095	389·8	109·0	284·7	58·9
1913	15,979	9,008	524·7	130·0	365·0	105·4
1914	17,933	10,678	673·0	157·7	466·0	128·0

The Moscow Narodny Bank, founded in 1912, became the central credit institution of the co-operative banks. By 1917 it had fourteen branches in Russia and commission agencies in London and New York. All co-operatives and their regional unions held shares of the Moscow Narodny Bank.[45] The credit co-operatives also received short-term credits from the Joint-Stock Commercial United Bank in Moscow.[46] The development of the rural co-operative movement was among the most promising of the social phenomena of peasant Russia. Unfortunately it was cut short by the Bolshevik Revolution, which substituted compulsory co-operation, in spirit not unlike the fiscal commune abolished by Stolypin's reforms of 1906–11.

Chattel credit was served by a number of pawnshops, of which two were state owned, eighteen joint stock, and 105 municipal.[47] The assets of the pawnshops were 68·2 million roubles in 1914, their liabilities 91·3 million.[48]

State savings banks

Although legislation introducing savings banks goes back to 1841, there were only two such banks in 1862. Until the 1880s development was very slow. The expansion of the savings banks owes much to the drive initiated by Finance Minister N. K. Bunge. In 1881 he raised the interest rate on deposits to 4 per cent. In 1884 the State Bank was authorised to open savings banks in each agency of the State Bank without waiting for the introduction of post office savings banks, whereby the rural population would be reached. These were introduced in 1889, and they led to a vast increase in savings, which continued even after interest was reduced to 3·6 per cent.[49] Table 5.13 shows the evolution of savings in the state savings banks.[50]

The breakthrough occurred, as with so much else, under Witte in the 1890s. Witte substantially simplified the opening of new banks and at the same time offered the depositor many important facilities. The most important factor in encouraging savings however was the stabilisation of the currency under Witte from 1894 onward.

TABLE 5.13   Growth indicators of state savings banks in Russia, 1870–1914 (m. roubles)

Year (1 Jan)	No. of banks	No. of books (thousands)	Balance of money deposits	Balance of deposits in securities
1870	64	67	4·8	–
1880	75	97	7·6	–
1890	871	638	111·3	–
1900	4,781	3,145	608·3	90·0
1910	7,051	6,940	1,282·9	279·0
1911	7,365	7,436	1,396·8	287·0
1912	7,705	7,973	1,503·0	300·0
1913	8,005	8,455	1,594·9	318·0
1914	8,553	8,992	1,835·4	349·0

Depositors could purchase securities through the banks without commission by means of their deposits. By 1912 2·5 per cent of all savers held securities. For some of the savers the purchase of securities was a means of continuing saving beyond the statutory maximum on deposits, which was 1000 roubles for individuals and 3000 roubles for institutional savers. However the majority of those who purchased securities were small-scale savers.[51] The average deposit in 1912 was 182 roubles; the average for rural savers was 190 roubles, for urban savers 173 roubles. The poorest elements – peasants and cottage workers, industrial workers and craftsmen, domestic servants and minor public servants – accounted for over 60 per cent of all books and 55 per cent of the deposit balances, the average deposit in this class being 166 roubles.[52]

Life insurance through the savings banks was introduced in 1905. Less than 13,000 people were insured in 1912; nearly a quarter of those insured, the highest proportion for any group, were government officials.[53]

The deposits in the state savings banks were an important element in the development of a capital market in Russia. It was in large part owing to them that the Imperial government could begin to issue loans internally from the 1890s onward. Furthermore they were of great assistance in temporarily accommodating government securities before their firm placement, whether abroad or in Russia. Until 1910 savings banks deposits were invested in securities (chiefly state funds), mortgages, and railway loans guaranteed by the government. In 1912 the proportions were 39·2 per cent in state funds, 38·2 per cent in mortgage bonds, and 22·6 per cent in guaranteed railway bonds.[54]

Such channelling of voluntary savings of small savers into the area of state interest or mortgage credit undoubtedly reduced the scope for private interests' bid for a share of these savings. However all the types of securities mentioned were favoured forms of investment of the general public. Mortgage bonds were in Russia a popular collateral as they were in other countries. Government and government guaranteed securities were also much more easily negotiable and liquid than industrial securities. Coupons of the state *Rente* were accepted as cash at par in payment of taxes, customs dues and in general in government transactions. They constituted a more appropriate field of investment for deposits of small savers which could be withdrawn at short notice.

Mortgage banks

In 1914 long-term credit operations on real estate were conducted by fifty-six institutions. Two were state banks for particular classes – the Peasants' Land Bank, founded in 1882, and the Land Bank for the Nobility, founded in 1885 – one was a *zemstvo* (district council) bank, and ten were joint stock banks. The remainder were chiefly the co-operative banks of land and property owners.[55] The rise in agricultural prices and the growth of the urban population led to an expansion of long-term mortgage credit, especially after 1906. Table 5.14 shows the development of the indebtedness of rural and urban real estate.[56]

On 1 January 1914 mortgage bonds represented over one-quarter

TABLE 5.14   Level of real estate debt in Russia, 1870–1913 (m. roubles)

	Rural real estate	Urban real estate	Total
1870–9	353·7	218·5	572·2
1880–9	776·5	416·1	1,192·6
1890–9	1,246·4	620·6	1,867·0
1900–9	2,123·7	1,168·6	1,392·3
1 Jan 1910	2,773·1	1,265·2	4,038·3
1911	3,051·7	1,393·7	4,445·4
1912	3,300·2	1,496·8	4,797·0
1913	3,478·8	1,642·6	5,121·2

of the total value of all Russian securities, 5300 million out of 21,600 million roubles, and nearly 38 per cent of the total value of securities held domestically. Only 5 per cent of the mortgage bonds were in foreign portfolios. Between 1908–9 and 1914 mortgage bonds absorbed a larger proportion of domestic capital than any other type of security. Of the 5300 million roubles in mortgage bonds only 1690 million were mortgages on urban properties.[57]

FUNCTIONS OF THE MAIN INSTITUTIONS OF COMMERCIAL CREDIT

The State Bank

The active work of the State Bank was based on the provisions of new statutes issued in 1894, three years before the introduction of the gold standard. Though there was an awareness that the 1894 statutes, as interpreted by contemporary orthodox financiers, were incompatible with the new rôle of the State Bank as a central bank of issue, those statutes were in force throughout the period under consideration.[58]

The statutes were prepared under the active leadership of Professor A. I. Antonovich of Kiev, a convinced supporter of the policy of financing intensive economic growth through paper issues. He was critical of the 1860 statutes of the State Bank, which allowed only discounting of commercial bills, because he felt that they did not correspond to the specific character of Russian economic life. He spoke of 'currency of honesty and intelligence' which could be used as collateral. S. Y. Witte, who took office as finance minister in August 1892, was greatly impressed by Antonovich, whom he brought to participate in the special committee set up to reconsider the rôle and functions of the State Bank.[59] Initially, under Antonovich's influence, Witte even contemplated discontinuance of his predecessors' work of preparing for the introduction of the gold standard. Ultimately however he decided that, given the unhappy history of Russian currency and the pressing need for foreign capital, a currency based on gold was more likely to further his plans for activating the economy.

In taking over the ministry of finance in 1892 – Witte wrote to the Tsar – I felt obliged to make clear to myself the foundations of the commercial and industrial policy of my predecessors and to bend all efforts towards confirming and finishing what they had begun or had taken over from their predecessors. The necessity of such succession and continuity seemed to me so paramount that I relinquished my own personal views.[60]

The main aim of the statutes was to increase credit to all branches of the economy where private credit was deficient. The Bank could discount not only six-months' bills but also in certain circumstances those running up to nine and twelve months, and not only bills based on commercial transactions but also those for 'industro-commercial purposes'. The most characteristic innovation of the statutes was the industrial loan on a *solo* bill secured by real estate, agricultural or factory equipment, 'respectable guaranty', or 'other creditworthy security'. The aim of such credits was not only 'provision of working capital but also of industrial equipment'. The maximum credit to any one industrial concern could not exceed 500,000 roubles. While original credit for this purpose could only be granted for twelve months, the statutes allowed for renewal upon expiry. Similar loans could be granted to agricultural producers, artisans, *kustars*, etc.

The 1894 statutes also authorised the Bank to grant credits on goods and on commercial paper for up to fifteen months with right of renewal for a further three months upon expiry. In certain specified cases the goods could remain in store with the debtor, and could even be passed on for manufacture or processing. The statutes envisaged opening up special accounts for bills and securities, the supply of working capital to county and municipal authorities, and grants of credit through a variety of intermediaries.[61]

In practice the State Bank did not develop its operations on the scale envisaged by the statutes, though the substantial increase in discount and loan operations and especially its credit to industry during 1893–96, as well as loans to estate owners, greatly contributed to the boom of the 1890s. There was in particular an increase in advances against goods. The introduction of the gold standard in 1897 forced the Bank to restrict its programme temporarily, but this retrenchment was not felt acutely in the economy because these were years of unprecedented expansion in connection with railway construction and large-scale foreign capital imports directly into industry. Furthermore, as the Bank no longer had to advance credit to the treasury and to the state mortgage banks, it was able to increase its ordinary commercial operations.[62]

When the slump came in the autumn of 1899 the State Bank began to apply in practice the provisions of the 1894 statutes, stepping up its advances on non-guaranteed securities especially. Even during the years when the State Bank acted more on the lines of an orthodox bank of issue, its promotion of the Russo–Chinese Bank and of the Chinese Eastern Railway Company, and its subsidies to the Loan and Discount Bank of Persia, were significant departures even though they were measures which the Bank carried out on behalf of the government in accordance with the government's programme of what Witte termed 'peaceful economic penetration' into colonial territories.[63] During the slump the State Bank also advanced direct credits to industrial undertakings on a large scale. These were known as 'infra-statutory' loans and they needed the sanction of the finance minister in each case. These loans will be discussed later in another connection.

Viewing the overall lending policy of the State Bank after 1897, it can be seen that commercial discounting represented on the average only 50 per cent of its activity, against e.g. 70–90 per cent of that of the Bank of France and the Reichsbank. The average duration of bill discounts was 43·68 days as against fifteen to twenty days in France and Germany. About 50 per cent of the bills discounted were one to three-months' bills; 30 to 40 per cent were three to six-months' bills. A large proportion of discounts applied to securities.[64] The Bank also made loans of various terms and designations – industrial, agricultural, on bonds, and on goods. Loan operations on goods took the form of pledging agricultural and industrial products for terms up to nine months, of metals up to fifteen months. Loans secured by various commercial documents, such as bills of lading and railway duplicates, were usually of three months' duration. Loans with securities as collateral (mortgage bonds were a very popular collateral) were granted up to nine months, or special current accounts were opened. Loans to small industrial concerns, agriculturalists, artisans, and small traders were advanced on bills with one signature for terms up to twenty-four months if secured by movable or immovable property, or a guarantee of other persons already enjoying credit.

Somewhat similar in character were the loans to small rural co-operative banks. They were issued on the security of bills for periods up to twelve months. In addition to these different kinds of credit, the State

Bank after 1911 undertook the construction of grain elevators for the improvement of the grain trade in the country. Grain stored in these elevators could be pledged at the Bank.[65]

Thus the State Bank continued to play an important part in supporting the credit organisation of the country even during the latest phase of the period under consideration, i.e. during 1908–14, when the private credit organisations were much stronger. It acted not merely as a clearing house for all kinds of settlements and as a keeper for the national reserves, but as an active credit institution which compensated for the weaknesses of the Russian money market.

The State Bank was able to continue its active credit policy after the introduction of the gold standard because of the manner in which the reform was implemented and because of the special budgetary and foreign exchange policies which were followed to assist its operation. According to the 1897 reform, the laws governing note issues of the State Bank required 100 per cent backing of notes over and above 600 million roubles, up to which amount 50 per cent backing was required. The inelasticity of the country's monetary system as established in 1897 was the subject of much contemporary criticism. The council of the State Bank, and the finance committee responsible for over-all financial policy, made no attempt to allay this criticism by drawing attention to the operations of the State Bank, because they themselves adhered to orthodox concepts of what the policy of a bank of issue should be. Even the more adventurous spirits, like Witte, preferred not to attract any publicity that might damage the very delicate and sensitive pattern of monetary and credit relationships that was gradually evolving.[66]

In order to secure the necessary elasticity of the system, the Russian government maintained gold reserves far in excess of legal requirements and refrained from fully exercising its right to issue uncovered notes. The Russian rouble was thus more in the nature of a gold certificate than a banknote. The maintenance of this large gold reserve was a luxury for a country so deficient in capital. It was thought necessary however because Russia was a large-scale debtor. Russia had always had a balance of payments problem and was exposed to gold drains continually, not just during periods of economic and political crisis. The large gold reserve, especially the gold balances of the Russian treasury and of the State Bank held abroad, helped to maintain the stability of the exchange rate. Furthermore, because most exports were of agricultural products, Russian export earnings had a seasonal character, and the government found it necessary to pay close attention to that fluctuation, as it also affected the stability of the exchange rate. The large gold balances also added to Russia's financial prestige and enabled Russian financial authorities to choose the most propitious moment for seeking foreign credits.[67]

Side by side with the accumulation of the gold reserve went another process, an integral part of the first – namely, the stabilisation of the budget. Witte followed a policy, which was continued by his successors (except during the Russo–Japanese War and the Revolution of 1905), of accumulating large budgetary surpluses from year to year. Part of these surpluses together with unemployed balances from credit operations were the so-called 'treasury balances', which were kept on Treasury account with the State Bank and represented a very substantial proportion of the resources not only of the State Bank but also of the joint stock banks. After the monetary reform, had there been no government deposits to be drawn upon, the State Bank would have been forced to reorganise its credit policy completely, in the direction of strictly short-term operations with full security. Because of the 100 per cent gold cover for banknotes and the appearance of a stable source of funds for credit operations in the form of treasury balances, the character of banking operations did not change after 1897, except for a short interval, in the direction of more orthodoxy. On the contrary the Bank was able to assume the rôle of an economic development agency in accordance with the objectives of the government in the economic field.[68]

There was undoubtedly a danger that, with political complications, public deposits might suddenly be withdrawn and the State Bank would be deprived of the larger part of its working capital. Treasury deposits exceeded the Bank's total authorised fiduciary issue of 300 million roubles. The upheaval of 1905–7 also proved the Bank's inability to attract private deposits to compensate for the withdrawal of treasury balances. This indicates that, in Russia's circumstances, political stability was a *sine qua non* for the success of her measures of modernisation.

Though the quantity of currency in circulation more than doubled between 1897 (when the gold standard was introduced) and 1914, from 1133·8 million roubles to 2281·6 million,[69] this obviously was not sufficient to meet the demand for money of a rapidly expanding economy in which whole regions, theretofore almost self-sufficient, were being drawn into the sphere of money exchange.[70] The various transfer and clearing operations introduced by the State Bank went a long way to offset the demand for currency. The opening of banking operations in the branches of the state treasury led to a very large turnover in book transfers and in bills of exchange which had to be sent to other towns for payment. The introduction of postal money orders in 1906, the organisation of clearing houses in the principal commercial and industrial centres, the creation of a special clearing house for the railways, and the opening of special current accounts for railways worked in the same direction.[71] During the first decade after the introduction of the gold standard the proportion of specie in circulation was kept high in order to induce public confidence in the new monetary system. After 1906 the ratio of specie to total money in circulation fell from 54·6 per cent on 1 January 1906 to 27·1 per cent on 1 January 1914.[72]

TABLE 5.15   Money and specie in circulation in Russia
(m. roubles 1 January)

Years	Total	Gold	Silver	Notes
1865	664	–	–	–
1866	662	–	–	–
1867	697	–	–	–
1868	675	–	–	–
1869	703	–	–	–
1870	694	–	–	–
1871	695	–	–	–
1872	752	–	–	–
1873	748	–	–	–
1874	774	–	–	–
1875	764	–	–	–
1876	752	–	–	–
1877	767	–	–	–
1878	1,015	–	–	–
1879	1,153	–	–	–
1880	1,130	–	–	–
1881	1,085	–	–	–
1882	1,028	–	–	–
1883	973ᵃ	–	–	–
1884	959	–	–	–
1885	900	–	–	–
1886	907	–	–	–
1887	941	–	–	–
1888	971	–	–	–
1889	973	–	–	–
1890	928	–	–	–
1891	907	–	–	–
1892	1,055	–	–	–
1893	1,074	–	–	–
1894	1,072	–	–	–
1895	1,048	–	–	–
1896	1,055	–	–	1,055
1897	1,134	36	30	1,068
1898	1,128	148	79	901
1899	1,235	451	122	662
1900	1,277	641	145	491
1901	1,384	683	146	555
1902	1,376	694	140	542
1903	1,424	732	138	554

Years	Total	Gold	Silver	Notes
1904	1,486	775	133	578
1905	1,661	684	123	854
1906	2,179	838	133	1,208
1907	1,957	642	120	1,195
1908	1,897	622	120	1,155
1909	1,759	561	111	1,087
1910	1,867	581	112	1,174
1911	1,992	642	116	1,234
1912	2,100	656	118	1,326
1913	2,244	629	120	1,495
1914	2,282	494	123	1,665

[a]The contraction in the currency supply during the 1880s following its expansion in connection with the Russo–Turkish War might have delayed the industrial 'take-off' according to Barkai. He may be right about deflationary effects during the 1880s because the money supply via the banking system did not expand significantly, mainly because Vyshnegradsky used resources of the State Bank to buy gold which not being legal tender could not be put into circulation. However, for the 1870s and 1890s Barkai underestimated the stock of money by taking into account only deposits of joint stock banks.

The functions of private commercial banks

Municipal banks and mutual credit societies, although the mainstay of small business in providing commercial credit, played a relatively minor role in the progress of industrialisation. The nature of their operations reflected the weakness and lack of initiative of small business, especially outside the main urban centres. While they provided short-term commercial credit by discounting bills and promissory notes, they devoted relatively large resources to credits secured by real property. On 1 January 1914 the mutual credit societies had outstanding credits secured in this fashion of 56 million roubles and the municipal banks 87 million roubles, compared with 563 million and 126 million, respectively, devoted to discount operations.[73] Furthermore loans to individuals rather than to business represented a large part of the credits granted. The setbacks that they suffered during the early stages of their activity were, for both the bank directors and the public, an object lesson in the very delicate task of rational utilisation of commercial credit.[74]

The relative weakness of the municipal and mutual credit banks was a reflection of the underdevelopment of small urban centres and of the provinces in general. It was consistent with the pattern of Russia's industrialisation, which excepting a few consumer goods industries was geographically concentrated in a few regions and only very slowly percolated into others.[75] The expansion of railways and improvements in the agricultural sector contributed to a quickening tempo of economic life in the provincial towns, but, given the size of the country, areas removed from the main trunk lines remained only marginally touched by these new developments.

Thus it was left mainly to the joint stock commercial banks to perform the most important functions of providing short-term credit for all branches of the economy as well as long-term credit to industry for the acquisition of fixed capital.[76] The joint stock banks also engaged in promotional activity on an appreciable scale. Until the 1890s almost all the funds that flowed into the joint stock banks were utilised in the form of discounts, advances on goods, and credits *en blanc* to industrial and commercial firms whose activities were almost entirely based on credit. 'Aucune entreprise', wrote the experienced E. Epstein, 'industrielle ou commerciale, la plus grande comme la plus petite, ne pouvait pas se passer d'avoir recours au crédit, sur la plus grand échelle.'[77]

Commerce in particular resorted to intensive use of credit. Merchants bought goods from producers and wholesalers with promissory notes or bills drawn by their suppliers and, in very rare cases, with cash obtained from banks by discounting promissory notes. In consequence almost all commercial bills and notes accumulated in the banks.[78] In the 1890s the general progress of the Russian economy, connected mainly with railway construction, and the substantial increase in the resources of the joint stock banks, which increase was partly a consequence of this general improvement and partly a result of the policy of the State Bank of encouraging the flow of deposits into the joint stock banks, enabled the banks to turn to other forms of credit. Nevertheless as late as 1914 discounts and advances against commercial bills and notes represented a very important though declining proportion of their total assets, and bills of exchange discounted with banks seemed to have increased at a greater rate than the estimated commercial turnover.[79] According to Gindin the relative importance of the joint stock banks in discounting bills of exchange rose from 30 per cent in 1881 to 47 per cent in 1893, 52 per cent in 1900, 54 per cent in 1908, and over 58 per cent in 1914.[80]

The rôle of the joint stock banks in making advances on goods was even greater. The State Bank and the joint stock commercial banks were the only banking institutions granting such credit. Until about 1905–6 the State Bank took first place; then it was overtaken by the joint stock banks. The State Bank tended to concentrate on rediscount and direct credit on goods to specific sectors and areas. The joint stock banks' credits against goods applied to a greater variety of merchandise. All evidence seems to indicate that commerce in general was well served by the banks, though certain regions were neglected, as is shown in

Agahd's biting criticism of the joint stock banks' activities in the Far East.[81]

There was a tendency among Russian economists to blame the joint stock banks for the backward commercial structure and habits of the country and for the failure to wrest Russian foreign trade, especially import trade, from foreign firms. This criticism seems to be only partly valid. The banks failed to reduce the many intermediate stages through which a commodity passed before it reached the final consumer. This was partly a matter of transport facilities and partly a matter of organisation. With regard to foreign trade, the joint stock banks could, given the experience and information available to them through their foreign branches, advise Russian merchant firms on foreign markets, sources of supply, etc., but the business of selling or buying was primarily that of the merchants. It would appear that the joint stock banks were blamed for what were essentially shortcomings of the Russian merchant class. Indeed, where the joint stock banks took upon themselves direct trading activities or when they undertook selling and buying on a commission basis, they were very successful indeed.[82]

Joint stock banks and industry

The credit policy of the joint stock banks with respect to industry falls into two periods. From the 1860s until the 1890s the joint stock banks mainly provided working capital by discounting bills of industrial firms and by advancing documentary credits for the importation from abroad of machinery, raw cotton, chemical products, etc. There was an essential difference between the commercial bills and the majority of industrial bills offered for discount. Commercial bills represented almost exclusively bills drawn by the firms' suppliers, while bills presented by industrialists were really promissory notes which bore two signatures : the first, that of the firm to whom credit was granted, and the second, that of one of the directors of the same concern, as a personal guarantee. In certain industries, such as textiles or sugar, where the director was the principal or even the sole owner of the concern, his signature was even more important than that of the concern itself. This special character of industrial bills was due partly to the fact that the purchase of raw materials did not coincide in time with the firm's receipt of cash or bills for the products sold. Furthermore the most important purchasers usually did not pay in bills, but by bank drafts, for which their accounts were debited on the basis of contracts with the banks.[83]

From the 1890s onward, at first gradually, and then on an increasing scale, the joint stock banks added to their existing activities a new branch – namely, provision of fixed capital for the formation of new concerns or the redevelopment of old ones. In this way the largest joint stock commercial banks added investment banking, on an appreciable scale, to their ordinary deposit banking business. Most of the St Petersburg banks were of this 'mixed Continental' type, except for Volga–Kama Bank, which for this reason is listed separately in the statistical tables showing the evolution of the assets and liabilities of Russian commercial banks. The Moscow joint stock commercial banks, on the other hand, tended to be of the 'English' type advancing (in principle) only short-term, strictly commercial credit.

Like the majority of textile firms in the Moscow region, the banks there were unincorporated share companies. The directors of the banks were all local textile manufacturers and merchants. The directors of the St Petersburg banks included retired government officials of high standing, promoters of railway companies, stock exchange dealers, and a few rich landowners.[84] The largest Moscow bank, the Merchant Bank of Moscow, was from its foundation in the 1870s to its dissolution in 1917, the property of fifty families. The number of partners changed only with changes in family membership through death or marriage. The membership of the board was remarkably stable; only one man held the post of chairman from 1891 to 1917.[85]

In the financial practice of the Moscow banks, credits to commerce and industry by bill discounts took first place, while in St Petersburg, except for the Volga–Kama Bank, they represented only half of the bank's total operations. Advances on securities, if practised at all, as during the depression of the 1880s, were very sparing and were granted on security of state bonds and state-guaranteed bonds in the main. Industrial shares accounted for a very small fraction of the total, and the advance when given was not more than 50 to 60 per cent of the market value. St Petersburg advanced 70 to 80 and even 90 per cent of the market value.[86]

A study of the Moscow Merchant Bank shows that it kept aloof from lucrative contacts with founders of private railway companies (railways were a favourite form of investment of St Petersburg banks). It even voted against participation in the capital of the government-sponsored Russo–Chinese Bank, as 'money will get stuck for six months'.[87] It also refused to take an interest in the officially supported Loan and Discount Bank of Persia[88] On the other hand, as early as 1873 the Moscow Merchant Bank granted loans against the shares of large Moscow firms, officially for nine months but in practice for several years. During the crisis of 1899–1901 large credits were granted to manufacturing firms, mainly in Moscow, on security of shares or by continuous renewing of bills.[89] After 1907 there was an increase in industrial credits and a change in their form. In addition to credits granted against shares and debentures of large Moscow concerns, the bank's branch in Kiev made loans to sugar refineries against *solo* bills plus additional security of shares. Substantial credits were also advanced through the bank's St Petersburg, Rostov, and Kiev branches on security of municipal property by discounting finance bills without additional security.[90]

A distinguishing feature of these credits, compared with similar operations by St Petersburg banks, was the fact that they were not used for fixed capital but used to supplement the working capital of concerns. The credits were given, in accordance with the bank's charter, for nine months, but many of them through frequent renewal were held for five or six years. The nature of the industries that Moscow banks served may also explain the difference in practice between the Moscow and the St Petersburg banks. The Moscow banks served the textile and sugar refining industries, in which working capital represented a high proportion relative to fixed capital whereas the St Petersburg banks served the mining, metallurgical, and similar industries, in which working capital in contrast represented a low proportion relative to fixed capital. Furthermore the textile mills of the Moscow region developed gradually over a fairly long period, and firms could rely on their own internal accumulations for fixed capital requirements.[91]

Another distinguishing feature of the Moscow banks was that they made no attempt to control or to interfere with the running of any concern to which credits were granted. Bank representatives did not as a rule sit on boards of the industrial firms; on the other hand, the majority of the borrowers did hold shares in or were directors of the Moscow banks. As industrialists they did not want bank interference. As bankers they knew their credits to be so secure that intervention was superfluous. The intimate connection between Moscow banking and industrial interests meant that the banks were in fact associations of several manufacturing concerns, and the first-hand knowledge of the credit standing of the firms made it possible for the banks to lend in this manner. Moscow banks also did not as a rule branch out; they operated within fairly closely knit communities, and did business with firms of long standing and solid reputation.[92]

Unlike the Moscow banks and the Volga–Kama Bank of St Petersburg, all other large joint stock banks engaged in transactions with non-guaranteed securities on a significant scale. The St Petersburg banks were most active in this respect. In 1893 they accounted for 37 per cent of the value of transactions on non-guaranteed securities of all joint stock commercial banks; by 1914 they accounted for 76 per cent.

Gradually these joint stock banks evolved a mechanism for financing industry. This mechanism is reflected in Table 5.16.[93] The 'special current accounts' (*onkol'*) and the 'correspondents' *loro*' (items 3 and 4 in Table 5.16) were most significant, and they provide a key for understanding the mechanism. Through the special current accounts which were a form of overdraft the banks opened credits to the public to enable them to acquire shares which a given bank had issued, or had placed in association with other banks in so-called 'syndicates', on behalf of various industrial concerns. Credits given directly to a concern under a bank's patronage (i.e. a concern for which the bank made an issue) are chiefly reflected in item 4, 'correspondents' *loro*'. Even when concerns were connected with the banks in this way (*konzernunternehmung* was the term used in German banking parlance to describe financing of this type), the banks tended to advance short-term credits to them on security of their shares rather than by discounting bills or lending against goods. This can be seen in items 5 and 6, which show the limited credits granted in the two latter fashions.

TABLE 5.16 Russian joint stock banks' accounts of non-guaranteed securities[a] and accounts *loro* on bills and goods (m. roubles, 1 January)

Designation of account	1895	1900	1908	1914
1 Banks' own non-guaranteed securities				
St Petersburg banks	6·6	20·0	17·8	91·7
Volga–Kama	0·9	1·4	1·5	3·1
Moscow banks	1·4	3·7	3·2	20·6
Provincial banks	6·0	12·3	10·6	21·3
TOTAL	14·9	37·4	33·1	136·7
2 Loans on non-guaranteed securities				
St Petersburg banks	0·8	1·7	2·1	12·8
Volga–Kama	1·9	2·8	2·4	2·6
Moscow banks	6·7	11·7	6·0	11·9
Provincial banks	8·6	14·4	4·4	3·7
TOTAL	18·0	30·6	14·9	31·0
3 Special current accounts under non-guaranteed securities (*onkol'*)				
St Petersburg banks	57·0	69·8	85·8	534·5
Volga–Kama	16·8	36·0	26·8	70·5
Moscow banks	20·3	30·7	27·0	137·4
Provincial banks	25·8	42·0	28·5	67·4
TOTAL	119·9	178·5	168·1	809·8

Designation of account	1895	1900	1908	1914
4 Correspondents' *loro* secured by non-guaranteed securities				
St Petersburg banks	26·8	70·1	27·6	589·6
Volga–Kama	0·5	1·2	0·8	5·4
Moscow banks	1·6	2·9	1·6	31·7
Provincial banks	4·3	7·7	8·5	14·9
TOTAL	33·2	81·9	38·5	641·6
Total on accounts with non-guaranteed securities				
St Petersburg banks	91·2	161·6	133·3	1,286·6
Volga–Kama	20·1	41·4	31·5	81·6
Moscow banks	30·0	49·0	37·8	201·6
Provincial banks	44·7	76·4	48·7	107·3
TOTAL	186·0	328·4	251·3	1,619·1
5 Correspondents' *loro* secured by bills and commercial bonds				
St Petersburg banks	9·0	35·1	75·4	219·5
Volga–Kama	0·5	2·7	5·4	9·9
Moscow banks	0·4	1·8	0·5	9·6
Provincial banks	13·2	19·2	35·4	79·7
TOTAL	23·1	58·8	116·7	318·7
6 Correspondents' *loro* secured by goods and commercial documents				
St Petersburg banks	6·5	12·6	49·5	54·1
Volga–Kama	–	0·9	0·7	1·3
Moscow banks	4·5	5·8	7·2	6·5
Provincial banks	2·2	7·5	6·3	16·1
TOTAL	13·2	26·8	63·7	78·0

*Non-guaranteed securities were shares and bonds, the interest payment on which was not guaranteed by the government, in contrast to government guaranteed securities, among which were the majority of railway bonds, the mortgage bonds of the Peasants' and Nobles' Land Banks, and a small number of railway shares.

The placing of securities through special accounts reflected the narrowness of the Russian capital market and the preference shown by the investing public for fixed income securities such as mortgage bonds and those emanating from or guaranteed by the government. The banking houses were therefore performing an important function of encouraging the public to invest in shares through the *onkol'* accounts and thereby contributing to the formation of a stock market.

It is evident from Table 5.16 that the mechanism here described did not evolve fully before 1908, and that its heyday came during 1908–14. The placing of industrial shares through *onkol'* accounts started in the 1890s.[94] It would appear that, with the recession of the autumn of 1899, the joint stock banks found themselves with holdings of industrial securities that immobilised a large proportion of their resources. The banks immediately stopped all further credits to industry, but this did little to solve their predicament, as foreign banking houses, the French in particular, drastically cut their short-term credits, both to Russian firms directly and to Russian banks. There were no buyers for industrial shares either in Russia or abroad.[95]

The banks' survival and ultimate growth were mainly due to prompt action on the part of the State Bank, which adopted a very liberal policy of advances to joint stock banks on the non-guaranteed securities owned by the banks themselves. To enable the banks to attract more deposits, Witte instructed the State Bank to reduce interest payments on its private deposits and to cease payments on current accòunts. The State Bank was authorised to accept for rediscount bills up to eight months' duration.

Upon the initiative of the State Bank, and with its capital, a special banking syndicate was set up, with the object of purchasing securities of 'sound' concerns which had liquidity problems to prevent their further depreciation and to allay panic. This so-called 'Red Cross of the Bourse' was in operation throughout the worst period of the crisis, and it proved a very effective weapon. In particular it helped to raise morale in a society in which, as the pre-revolutionary expert on Russian banking, I. I. Levin, expressed it, 'the industrial psychology of the nation was still in its infancy.' The 'Red Cross' was resurrected again in 1912 to allay panic connected with the disturbed international situation due to the Balkan Wars.[96]

Both the State Bank and the treasury substantially increased their deposits in private banks and in the banks' foreign branches, and continued to maintain them on a high level, except during the Russo–Japanese War and the Revolution of 1905. Finally the State Bank practised on a large scale the policy of 'infra-statutory loans' to industrial concerns directly. Such loans required the special sanction of the finance minister and were entered on special accounts of the State Bank. These loans, given to 'sound' firms in temporary difficulties, reached very large dimensions.[97] The essence of the infra-statutory loans from the point of view of the banks lay in freeing a portion of their immobilised resources. The credits of the State Bank enabled the industrial concerns involved either to resume their normal payments or to effect a partial settlement with their creditors immediately and pay the balance, under government supervision, within a specified time.[98]

On the whole, thanks to the timely intervention of the State Bank, both the banks and industry weathered the drastic withdrawal of foreign credits which followed the crisis. Partly because of the need to cope with the new situation arising from the withdrawal of foreign credits, and partly because the banks had on their hands large blocks of industrial shares,[99] they began to take a much more direct interest in industrial firms, and began to reorganise them, giving them greater efficiency and better technological equipment.[100] Short-term foreign credits resumed as soon as the situation became stabilised, but direct foreign investments in Russian industry practically ceased. They were resumed only after 1908, and then in a radically different form.

A further evidence of the government's solicitude for the joint stock banks was shown when it took over the two weakest ones to prevent them from declaring bankruptcy and thereby weakening the standing of private banking in general. This policy of the State Bank, which was of great importance in strengthening banking in Russia, had its obvious dangers. It encouraged favouritism, graft and bureaucratic intervention. It also could, and on occasion did, encourage improvidence and a claim on government assistance when things went wrong. It was however consistent with the Russian government's determination to modernise the economy speedily; it was also consistent with Russia's reliance on foreign capital.[101]

Industrial finance after 1908

After 1908 a change took place in the pattern of industrial investment. Foreign financiers, having sustained serious losses on their direct investments in Russian industry during the slump because of their abysmal ignorance of Russian conditions, began to realise that in a country like Russia direct investment in industry was fraught with dangers. They also became aware, through their experience in the slump, that behind the Russian joint stock banks stood the Russian treasury with its enormous resources.[102] Consequently there was a growing tendency on the part of foreign bankers, the French in particular, to acquire shares of Russian joint stock banks, either by purchase, or by participation in new issues of their capital, or by taking part in the financial reorganisation of the weaker ones (including the two banks under the patronage of the State Bank).[103] By 1916 foreign participation in the capital of the ten largest joint stock commercial banks, aggregating 420 million roubles, accounted for 45·1 per cent of the total. Of the 189·7 million roubles invested by foreigners, 50·5 per cent was French, 37 per cent German, 9 per cent British, and 3·5 per cent other nationalities.[104]

In addition to acquiring bank shares, French banking houses, especially the Banque de Paris et des Pays Bas, the Société Générale, the Union Parisienne, and the Crédit Français, began to form syndi-

TABLE 5.17 Foreign participation in Russian joint stock banks, 1916–17 (m. roubles)

Bank	Capital	French Absol.	French %	Foreign participation German Absol.	German %	British Absol.	British %	Other Absol.	Other %	Total foreign Absol.	Total foreign %
First group											
1 Russo–Asiatic	55	36	65·4	2	3·6	4	7·2	1·5	2·7	43·5	79·0
2 United	40	18	45	1	2·5	0·5	1·2	0·5	1·2	20	50
3 St Pet. Priv. Comm.	40	22·8	57	0·2	0·5	0·2	0·5	–	–	23·2	58
4 Russo–French, Moscow Priv. Comm., & Rostov–Don Merchant	35·5	14	39·4	–	–	–	–	–	–	14	39·4
TOTAL	170·5	90·8	53·2	3·2	1·8	4·7	2·7	2·0	1·1	100·7	59·6
1–3 only	135·0	76·8	56·8	3·2	1·8	4·7	2·7	2·0	1·4	86·7	64·4
Second group											
5 Russian Bank for Foreign Trade	60	–	–	24	40	–	–	–	–	24·0	40·0
6 St Pet. Intntl.	60	1	1·66	20	33·3	0·5	0·8	2·5	4·1	24·0	40·0
7 Warsaw Comm.	20	–	–	6	30	–	–	–	–	6·0	30·0
8 St Pet. Loan & Discount	30	–	–	4	13·3	–	–	–	–	4·0	13·3
9 Four Polish and Baltic banks	35	–	–	11	31·4	–	–	–	–	11·0	31·4
TOTAL	205·0	1	0·4	65	31·7	0·5	0·8	2·5	2	69·0	33·6
5–8 only	170			54	31·7					58	34·1
Third group											
10 Azov–Don	60	10	16·6	8	13·3	2	3·3	2	3·3	22	36·7
11 Bank of Siberia	20	4	20	4	20·0	–	–	–	–	8	40·0
TOTAL	80	14	17·5	12	15	2	2·5	2	2·5	30	37·5
Fourth group											
12 Russian Comm. & Indust.	35	4	11·5	1	2·8	10	28·5	–	–	15	42·8
13 Anglo–Russian	10	–	–	–	–	8	80	–	–	8	80·0
TOTAL	45	4	8·8	1	2·2	18	40	–	–	23	51·0
GRAND TOTAL	500·5	109·8	21·9	81·2	16·2	25·2	5	6·5	0·1	222·7	44·4
The 10 largest only (1–3, 5–8, 10–11, 12)	420	95·8	22·9	70·2	16·7	17·2	4	6·5	1·5	189·7	45·1
% of total foreign participations	–		50·5		37·0		9·0		3·5		100

Source: V. Ol', *Inostrannyye kapitaly v Rossii* (Petrograd, 1922) pp. 146–250.

cates with Russian joint stock banks for joint financing of Russian industrial concerns. It seems clear from the contracts consulted that the aim of the French banks was to entrust to the Russian banks the tasks of seeking out investment opportunities, acquiring concessions from the government where appropriate, and taking the general responsibility for the practical side of the business arrangement in Russia. The French banks for their part undertook to underwrite the capital for the ventures and (what was very important from the Russians' point of view) to place the shares on the French market.[105] Placing industrial shares was still a prolonged and laborious business in Russia; moreover the Russian banks, which were usually allowed about one-third of the underwriting profits on issues, could count upon higher profits when shares were sold on the Paris market. Therefore Russian banks tended to introduce Russian shares on foreign markets, even though they could have placed them domestically, and even though such shares were subsequently purchased by Russians.[106]

The French passed on responsibility for the industrial firms to the Russians and thereby secured participation in business which the Russian government by preference entrusted to Russian banks. During the period 1908–14 the French were attracted by the Russian armaments industry, shipbuilding, and the debentures of the private railway companies, twenty-three of which had been authorised by the Russian government. Russian banks in conjunction with foreign banking houses raised practically all of the capital for these companies, as well as new capital for the large old companies which had survived the nationalisation of the lines during the 1890s.[107]

The usual procedure was for a Russian bank to buy up the concession from the original founder by offering him a place on the board, or by acquiring concessions in the name of bank directors. (By law a company could not be a promotor of another company.) Second, a technical committee was set up, or, if the issue in question was on behalf of an already existing company or a reorganised concern, expert opinion was enlisted. Third, a financial syndicate was organised. Sometimes the technical committee and the banking syndicate were set up simultaneously, as was the case with the project for the electrification of the Moscow horse-tramcar service.[108]

Enumeration of the various investment projects considered and implemented in this way would take too much space. Suffice to say that there was large-scale financing in various branches of industry, municipal services, railway construction, etc.[109] Share issues of Russian railway companies did not attract the banks greatly, because there was no market for them before the line was in operation and had proved profitable; only then could the banks introduce the 'matured' shares to quotation. To encourage Russian joint stock banks to undertake share issues of railway companies, the government had to agree to guarantee 3 per cent interest on the shares during construction.[110] On the whole the initiative with regard to railway financing came from foreign banks. The Russian banks were interested however in securing profitable 'railway deposits' which they were allowed in proportion to their share in the syndicate. In this way, as the funds for construction were utilised gradually over four to five years, substantial deposits were put at the disposal of the banks.[111] Eighty per cent of the debentures for construction were raised in France alone. The British, through a firm of brokers, C. P. Crisp & Co., took up debentures of several railway companies.[112]

Excepting railways, armament works and shipbuilding, the tendency of Russian banks was to finance business by means of financial reorganisation, or by enlarging the capital of existing companies, or by transforming individually owned firms into companies. Shepelev estimates that out of some 1087 companies that commenced activity during 1910–13 only 30 per cent by number and 35 per cent by capital were entirely new. During the same period only 49 per cent of the total net capital issued on behalf of joint stock companies (railway companies excluded) was on behalf of newly formed companies.[113]

Looked at from this angle, the entrepreneurial activity of the joint stock banks seems to have been restricted to the most profitable kind of business and/or that involving the least risk because of its connection with the government. There is voluminous evidence however showing the expansion of banking activity involving innovation and risk. For example the region of the Urals was stagnant throughout the nineteenth century, and 'the renaissance of the Urals', as contemporaries called it, was in part a result of the activities of the banking houses. Inadequate transport was among the factors which caused stagnation in the Urals, and the banks, seeing a potential market, undertook railway construction in this region.[114] Joint stock banks also branched out into financing cotton growing, ginning, and transportation to the cotton mills, thus freeing cotton growers from dependence on a few large mercantile firms. They thus contributed to the increase in the proportion of home grown cotton used for manufacture.[115] Furthermore the joint stock banks were closely connected with the glass and cement industries, which, during the building boom associated with Stolypin's land reforms, 1906–11, registered the highest rates of growth of all Russian industries.

Nevertheless there is evidence, confirmed by the recurrent clamour for special industrial banks, that smaller concerns and those in light industry did not get enough credit from the joint stock banks. This was in part due to the manner in which the joint stock banks granted credit. They usually gave credit by discounting finance bills guaranteed by persons of standing or enjoying credit with the banks. Such credit was usually not accessible to the smaller concerns, unless they were among the circle of concerns under banking patronage, i.e. those connected through issues.[116] A further criticism that was commonly levelled at the credit mechanism devised by the joint stock banks was that they favoured issues where ordinary credits would have sufficed because they could make bigger profits and because such issues gave them control over the concern. There were complaints that banks ran the firms, interfering with every detail and ordering business managers about 'as if they were bank officials'.[117]

The joint stock banks were able to engage in promotional activities because of the special nature of the resources of the Russian credit system. In the earliest stages, when current accounts were still under-developed, this was a reflection of the backwardness of the system. Later however when relatively long-term resources, such as the banks' own capitals and time deposits, were on the increase, current accounts grew as well (from 300 to 500 million roubles from 1893 to 1900, to 900 million in 1908, and to 2415 million in 1914).[118] Funds which in other countries went directly into securities or into savings banks in Russia went into commercial banks. Deposits in savings banks during the latest phase increased by only a slightly higher amount than those in the joint stock banks, and were less than deposits in the commercial credit system.[119]

Even deposits in current accounts – according to Epstein – repre-sented a profitable investment of capital in Russia. This is confirmed by the restricted turnover of current accounts. In 1913 the average turn-over was twenty-three times in the State Bank, which paid no interest on current account deposits, but it was only six times in provincial banks, seven times in Moscow banks, and under ten times in St Peters-burg banks. Therefore *de facto* long-term capital resources were much larger than the banks' own capital and time deposits together would suggest.[120] It was this structure of the banks' liabilities which enabled the banks to concentrate their funds in relatively illiquid assets with less than the usual risk inherent in the resulting immobilisation of banking funds.

A further factor in the same category was the large relative weight of treasury funds in the totality of banking resources. The treasury funds available to joint stock banks *via* the State Bank have already been mentioned. Large treasury funds were also available directly to the joint stock banks. A large proportion of the gold balances of the treasury which were on the accounts of the credit office of the finance ministry did not pass through the State Bank accounts at all. Some were deposited by the credit office in foreign branches of Russian banks, where they were entered into 'correspondents' account'. The treasury charged only 3 per cent interest on the foreign balances, which were *de facto* long-term. Then there were the 'railway deposits', of which the joint stock banks held over 333 million roubles on 1 January 1914.[121] Altogether, out of the aggregate amount of resources in the commercial credit system (6900 million roubles on 1 January 1914) 1500 million roubles were treasury funds of one kind or another.[122]

A lion's share of the long-term deposits in general and of treasury funds in particular went to St Petersburg joint stock banks. They also had at their disposal short-term credits of foreign banks. Table 5.18 shows the availability of funds emanating from the State Bank, the treasury and the foreign banks to joint stock banks.[123] Altogether the resources of the joint stock banks in 1914 reached 4900 million roubles, accounting for 68 per cent of the resources of the commercial credit system.[124]

TABLE 5.18   Some sources of Russian joint stock bank funds, 1 January
1910–14 (m. roubles)

Year	Debt to State bank	Railway deposits	Treas. deposits in for. brs. of Rus. banks	Total govt funds	Foreign credits	Total
1910	61·6	52·8	76·4	190·8	209	399·8
1911	208·7	154·9	155·5	519·1	268	787·1
1912	378·4	130·7	226·1	735·2	446	1,181·2
1913	386·6	221·5	191·5	799·4	500[a]	1,299·4
1914	386·6	333·6	202·6	924·8	546	1,470·8

[a]Estimated.
Source: *Vestnik Finansov*, No. 6, 1928.

The concentration of relatively long-term resources in the banks was in a sense a reflection of economic backwardness. The funds which in other countries were used by the private investor to purchase securities directly were at the disposal of the banks because the Russians preferred depositing their funds in banks to holding securities. The banks used these funds, together with others, for the widening of their *onkol'* operations, whereby they assisted and encouraged other private investors to buy industrial securities issued by them.

A further point should be made. Though the resources of the commercial banks reached 6900 million roubles in 1914,[125] the effectiveness of these resources was much less in Russia than a similar amount would have been in a more developed country, because of the slower circulation of goods, longer tenor of bills, and less developed clearing operations. Therefore more credit was required for the realisation of returns on goods in Russia than on goods of the same value elsewhere.[126]

TABLE 5.19   Average value and period of commercial bills

Average value of commercial bills (roubles)		Average period of commercial bills (days)	
1860–79	1,866	1860–74	156
1880–4	1,769	1875–9	138
1885–9	1,071	1880–4	149
1890–4	777	1885–9	149
1895–9	582	1890–4	137
1900–4	475	1895–9	109
1905–9	428	1900–4	96
		1905–9	92

CONCLUSION

In a final assessment of the rôle of banking in the industrialisation of Russia, it must be stressed that the development of the Russian banking system was itself part of the industrialisation process. Banking had to be brought into being, and not just adapted and expanded to serve new needs as was the case in most of Western Europe. E. Epstein, the Russian expert, even goes so far as to claim that, while elsewhere banking was the product of economic evolution, in Russia economic evolution was the product of banking.[127] Though this assertion is exaggerated, it nevertheless remains true that in many spheres of economic activity in Russia the banker was the initiator and not simply the servant.

As many contemporary underdeveloped areas are in a position similar to that of Russia in 1860, the Russian experiment may be highly relevant. On the other hand, Russia was unique in having 'a very rich state in a very poor country', and once the state set itself the task of making the country richer it could mobilise enormous resources for the job. The banks undoubtedly succeeded in mobilising resources previously lying idle or used less productively; however the first spurts of industrialisation and the investments connected with them before 1890 took place largely independently of the Russian banking system. A high proportion of investment in the railway system was financed by the state, either directly through the budget or indirectly by guaranteeing interest payments on railway bonds issued abroad. Banks were instrumental in this, but they were foreign banks in the main until well into the 1890s. Moreover the new growth industries – the oil industry in Baku, the iron industry in Krivoy Rog, the coal mining industry in the Donetz Basin, the metallurgical industry in Russian Poland – all came into being through direct foreign investment, which had begun in the 1870s but which fully evolved only during the 1890s.

On the other hand, from the very start of their activity both the State Bank and the joint stock banks, especially the latter, and within their sphere of activity the municipal banks and the mutual credit societies as well, did provide working capital for industry. Furthermore from the 1890s onward both the joint stock banks and the savings banks began to play a more active part, the joint stock banks by making advances not only against state securities and state guaranteed securities but also against shares in debentures of industrial concerns, the savings banks by accommodating issues of state securities before final placement.

In the 1890s the joint stock banks began to contribute to the widening of the capital market by operations with dividend bearing securities through the _onkol'_ accounts. The St Petersburg Bourse, though its importance as a market for Russian securities was undoubtedly growing, especially during the years 1908–14, still played a secondary role to the Paris Bourse, and even to that of Brussels; moreover it leaned heavily on the St Petersburg banks, whose creation it largely was. A large number of Russian securities, though quoted in St Petersburg, were involved in active dealings only in foreign bourses.[128] The Paris, Brussels, and other foreign bourses had become major dealers in Russian securities in the 1890s and earlier, while St Petersburg began to gain strength in the 1900s only. Even then the preference of the Russian public for mortgage bonds, and the large issues of these bonds during 1906–14 in connection with Stolypin's land reform, meant that foreign investment in Russian industrial securities represented a higher proportion relatively to their total investment during this period than domestic holdings did.[129] Gindin estimates that by 1 January 1914 out of a total of 21,600 million roubles (nominal) of Russian securities, 7800 million or over 36 per cent were held abroad. This proportion rises to over 47 per cent if one excludes mortgage bonds, for which there was practically no market abroad (only 5 per cent of the mortgage bonds issued). The 13,775 million roubles of securities estimated to be in Russian portfolios were, according to Gindin, distributed in the proportions indicated in Table 5.20.

After 1908 a preponderant proportion of foreign investment in Russian industry entered Russia through the St Petersburg joint stock banks, as did short-term credits from abroad. It can be argued that French banking houses would not have resumed their investment

TABLE 5.20   Per cent distribution of Russian holdings

State and railway bonds	38·4
Municipal bonds	2·2
Mortgage bonds (urban property 12·2 p.c.)	37·7
Shares and debentures of joint stock companies	21·7[130]

activities in Russia had it not been for the Russian banking houses which were prepared to shoulder responsibilty. On the other hand, Russian joint stock banks, because the State Bank assured their liquidity, could act as promoters and even engage in entrepreneurial activity, which was still inadequate in Russia. Behind the State Bank stood the treasury with its vast resources and still vaster potential, and with an extremely elastic fiscal system – if one ignores the fact that political instability was likely to prejudice its effectiveness. As Agahd expressed it so graphically : 'Between the [Russian] industrial share and the Paris bank is the *giro* of a St. Petersburg bank; between a St. Petersburg bank and the Paris bank is the *giro* of the Russian finance ministry.'[131]

Of inestimable importance in enabling the credit system to play its part was the alertness of the State Bank (with the finance ministry behind it) in averting disaster, the flexibility of the Bank's lending policy, and the Bank's awareness of the weakness of the credit structure and readiness to fill the gaps left unattended by other banking institutions. Unlike the governments of some contemporary underdeveloped countries, who use the money creating facilities of the banking sector as an alternative to taxation, the government of Russia like that of Japan transferred resources obtained by taxation to the banking system. In effect they used a combination of the tax power of the state and the specialised talents of bankers to shift resources from consumption to production. This policy was not always consistent. Sometimes paradoxical situations arose, as when deposits of small rural savers were invested in mortgage bonds of the Nobles' Bank. With some reservations it can be said that the Russian State Bank played the role that, in E. Nevin's opinion, should be played by a central bank in an underdeveloped territory.[132] Within limits it provided direct finance of development; it certainly provided indirect finance and it provided the financial infrastructure. Like Nevin's central bank, the Russian State Bank held a certain proportion of its assets externally 'in order to guard against contingencies involving an external drain of funds'.[133] Unlike Nevin's model, in which the central bank does not engage in ordinary commercial banking because of the risk of compromising the bank's moral position,[134] the Russian State Bank was a large commercial bank – until the 1890s the largest – and up to a point it competed with private banks in attracting deposits. Both the public and the business community apparently found its moral position beyond reproach.

Opposition to and a certain self-consciousness about the unorthodox policies of the State Bank, especially after it became a bank of issue, came from people who felt that the departure from the current practice of major banks of issue was an admission of inferiority. The financial authorities themselves, except for a few bold spirits like Witte, were shamefaced about it.

The large proportion of resources taken up by mortgage credit was a negative feature of the Russian capital market, especially as, to judge by literary evidence, the credits obtained by estate owners were used for conspicuous consumption, often outside Russia. It could also be argued that the availability of credit for land purchase kept peasants on the land who would have otherwise looked for other sources of income, and that easy land credit impeded urbanisation. The agrarian problem was not however one which could be approached from a strictly economic point of view, at least in the short term.[135] The inter-related complex of measures and policies followed after 1906 augured well for the solution of the agrarian problem. From the point of view of industrialisation, there is much evidence that mortgage bonds were used as collateral when obtaining loans for industrial purposes. This was widespread prior to the 1890s and continued throughout that decade, especially where Moscow banks were concerned. Furthermore many landowners used the funds they obtained by mortgaging their estates to buy shares of joint stock companies as well as government bonds. Finally the land banks contributed to a redistribution of real wealth and rendered it more liquid.[136]

A final point must be mentioned. The Russian experiment in modernisation had, after some hesitation, been made not by using money inflation, but on the contrary by using a very rigid system of note issue. Russia's earlier unhappy experience with paper currency would have been reason enough to impose rigid checks upon an improvident government, but as already explained there were valid reasons – connected in the main with the need for foreign credits – why Russia should have adopted the system it did. The generous provision of means of payments *via* the credit system partly corrected the inadequacies of the currency supply.

It may be appropriate to sum up by paraphrasing Nevin : solvency and sound finance cannot be provided by statute. Whatever the statutory provisions, central bank credit will be misused unless the bank exercises good judgement and the government uses wise abstention. Otherwise the central bank will become the milk cow of an improvi-

dent government.[137] On the whole, during the period under consideration and especially after the 1880s, both the State Bank and the
Imperial government acted with wisdom and restraint. There were
departures from this line : the State Bank was used indirectly to finance
Russian adventures in the Far East and in Persia. The lack of parlia-
mentary representation before 1906 and the circumscribed competence
of the duma after 1906 were serious drawbacks. The large foreign
debt and the government's intense concern for its financial reputation
abroad however had a very salutary restraining effect upon government action and upon officials responsible for financial policy.

Table 5.21 attempts to assess financial ratios as of 1900 and 1914.

TABLE 5.21   Financial ratios in Russia on 1 January 1900 and 1 January 1914
(m. roubles)

GNP, 1900[d]	6,580·0
Principal assets of the commercial credit system	
(ratio to GNP: 0·30)	1,990·0
GNP, 1914[d]	11,805·0
Principal assets of the commercial credit system[a]	
(ratio to GNP: 0·61)	7,203·0
Assets of other financial institutions,[b] 1914	8,041·2
Total assets of all financial institutions	
(ratio to GNP: 1·29)	15,244·2
Specie in circulation, 1900	786·0
Paper currency in circulation, 1900	491·0
TOTAL	1,277·0
Income velocity of specie and currency, 1900	5·16
Specie in circulation, 1914	616·9
Paper currency in circulation,[c] 1914	1,664·7
TOTAL	2,281·6
Income velocity of specie and currency, 1914	5·19

[a]The State Bank, joint stock banks, mutual credit societies, and municipal
banks; see Table 5.4.
[b]Bourse banks, savings banks, small credit institutions, mortgage banks and
pawnshops.
[c]From Katzenellebaum, loc. cit., p. 6, and Raffalovich, op. cit., p. 359. Table 15.
[d]Prokopovich, 'Über die Bedingungen der Industriellen Entwicklung
Russlands', loc. cit.

Unfortunately data are lacking for the gross national product before
1900, for comparative purposes. It is evident however that Russia like

Japan, both latecomers to industrialisation, achieved a relatively high ratio in a very short time. A high rate of growth in the ratio can be inferred from the fact that the assets of the commercial banking system grew from less than 1000 million roubles in 1875 to more than 7000 million in 1914.

6 French investment in Russian joint stock companies, 1894–1914*

The Russian industrialisation drive was accompanied and made possible in the decade of the 1890s and in the first decade and one-half of the twentieth century by an unprecedented influx of foreign capital into various types of investment : into government bonds, into railway bonds with government guarantee, into municipal enterprise and into industry. By 1914 foreigners held nearly one of every two Russian bonds of a public nature in circulation and in addition they held almost half of the shares of the joint stock companies.[1] The French alone held about two of every three Russian bonds abroad, and nearly one of every three Russian bonds issued. They also accounted for about one-third of foreign holdings of Russian company shares and for about one-seventh of the total nominal Russian joint stock capital issued. Though relative to French holdings of Russia's public debt French investment in Russian company shares was fairly modest, its importance in the context of the Russian economy was much greater than the mere absolute amount would suggest, as French capital went primarily into Russia's basic industries such as mining and metallurgy, and into banking.

The mass influx of French capital into Russian industry had begun after 1894. Political factors acted as a stimulus, but factors of a non-political nature seemed to have been more important in shaping French investment decisions. French interest in Russian industry coincided with the industrial boom in France in the years 1896–9, which Clapham has called the 'period of the real French Industrial Revolution'.[2] It was connected with a temporary disillusionment of the French public with the low yield of government securities, hitherto their favourite form of investment, and their consequent desire to look for more remunerative employment of capital in the industrial field.[3]

Simultaneously such factors as large government orders for military

* From *Business History* (Liverpool), vol. II (June 1960). Reprinted by permission.

and naval stores, the new tariff policy, the hopes connected with the construction of the new urban and suburban electric transport and the preparations for the 1900 exhibition, had brought about a rise in prices of basic industrial products and opened up prospects of rich rewards to the investor. Financiers and stock exchange dealers were not slow to profit by the new situation and began to circulate industrial securities which were eagerly taken up by the French public. Soon the enthusiasm for dividend bearing securities was extended to Russian industrial securities which had not previously greatly interested the investing public.[4] Though the average rate of interest on Russian government bonds, conversions notwithstanding, was still relatively high, the exceptionally high profits made on the purchase of these bonds during 1888–94 were obviously a thing of the past, and Frenchmen were eager to avail themselves of the opportunities of higher profits which Russian company shares seemed to offer. The wide publicity given to a handful of Russian concerns which distributed uncommonly high dividends acted as a further inducement, and Russian industrial securities were flowing on to the Paris Bourse where they were appreciating in value like their French equivalents.

French interest in Russian industry was further encouraged by the attitude of the Belgians who, stimulated by the high prices which the products of mining and metallurgy commanded at that time in Belgium, either directly took the lead in the opening up of the mineral wealth of the Dnieper region in South Russia, or did so on behalf of French capital. Much French capital had thus entered Russia under a Belgian cloak, partly owing to the more liberal Belgian company law, partly because Belgian taxes were lower than French, and partly because Belgians traditionally pioneered new ventures which they subsequently passed on to others at a profit.[5]

More important than the forces at work in France in favour of Russian industrial securities were the measures of reform undertaken by the Russian government. First there was the tariff policy, which culminated in the highly protective tariff of 1891, and which by virtually eliminating the competition of foreign imports opened up for the prospective owners of new Russian industries a market of over 100 million people. Second came the currency reform, 1894–7, which put an end to the violent fluctuations of the exchange rates and made long-term foreign investment in Russia more attractive. Finally there was the intensive programme of railway construction, which resulted in almost doubling the network between 1892 and 1902, and created a steady demand for the products of the mining and metallurgical industries.[6]

Much of the expenditure for railway construction and equipment emanated from the Russian government, and this was a very important factor in attracting French investment into the metallurgical and mining industries. Government orders were given for several years in advance and at prices which had an element of subsidy in them. The patronage of the government conferred upon the shares of the enterprises connected with railway construction a special security, and the kind of official guarantee so dear to the heart of the French investor. This may explain the obvious bias of the French for investment in mining and metallurgy, for by 1900 they had sunk about 70 per cent of the total invested in Russian industry in that direction, as well as the large concentration of French capital in South Russia, which specialised in the production of rails.[7]

The evolution of French capital investment followed that of the Russian economy in general. The years 1895–1900 and 1909–14, the boom years in Russian industry, were also years of the largest influx of French capital, whereas the intervening years of crisis and depression, protracted by the Russo–Japanese War and the 1905 Revolution, meant a virtual cessation of the influx of French capital into Russian private enterprise.

By 1900 the French had invested in Russian joint stock companies (commercial and railway companies not included) a total of 692,371,823 francs. In addition some 100 million francs of French capital went into Belgian firms engaged in mining and metallurgical activities in South Russia. This capital was distributed between ninety companies, forty-nine of which were engaged in mining and metallurgy and another nine in the manufacture of machines and metal goods.[8] During the decade of the 1890s the rate of growth of French capital investment exceeded both the rate of growth of total foreign capital and that of domestic capital invested in joint stock companies in Russia.[9] Not all this capital entered Russia as investment in French concerns. As much as 44 per cent of French capital took the form of participations in forty-two Russian companies.[10]

French investment in foreign companies was due to several causes. While French companies operating abroad had to pay French taxes on their total share and debenture capital, those which worked on the basis of foreign statutes were liable to taxation only on the portion of their securities estimated to be in circulation in France, a portion difficult to ascertain, thus providing opportunities for tax evasion.[11] Another reason for the 'naturalisation moscovite' was the lengthy, cumbersome and frequently costly formalities connected with the foundation of a new company, which in Russia still required Imperial authorisation.[12] The tendency of French capital in Russia to abandon its nationality was due also to the hostility with which certain sections of public opinion in Russia viewed the 'foreign conquest' of the mineral wealth of their country and to the desire on the part of the French to share in the favours which the Russian administration accorded more readily to Russian concerns.[13] Finally, foreign companies in Russia were subject to a clause which entitled the Imperial government to withdraw its authorisation at will, and in order to forestall such a possibility, French capitalists preferred to use Russian registry.[14]

French capital, like foreign capital in general, had in the main entered Russia in the form of participation in share capital. Exact figures for the amount of French participation in debenture capital are not available. It is known only that total debenture capital in Russian industry in 1899 was 176 million roubles of which 80 million was in metallurgy and machine construction alone. Two-thirds of this debenture capital was estimated to have been placed abroad.[15] In the early period of Russian industrial expansion it was necessary to resort to debenture issues because many companies found it difficult to secure short-term credit. However issues of debentures required permission of the finance minister, who granted such authority sparingly. He was afraid that the possible failure of industrial concerns to meet the interest on their bonds would unfavourably affect the government bonds and railway bonds with government guarantee. Moreover, under Russian law, industrial bonds were a priority mortgage claim, and this made such issues inaccessible to many mining concerns, which were for the most part tenants of their respective sites.[16]

Geographically over 40 per cent of the French capital invested in 1900 was in South Russia; second and third in order of importance were the Polish region and the Urals, and the territorial bias in favour of these three regions reflected French preference for mining and metallurgy.[17] Historically the first to attract French capital was the Sosnowica–Dombrowa region of Russian Poland, situated in the extreme south-western corner of the Kingdom of Poland, where originally most of the foreign capital was German and where many firms were simply branches of equivalent concerns in Germany. Most of the German works here specialised in metal working and engineering, and employed pig iron imported from Germany. This was stimulated by the provisions of the 1868 tariff which retained low duties on pig iron while raising substantially those on imported iron. The German manufacturers also availed themselves of the right of duty free imports of iron from Germany for machine construction work. During the 1880s the import duties on pig iron were gradually increased and, what was more important, much higher duties were imposed on goods entering by land, making imports of German pig iron prohibitive. This fact, joined to the construction of the Ivangorod–Dombrowa railway line, which connected the coal of the Dombrowa basin with the iron ores in the east, encouraged the development here of basic metallurgy into which foreign capital began to flow.[18]

Though German capital was still predominant, the laws of 1887 and the insistence of the Russian government that the shareholders of joint stock companies outside towns in Poland must be of Russian nationality, resulted in a tendency on the part of German entrepreneurs to accept Russian nationality, and also led to a certain slackening of German capital imports.[19] Simultaneously there was a gradual penetration of French capital into this region, a development which was undoubtedly viewed favourably by the Russian authorities, although there is no means of proving that it was consciously encouraged by them.

While French capitalists had undoubtedly made their contribution to the higher rates of growth and higher levels of productivity of this region, notwithstanding its slender resources, much larger was their contribution to the development of the South Russian industrial region, of which they may be considered, with some qualifications, the founders and pioneers. The South Russian industrial district with its coal deposits in the Donetz Basin, the iron ores of Krivoy Rog in the Yekaterinoslav *guberniya* on the Upper Dnieper, the resources of limestone, dolomite and fire clay in the vicinity, and manganese ore in the Nikopol-Maryupol region, had become by the end of the nineteenth century the principal source of coal and iron for the whole country.

The mineral wealth of this region had attracted the attention of the Russian government at an early date, but all attempts to set up a state owned metallurgical industry proved ineffective. Government attempts to stimulate private initiative by grants of concessions and subsidies also met with failure. Either the necessary capital could not be assembled, or the choice of the site for exploitation proved wrong, or simply the subsidies and privileges accorded by the government were used for personal purposes.[20] Moreover in all attempts at promoting a metallurgical industry in this region use was made of the inferior local ores. Even the Welshman, John Hughes, who in 1871 had built the metallurgical works of the New Russia Company (incorporated in London in 1869 with a capital of £300,000), established himself on the coal fields of the Donetz Basin and used local impure ores. He would have succumbed in the long run had he not been saved by the discovery of the ores of Krivoy Rog. The merit of the discovery lay with a Russian landowner, A. N. Pol, who however failed to enlist interest or financial backing in Russia. He found the necessary backing in Paris, and the outcome was the Société Anonyme de Mineral de Fer de Krivoy Rog, founded in 1880 with an initial capital of 5 million francs.[21] One by one French, Belgian and Russian firms followed suit, some setting up their works on the ore, some on the coal, still others between the two. By 1898 there were in South Russia seventeen large works for the smelting of pig iron, with twenty-nine blast furnaces in operation and a further twelve in course of construction. Only one of these works was entirely Russian. In addition to these major metallurgical works, the main characteristic of which was the production of pig iron in the companies' own blast furnaces, and its further manufacture into iron, steel, pipes, rails etc., there sprang up in South Russia a number of metal working and engineering works using local pig or wrought iron.[22]

The French had also contributed indirectly to the development of metallurgy in South Russia by large investments in the coal industry of the Donetz Basin. They had a controlling interest in six large concerns, which accounted in 1899 for over 34 per cent of the coal output of the region. In addition French capital was employed in a number of smaller concerns. By 1913 concerns with French capital participation accounted for about 51 per cent of the coal output and for over 78 per cent of the pig iron output of South Russia.[23]

The large demand for metallurgical products, and the fears of the near-exhaustion of the Krivoy Rog ores, induced French investors to turn their attention to the Urals. In the eighteenth century this had been the principal centre of Russia's iron industry, but was stagnant throughout most of the nineteenth century. In 1896 and 1897 two companies, both effectively French, had been founded here. The first, incorporated in Paris, the Société Metallurgique de l'Oural–Volga, with a capital of 18 million francs, decided to build a steel mill at Tsaritsyn on the lower Volga, in order to use the ore of the Urals and the coal of the Donetz Basin. The second, Volga–Vishera, was founded as a Russian company and had a capital of 25 million francs. The programme of the company was to smelt the ore in the northern Urals using timber, which was still readily available in the north, and to construct a steel works near Kazan in Paratov. Though the companies did not meet with outstanding success, nevertheless the initiative of the French had shaken the Ural industrialists out of their customary inertia, as witness the deliberations of the Congress of the Metallurgists of the Urals held in Yekaterinenburg in the winter of 1897.[24]

The crisis which hit the Russian economy at the turn of the century affected a number of French companies. Though cases of declared bankruptcy and liquidation were rare, some companies were placed under court administration, the most notable case being that of the Société de l'Oural–Volga. In a few cases the Russian State Bank afforded assistance to French or French financed companies.[25] On the whole the French suffered much less than the Belgians, and this was especially true of the coal enterprises.[26] This was due partly to the larger size of the French concerns and partly to the fact that, though the flow of short-term capital from abroad to Russian banks had practically ceased during 1900–2, the French banks continued to provide short-term credits to a number of concerns in Russia.[27]

By 1903 there were signs that the crisis was subsiding. However the outbreak of the Russo–Japanese War in February 1904, though it created demand for certain types of industrial products, introduced an element of risk which restricted foreign credit. The revolutionary disturbances, strikes and outbreaks of violence, which were most pronounced in the industrial regions, could not but frighten away the prospective investor. In addition the precarious financial position of the state and the danger of a return to an inconvertible currency deterred foreign capital further. By 1906 things began to improve a little, and several transactions involving French capital imports were being considered. The monetary crisis in Western Europe in 1907 acted as a temporary check, but from 1909 onwards there was a constant stream of capital which both contributed to, and was stimulated by, the boom in the Russian economy. By 1914 the aggregate nominal value of French capital estimated to be employed in Russian companies was little short of 2000 million francs. The market value was about 3000 million.[28]

No essential changes occurred in the pattern of distribution of French capital between various types of industry. Mining and metallurgy still accounted for over 60 per cent of the total capital invested, though within this large group there was a new emphasis on the oil industry (French capital going into English and Russian companies), and on metal working and engineering. This change made for better distribution of risk. One of the reasons for the change was the growing French interest in Russian concerns producing military and naval stores, the demand for which had increased in connection with the reconstruction of naval and military equipment after the Russo–Japanese War.[29] The growth of French investment in oil was due to the high prices for oil and oil products in the years preceding the 1914 War. The French had further strengthened their position in South Russia through new investment in former Belgian and in Russian companies, and had sunk new capital into the re-equipment of old concerns.[30]

To an even larger extent than in the 1890s French capital entering Russia did so under a Russian label. The number of companies working under French registry remained practically unchanged. With a few exceptions the companies of French nationality were founded specifically for activity in Russia. This applied to an even greater extent to Belgian and British companies.[31]

In response to the crisis the industrialists of South Russia, upon French initiative and under French leadership, organised themselves into syndicates, of which the most important were the *Prodameta* and the *Produgol*. In the changed conditions of the boom after 1909, the competition between the various syndicates, in particular between the two largest ones, and the conflict of interest between various firms in each syndicate, indicated that they had outlived their usefulness. Among the largest firms there was a tendency towards vertical integration, reflected in the acquisition of ore and coal mines by metallurgical companies.[32]

A feature of all French as of other foreign concerns in Russia was their large size.[33] Another important feature of the foreign enterprises was their relatively high level of technical equipment. Indeed many of the foreign financed plants were, from the technical point of view, superior to those of the country from which the capital originated. The new plants in Russia had benefited from the latest achievements of contemporary technique and industrial organisation and the accumulated experience of Western engineers and technicians.[34] Foreign and foreign financed firms were also in a better position to apply technical improvements, as they had more and cheaper capital at their disposal. On the other hand, Russian owned enterprises, even in the leading and nationally important industries, as for example the state owned Obukhovo armament works or the privately owned Putilov engineering works, suffered from chronic shortage of resources and had to employ equipment half a century old.[35] Even labour productivity, though notoriously low in South Russia as compared with Western Europe, was nevertheless much higher there than in the country at large.[36]

Though the 'newness' of much of the industry set up by foreigners was from the technical point of view an advantage, there were attendant difficulties. The new industries in South Russia were set up amidst the wild steppe. This meant that French entrepreneurs had to take into account not only the outlay on the enterprise proper, but also the cost of laying roads and building bridges, establishing water supplies, attracting and training the labour force, building houses, hospitals, churches, communal baths, introducing postal, telephone and telegraph services, and providing police protection. In most countries in similar circumstances there would have been estate agents, contractors and others eager to provide such services. In Russia initiative of this kind was lacking. Moreover it had been customary in Russia since the eighteenth century to place upon the plant owners responsibility for various services, which elsewhere fell within the scope of the municipality or the state.[37]

The available evidence would suggest that the French, like most other foreign entrepreneurs in Russia, acquitted themselves reasonably well in these additional tasks. We find in the balance sheets of the various companies large allocations for the construction and maintenance of houses, schools, churches, communal baths, etc. The rents charged for accommodation compared favourably with those prevailing on the market. In South Russia, where building material had to be shipped over great distances from the north, the rents represented only a modest remuneration of the capital, especially as in view of the general lack of 'house pride' among the Russian workmen maintenance and repair costs were high.[38] The Belgian labour inspector Lauwick, who knew conditions in South Russia from personal experience, affirmed that rents just covered maintenance and repair costs and that the interest and amortisation of the capital were at the charge of the companies concerned.[39]

This explains why, apart from a few exceptions, the financial results of the majority of French companies in Russia were not spectacular. During the boom of the 1890s the average dividend was about 7 per cent, though some French companies like the Bryansk distributed more than 30 per cent. The successful concerns were those which had acquired the mineral bearing or construction sites before the boom of the 1890s at relatively low prices, or had the privilege of duty free imports of equipment. The companies founded in the latter part of the 1890s vied with each other in the acquisition of sites, and offered extravagant terms for them to local landowners or peasant communities, who were quick to exploit the situation.[40]

French and Belgian capitalists had committed several errors of judgement in their investment policy in Russia, especially with regard to the estimated capital expenditure required. 'Ce qui aurait coûté un pour le premier établissement en France, en Angleterre et en Allemagne est revenu à deux et même à trois en Russie,' wrote the French Consul in Kharkov.[41] Labour though cheaper was less productive. 'Plusieurs directeurs estiment', wrote the Belgian Lauwick, 'que leur établissements feraient en Belgique ou en France la même production avec un cinquième d'ouvriers en moins.'[42] The French chargé de mission in Russia, Maurice Verstraete, warned prospective investors not to entertain too many illusions with regard to the rates of pay, which were higher than one was led to believe because of the many stoppages and the lack of experience of the Russian worker.[43] The effective number of workdays per worker was not more than 230 a year for there were many feast days and various family celebrations.

The days following such festivities and Mondays were usually a total loss. Intemperance was a real scourge and the cause of many accidents. Then there was the difficulty of procuring labour, especially at harvest time, when workers tended to leave for field work. Fluidity of labour was a serious handicap and various stratagems had to be resorted to to combat it.[44] Finally 'l'ouvrier russe n'est pas toujours le collaborateur intelligent dont l'ingénieur a besoin.'[45] The low level of general education and the limited facilities for specialised technical training were partly responsible for this, but French owners were remedying the situation by providing primary and technical schooling in their concerns.

All these factors raised the cost of capital expenditure. To those already mentioned must be added bad roads and long distances over which materials and products had to be shipped, the high costs of raw materials and equipment – especially for those concerns which did not have the privilege of duty free imports – and the failure of many concerns in the fever of promotion to prospect the sites thoroughly, which involved loss of precious time and capital.[46] Finally 'beaucoup de papier d'apport ou de parts de fondateurs ont été créés par des financiers avides qui ont compromis par ce balast l'avenir de certaines sociétés par actions'. In this way the initial capital was quickly absorbed and additional issues of capital had become necessary. More-over in most cases the companies found themselves short of capital for operating purposes, and were forced to resort to bond issues or to bank advances. Given the necessity to remunerate such large capital only few French companies distributed large dividends.[47]

The costs of production also proved higher than anticipated. The factors which had contributed to high capital costs were here at work as well. Many of the works were set up hastily, and their erectors over-looked the disadvantage of having to ship fuel and other raw materials over great distances, which might seriously detract from the advantage of a site near the richest ore deposits. The coal industry was handi-capped by a shortage of railway transport, which was in the main mobilised for carrying grain to the Black Sea ports. The special com-mittee in Kharkov for the allocation of railway transport failed to put things right, as the concerns were required to place orders for wagons well in advance, and were liable to heavy fines if they failed to utilise the transport thus allocated. They tended in consequence to be sparing with their orders and this, in turn, involved high interest charges, as stocks had to be stored till further transport facilities became available. This incidentally made for higher coal prices and affected metallurgical concerns without coal mines of their own.[48]

Finally the administrative costs of many French financed concerns were high. 'Il y a beaucoup trop de directeurs, commissaires, contrôleurs, reviseurs, agents commerciaux, secrétaires et employés,' wrote the French vice-consul at Kharkov to Delcassé. The number of directors in particular was excessive and their salaries high in relation to the concern's income, especially as they delegated responsibility to the managing directors, and sat simultaneously on the boards of several companies. Moreover they tended to abuse their position 'pour spéculer et escompter leurs propres effets avec l'argent destiné au fonds de roulement'; they were also reported to have made separate claims for expenses on each of the concerns in which they were involved when they made business trips to Paris. In addition it was necessary 'distribuer beaucoup d'or à ronger pour pouvoir faire des affaires et monter des entreprises'.[49]

On the whole a great many of French concerns were badly administered. In this respect the concerns built by foreigners had become not very different from the majority of Russian ones. 'Le milieu dans lequel l'étranger se meut ici l'absorbe très vite et s'impose à lui,' wrote the French Chargé d'Affaires Boutiron to Delcassé. The *laissez-aller* which prevailed in the French financed concerns was also due to the fact that in most companies, even where the members of the board of directors were foreign, the members of the management were Russian and 'apportent dans leurs fonctions le principal défaut du russe : la négligence du lendemain'.[50]

If the financial results of most French financed firms in Russia were not too spectacular in the 1890s, they were less so during the subsequent crisis and depression, to which French entrepreneurs contributed in no small measure by constructing two or three blast furnaces where one would have sufficed. Only in the Polish region concerns like the Huta Bankowa, Czeladz and Sosnowice gave substantial dividends, though during 1909–14 the position also improved in South Russia.[51]

The French had also to train Russian miners and workmen and educate Russian technicians and engineers. Some of the metallurgical workers, technicians and engineers were foreign, but the overall proportion in relation to the total workers and employees in any given concern was not large, and tended to fall as time went on; though the proportion of foreign foremen was rather large.[52] This was due to the lack of Russians with the necessary qualifications for this position; in fact purely Russian concerns often employed foreign foremen. Russian engineers were highly thought of as regards their theoretical knowledge, but in most cases chief engineers of foreign financed concerns were foreign.[53] However, as foreign employees had to be paid better than the Russian ones, and as the employers had also to bear the cost of repatriation of such men with their families upon the expiry of contract, there was a natural tendency to resort to local labour as soon as a substitute could be found. During the crisis and the revolutionary troubles of 1905–8 many foreign workers and technicians left Russia. They were replaced by Poles and Ukrainians in the main, who were thought to be more intelligent and adaptable, while Great Russians, though considered hard working and sturdy, were mostly employed in unskilled jobs.[54]

On the whole French concerns employed fewer non-Russian employees than other foreign firms in Russia, because when taking over already existing concerns they tended to leave their personnel and organisation undisturbed. Only the few concerns in Russia which were sister companies of those working in France had a relatively large French personnel. Thus the Lodz concern for the manufacture of woollen cloth, which was connected with Roubaix firms, employed some forty Frenchmen.

Foreign employees, though retaining their nationality, had frequently been born and brought up in Russia and spoke perfect Russian.[55] There were also some industrialists, engineers and administrative workers who had accepted Russian nationality.[56] Many were the Russified versions of French names to be found among those eminent in Russian industry. One of them, Goujon, ironically became the spokesman of 'truly Russian' interests in the Moscow district against the competition of the South Russian firms owned by his former compatriots. The acceptance of Russian nationality by Germans, Englishmen and Swedes was also fairly widespread.

The most important change in the pattern of French investment in Russia during 1900–14 was the increase of French investment in Russian banks, and the more intimate connection between French banks and Russian industrial concerns. Before 1900 the functions of French banks were confined to the issuing and placing of shares of the companies, and to the supplying of medium or short-term credits for a number of them. There was as yet no monopoly of the financing of Russian industry by a small number of banks. Though the Lyons financiers were particularly active, a number of other banks were also in some sort of relation with Russian industrial concerns, and the fact that consecutive issues of one and the same company were floated by different banks would indicate that the banks had as yet no permanent interest in the concern, but were solely concerned with the profit of the issue.[57]

During the period 1909–14 the Russian banks began to act as the vanguard of French banking houses in the financing of Russian industry. In the 1890s this function was performed by the Belgians, but after the crisis the Belgians, while still retaining some interests in South Russian industries, turned to business of a municipal nature in the main. The Swiss in other parts of the world tended to be active on behalf of French capitalists, but they had little contact with Russia and were known to have a special aversion for dealing with that country.[58] In the 1890s Russian banks were as yet too weak to perform such functions. Moreover the larger Russian banks were mainly under German influence and openly hostile to French interests.[59]

A very important reason for the interest which the French began to take in Russian banks was the obvious solicitude of the Russian finance minister for Russian banking houses during the crisis and depression. It became clear that the government was prepared to go to great lengths to aid the banks and save them from bankruptcy. This attitude of the Russian government offered the security minded French capitalists an excellent guarantee for the safety of their shareholdings in Russian banks, and for the various placings of capital in Russian concerns through the medium of Russian banks.[60]

Another factor in the growth of French interest in Russian banks was the desire to oblige the Russian government. The latter took upon itself, through the agency of the State Bank, the task of aiding the banks hit by the crisis, and found itself saddled with commitments which, in the strained financial situation after the Russo–Japanese War, it could no longer afford to meet. The government position was especially difficult because the State Bank became the target of attacks upon its policy of aiding the banks, which was considered incompatible with the latter's position as a bank of issue. It was in response to repeated requests on the part of Finance Minister Kokovtsov that French bankers undertook the fusion of the three 'Polyakov banks' and the reorganisation of the capital of the St Petersburg Private Commercial Bank in 1910 and 1909, respectively.[61]

French financial penetration into Russian banks was made easier by the weakening of the position of the German money market *vis-à-vis* Russian banks during 1909–14. The German connections with Russian banks were of old standing, and were formed on the basis of common dealings in the Russian paper rouble, for which Berlin was the only market outside Russia, and on the basis of financing industry in the Polish region. Russian bank shares were popular in Berlin and they accounted for nine out of the twelve types of bank shares quoted there. After 1909 however the Germans, owing to the relative narrowness of their money market, failed to strengthen their position in Russian banks, and even allowed the French to acquire shares in the banks hitherto under German influence. All nine types of Russian bank shares quoted on the Paris Bourse in 1913 were introduced during the years 1910–13, while only one Russian bank had introduced its shares to the Berlin Bourse during this period.[62]

The relative weakness of the German money market had forced Russian banks, in need of extending their capital, to turn to Paris. The tendency to enlarge capital became a widespread feature of Russian banking during this period. This was partly due to the expansion of economic activity, but equally important was the existing legislation under which loans against non-guaranteed securities could not exceed one-fifth of the capital. Furthermore there was a tendency for provincial banks to move to St Petersburg, where they could hold their own by extending their capital. Finally banks with larger capital found it easier to obtain short-term credits from abroad.

By 1916 the French had invested in the twelve main Russian joint stock banks an estimated 110 million roubles which represented about 22 per cent of the total capital of the banks, and 50·5 per cent of total foreign investment in Russian banks. The Germans held 16 per cent, and the British 5 per cent, of the total shares of Russian banks. The Russian banks fell into two distinct groups as regards foreign capital participation : four banks were of a pronounced French orientation and five of German orientation; in two other banks both French and German capital were represented in more or less equal proportions.[63] French banks also played an important part as suppliers of short-term credits to Russian banks. It has been estimated that the French accounted for about one-half of the short-term credits to seventeen Russian joint stock banks during 1909–11.[64]

The rôle of French capital in Russian banks was further emphasised by the fact that the banks with French capital participation were actively engaged in financing Russian industry. Thus the Russo–Asiatic, in which the French held about 65 per cent of the shares, had representatives on the board of sixty-two concerns. It was known to be particularly active in industries producing military stores and in the oil and tobacco industries. The Azov–Don had close ties with the metallurgical concerns in South Russia and the Urals, and with the cement, glass and sugar industries, etc.[65] On the whole the Russo–Asiatic with its 102 branches, a capital of 78 million roubles, and assets representing 17 per cent of the assets of the twelve main Russian joint stock banks, acted as the most powerful channel through which the French Société Générale and the Banque de Paris et des Pays Bas exercised their influence over the Russian economy. These two banks had also a formal *entente* with most other French banks interested in Russian institutions, such as the Banque Française pour le Commerce et l'Industrie, the Crédit Mobilier, the Union Parisienne and the Société Française de Banque et de Dépôt.[66]

However French financiers were not concerned with gaining power. By strengthening their position in Russian banks, they desired to delegate the task of seeking out new business opportunities to Russians, and while fully sharing in the profits of any new venture, they hoped thereby to escape direct responsibility, diminish their risks, and make up for their ignorance of Russian conditions and language.[67]

By way of summary it may be said that the average French holder of Russian dividend bearing securities, if not actually a loser, did not gain enough to compensate him for the risk involved : in contrast French banking houses benefited all along the line. They made large profits on promotion and issues, they earned commissions of 10–15 per cent for the capital reorganisation of Russian companies and banks hit by the recession, and finally they benefited from the difference in the French and Russian discount rates through their short and medium-term credits.[68] Simultaneously they had at their disposal the foreign balances of the Russian government, very large by pre-1914 standards, on which they paid a nominal interest only, so that in the last resort it was Russian funds which they lent on short term at high profit to Russian industrial and financial concerns.[69] Given the structure of the French investing public, consisting largely of small savers, and the decisive rôle of the banking houses in shaping investment policy, it can be concluded that, from the point of view of the immediate interests of the French financiers, French investment policy in Russia justified itself. It is not within the scope of this study to consider the question, so ably put by H. D. White, as to the wisdom of diverting resources from French industry which could have benefited from a liberal supply of capital-seeking remuneration.[70] Much larger were the funds which had been diverted from a capital-starved French industry into fixed income securities, which represented about 80 per cent of France's portfolio.[71] In Russia too the French had invested a mere 15 per cent of their total capital in industry, while the balance went into securities of a public nature.[72] Therefore the question raised by White as to the wisdom of diverting resources from French industry, would have to be answered by way of analysis of the factors which shaped the investing habits of the French public; a problem which cannot be dealt with here.[73]

7 French investment and influence in Russian industry, 1894–1914*

By July 1914 the French had invested an estimated 12,452 million francs in Russian securities.[1] The bulk of it went into bonds issued or guaranteed by the Russian government, and only an estimated 1700–1900 million francs were invested in shares and bonds of Russian joint stock companies.[2] Though they represented only a fraction of total French investment in Russia, French holdings of securities in Russian companies were nevertheless important in that they represented over 14 per cent of the total joint stock capital in Russia and about 33 per cent of foreign investment in this type of security. Moreover French capital was particularly important in Russia's basic industries, such as mining and metallurgy, and in banking, which in Russia was closely connected with industry. By 1916 over 60 per cent of French capital in Russian joint stock companies was active in concerns which extracted iron ore and coal and smelted it into iron, steel, and steel products.[3] Works in which French capital participated accounted for over 60 per cent of the pig iron and coal output of Russia by 1913.[4] The French were holders of nearly 23 per cent of the total capital of the ten largest Russian joint stock banks, and they were also large suppliers of short-term credits to these banks.[5]

Given this very considerable importance of French capital in Russia's economy, the question inevitably arises as to what degree of control and power over Russia's economy French capitalists had attained. There were two main channels through which control and power could be exercised over the whole Russian economy as distinct from the influence in or through an individual concern. The two largest syndicates in Russian industry, that of the metallurgical industry known as *Prodameta* and that of the coal industry known as *Produgol* represented the first channel. The large Russian joint stock

* From *Slavonic and East European Review*, vol. xxxv (Dec 1956). Reprinted by permission.

banks represented the second channel through which French capitalists could wield considerable power over the Russian economy. In five such banks the French owned over 53 per cent of the joint stock capital.[6]

The Prodameta and the Produgol were incorporated joint stock companies, founded in 1902 and 1904, respectively, with the avowed aim of setting up collective organisations for the sale of metallurgical products and coal of the member enterprises. In reality the two syndicates had many of the features of trusts, as the production side of the constituent enterprises was indirectly affected by the marketing quotas allocated by the syndicates. Moreover bonuses were paid to companies which marketed less than their allocated quantum, and some concerns agreed to suspend production altogether on the undertaking on the part of syndicates that a minimum dividend would continue to be paid to their shareholders.[7]

The idea of the Prodameta came from Paris. The first negotiations took place in January 1901 in St Petersburg on the initiative of Baron Hely d'Oissel and Dorizon, the chairman and director, respectively, of the 'Société Générale pour Favoriser le Développement du Commerce et de l'Industrie en France'. The Société Générale of Brussels rallied immediately to the project. In Russia the 'Société Générale des Hauts Fourneaux, Forges et Aciéries' (Makeyevka), the creation of the Société Générale, was used as an instrument for spreading the idea and the urgency 'd'une entente commune en vue d'obtenir une meilleure répartition des commandes de l'industrie privée et une plus exacte adoption de la fabrication aux besoins du commerce et de la consommation des fers en Russie'.[8]

In November 1901 the Congress of the Mining Industry of South Russia in Kharkov gave its approval of the idea and accepted in principle the projects submitted to it. On 2/15 February 1902 a conference was held in St Petersburg, at which nineteen metallurgical companies of South Russia were represented. Six of these companies were, as regards their capital, entirely or almost entirely French; in addition French capital was represented in at least five more companies, Russian and Belgian, in one of them to the extent of 50 per cent of its share and debenture capital. In the commission for the allocation of quotas, which was to consist of nine companies, French capital accounted for 100·37 million out of a total of 266·29 million francs of the share capital and for 48·46 million out of the total of 79·99 million francs of the debenture capital.[9]

The negotiations were protracted because of the conflict of interests between various groups of enterprises, and the initial scope of an organisation, embracing all types of metallurgical products, had to be abandoned for more modest agreements on specific products.[10] Subsequently various changes took place and as a result a loosely knit association of some thirty metallurgical enterprises placed in the main in South Russia, but with a few also from the Polish and the central areas, eventually emerged. Within this association there was a number of more closely knit smaller groups, with specific and detailed agreements. These thirty enterprises, though they represented a mere 17 per cent of the total number of Russian metallurgical enterprises, acounted for 70 per cent of the share capital of the metallurgical industry, for 33 per cent of its labour force, for 88 per cent of its production of assorted iron, 82 per cent of the total production of sheet and ordinary iron and for 74 per cent of the output of tyres and axles. The contract of association did not embrace iron ore or pig iron, but indirectly affected them.[11]

By 1910 the French had become the dominant element in the Prodameta, as reflected in the appointment and subsequent continuous re-election of Darcy, the representative of the Banque de l'Union Parisienne, as chairman. The extension of French influence was due on the one hand to the full adherence of the French company of Druzhkovka and of a number of French financed Polish enterprises, and on the other to the increase of French capital participation in the Donetz–Yur'yev Company (from 10 per cent in 1900 to over 75 per cent in 1910) and in the two largest Belgian companies.

The second syndicate, the Produgol, was run from the beginning of its formation in 1904 by a Paris committee. It was confined to the Donetz basin alone, and its constituent enterprises accounted for 60 per cent of the country's output.[12] The members of the Produgol were not interested in drawing the coal enterprises of the Polish region into the syndicate as, given the distances involved and the high transport costs, the coal of the Polish Dombrowa basin could not compete with the Donetz coal on the Russian markets. The time lag between the dates of the formation of the Prodameta and the Produgol was due on the one hand to the fact that the coal industry had begun to feel the impact of the crisis later than the metallurgical industry. On the other hand its formation was for some time frustrated by dilatory action on the part of the directors of a number of enterprises under the patronage of the Société Générale who made a handsome personal income out of commissions on sales of coal and stood to lose by the organisation of collective sales of coal.[13]

The formation of the two syndicates was prompted by the desire to remedy the disastrous position in which the enterprises, controlled by a large proportion of French capital, found themselves when struck by the crisis of 1900–3, followed by a depression lasting until 1909. It was thought desirable to create an agency which would be able to seek out new markets and reduce overhead costs, by rendering obsolete the separate sales agencies of the individual enterprises and by reducing transport costs over long distances, by means of the allocation of orders to enterprises nearest to the place of destination. These objectives were for the most part achieved. Expenditure on commission and commercial costs of the individual enterprise had fallen from an estimated average of 5–6 copecks per pood of iron to 1–2 copecks after the organisation of the syndicate.[14]

Equally important was the fall in the losses of individual enterprises arising from insolvency among commercial firms, a real scourge in Russian conditions, where everything had to be sold on credit and where longer terms of credit than customary in the West had to be granted.[15] The danger resulting from this practice was the more real for the French and Belgian enterprises in Russia, because of their ignorance of the language and of local conditions. The Prodameta dealt either directly with large-scale consumers such as railways and concerns outside the syndicate (which together accounted for over 40 per cent of the total sales effected by the syndicate) or with large scale commercial firms (which accounted for 55 per cent of the sales).[16] Moreover by concentrating the sales in one agency, the industrial concerns were in a better position to influence the terms of credit and the commissions of commercial firms than was the case when each firm had to negotiate separately.

However the immediate aim of the syndicates was to put an end to cut-throat competition between various concerns, which continued to produce notwithstanding falling demand and to throw stocks on to the market often below cost, thereby contributing to further depression of prices. The aim of the syndicates to prevent a further fall in prices was of the greatest importance from the point of view of the country at large. When Witte sought to attract foreign capital into Russian industry he was well aware of the fact that the protection of this industry by high import duties, which was to act as a stimulus to foreign capital, entailed a serious burden to the Russian consumer. He consoled himself however with the reasonable expectation that the enterprises created with the help of foreign capital would sooner or later create competitive conditions for industry, which would ultimately lead to a fall in prices.[17] This state of things had arrived sooner than Witte expected, but unfortunately in circumstances of acute crisis, which threatened the very existence of the newly created industries.

Though he formally disclaimed any responsibility for the plight of so many enterprises and though he publicly affirmed that the crisis of over-production was due to speculative promotion-fever, the imprudence, and the greed for dividends of the foreign and Russian entrepreneurs, Witte could nevertheless not afford to abandon them to their fate. The fear that an indifferent or negative attitude to the claims and complaints of these foreign entrepreneurs and financiers might have regrettable consequences, not only for Russian industrial securities but also for state bonds, was undoubtedly a very important consideration. In the majority of cases the same banks which had promoted industrial enterprises in Russia were also members of the so-called 'Russian Consortium' of banks which floated Russian government loans.

Moreover the French press had begun to attack Witte, whom it accused of having enticed millions of French capital with promises of fabulous returns and of failing to consider the legitimate desire of foreign capitalists and to defend their interests through a collective organisation.[18] The papers asserted that the *débâcle* of the foreign enterprises suited Witte, as Russians would thereby be in a position to acquire for a negligible price enterprises whose establishment had cost millions.[19] Witte could not ignore the unfavourable effect which the attacks in the French press might have on the multitude of French *rentiers* who at that time were holders of Russian government and government guaranteed securities to the extent of over 5000 million francs. He raised considerably the amount to be distributed in subsidies to the French press and commissioned the French financial writer Kergall to write a series of articles eulogising Russia's financial and economic position. This was not sufficient, and though articles in the Russian press seemed to indicate a negative attitude of the government to the project of the formation of syndicates, Witte formally announced that he would not oppose the project but would take action only if the syndicates adopted practices prejudicial to the interests of the Russian public.[20]

In so far as the French were the dominant element in Russia's metallurgical industry and the promoters of the idea of a syndicate, it can be said that the concession was wrung from a reluctant Witte. However the idea of trusts was not new in Russia. The well known *normirovka* of the Russian sugar industry, promoted by the Russian government itself, though it enabled Russia to expand sugar exports by dumping, was nevertheless achieved at the cost of high internal prices and ultimately meant reduced consumption for the Russian public. Witte himself had, at the beginning of 1902, inspired an agreement among glass manufacturers which resulted in the closing down of a number of works with excessive costs of production, though it provided for the remuneration of the capital of the shareholders of these enterprises.[21] Finally, with regard to the metallurgical industry, Witte had an agreement with six enterprises to deliver rails for state owned railways, which had fixed the price of rails at the 1899 level, and which stipulated for orders three years in advance. As the state owned a large part of the railway system of the country, the sums involved were very considerable, and by accepting the 1899 price for rails, notwithstanding the fall in the price of raw materials by at least a third, the government was in fact subsidising a selected number of enterprises at the ultimate expense of the Russian public.[22] It is interesting to note that these selected enterprises were all foreign or foreign financed. Indeed the clamour of a number of enterprises, inspired by the French Société Générale, for an association of Russian metallurgists, was prompted *inter alia* by the desire to extract from the *entreprises favorites*, i.e. those which benefited by government orders, an undertaking that they would refrain from producing metallurgical products for the general market. However these concerns opposed the suggestion of the Société Générale, because in view of the larger profits made on rails, they could afford to produce metallurgical products for general consumption at prices which other concerns could not afford without ruining themselves.[23]

It seems that the respective interests of the individual companies rather than French national interests were the driving force behind the policy of organising the collective sale of the products of the metallurgical and coal industries. French interests were in fact divided.[24] Thus the French Société des Aciéries du Donets of Druzhkovka, known for its close 'attaches avec le Boulevard des Italiens', i.e. the Crédit Lyonnais, originally abstained from participation in the syndicate together with the British company of John Hughes. Seventy-two per cent and 81 per cent of the output of the two companies, respectively, were taken up by the state, and both were averse from any undertaking limiting their output of other products, which, on the contrary, they desired to expand. The Société Générale on the other hand was interested in a number of companies, of which the most important was the Makeyevka Company, which did not have the good fortune to have guaranteed state orders.[25]

The Société Générales of France and Belgium were also concerned to arrest competition from a number of enterprises which, when faced with bankruptcy, had accepted the control of the courts. Such control, which in Russia exempted the companies concerned from the duty of making the statutory allocations to various funds and from paying creditors, afforded these companies superiority in competing with companies working under normal conditions by reducing their overheads. This may explain the initial refusal of the Donets–Yur'yev Company to join the syndicate.[26] Therefore, though the anonymous authors of a confidential note to the French embassy in St Petersburg boasted that 'les hommes qui gèrent en France et en Russie les capitaux Français engagés dans les entreprises métallurgiques russes . . . ont été les véritables initiateurs et guides du mouvement', the final success of which was due to their 'esprit de conciliation et la ténacité', it is almost certain that a purely Russian industry in similar circumstances would have chosen similar remedies.[27] A further point should be made which indicates the influence of the Russian environment on foreign entrepreneurs. The French, in leading the movement for the formation of syndicates, had no intention of imposing such syndicates on a reluctant Russian government or of negotiating from a position of strength. On the contrary they wished the government to undertake the organisation of the enterprises into a syndicate, the distribution of quotas, and the suspension of firms not fit for normal working.

As it happened, during the long years of crisis and depression, the policy of the syndicates could have little unfavourable effect on the economy. On the contrary we find that, though there had been a certain reduction in the output of pig iron by 1908, the output of manufactured metal products had increased. Moreover this increase was due almost entirely to the better equipment and mechanisation of the industries concerned.[28]

The policy of restricting production and raising prices had become a real danger during the boom of 1909–14, when it led to a virtual 'coal and pig iron famine' in the years 1911–12. The experiences of the over-production crisis, which had lasted for nearly a decade, could not easily be forgotten, and some entrepreneurs were obviously trying to make good the losses and frustrations of the preceding period. But the restrictive policies of the syndicates were not the only reasons for the shortages in coal and pig iron. Technical difficulties, in particular in the coal industry, made it impossible for the latter to cope with the unaccustomed demand. The high prices were among other things due to increased production costs as a result of the rise in wages, the cost of assistance to workers, and industrial taxation imposed by post-revolutionary legislation.

Whatever the position may have been, the Russian government was not unarmed vis-à-vis the syndicates, though the latter had grown considerably in power. In 1908 the government was instrumental in preventing the formation of a cartel of the metallurgical industry, which was sponsored by the Belgian and French banks.[29] Court proceedings were opened against the Produgol in 1914 and warnings were issued that, if production failed to catch up with demand, the government would proceed with the setting up of enterprises of its own to meet state needs, and moreover duty free imports of metallurgical products and coal were to be temporarily admitted.

The outbreak of war in 1914, which entirely changed the situation, makes it impossible to ascertain how matters would have developed. There is however no doubt that in face of an increasingly articulate public opinion, whose hatred of monopolies was, according to the French press, only exceeded by its hatred of autocracy, and in view of the improved credit-position of the Russian state, a strong line would have been taken.[30] Moreover it would appear that attacks in the Russian press on monopolies were not unwelcome to the government, for it thus saw the opportunity of checking the growth of agencies through which the claims of industrial interests could be voiced and pressure exercised – an undesirable phenomenon under a system of government of the Russian type.[31] Simultaneously, within the syndicates themselves and as between the two main syndicates, conflicts of interest arising out of the changed situation during the boom years were undermining the unity of industrial interests. The conflict between the Prodameta and the Produgol, both dominated by French capital, serves as an indication that there was no French national solidarity, unless the specific interests of the enterprise concerned demanded such solidarity.

The regional bias of French capital in favour of investment in South Russia had lent to what would normally have been a competition of regional interests the flavour of a struggle between foreign and national interests. This obtained in particular in the competition between the syndicate of the Ural iron manufacturers *Krovlya* and the Prodameta. The latter, by a policy of prices often below cost of production, had captured many of the markets formerly served by the Ural industries.[32] South Russian industrialists, convinced of their superior technical position and favourable natural conditions, viewed with impatience the solicitude shown by the Russian government for the metallurgical enterprises situated in the regions of St Petersburg and Moscow which, they believed, were doomed if left to their own devices.[33] The Russian government, on its part, showed great concern for the industries of these regions, not only because they were afraid of the resulting unemployment of thousands of workers if these industries were put out of business, but also because they thought it inadvisable from the economic point of view, given the size of the country, to concentrate industry in one region only.[34] In this sense French interests ran counter to Russian national interests, but, as already indicated, the French nationality of the capital was incidental to the regional interests involved.[35] We find also that in proportion to the penetration of French capital into the Urals, the regional interests of this area became more conscious and more vocal.[36]

The second channel through which French capital exercised influence over the Russian economy was French capital investment in Russian banks. Given the rôle which the Russian banks played in all spheres of economic activity and especially in large-scale industry, the French with their impressive capital participations in the largest Russian banks, with their considerable contributions in the form of short-term credits, and finally through their representatives on the boards of the Russian banks, were in a position to exercise indirect effective control over the economy at large.

Nevertheless the influence and control of French banks was much smaller than warranted by their position because of two basic factors. The first factor was that the French banks, in strengthening their position in Russian banks, did so in order to escape direct responsibility, to diminish their risks, and to make good their ignorance of Russian conditions and language by delegating the task of seeking out new business opportunities to Russians. Secondly the financial reorganisation of a number of banks, in which the French participated, proved a very attractive proposition affording to the French a commission of at least 10 per cent.[37] Also the interest on short-term credits, given the lower rate of discount in France and the large sums involved, furnished a substantial net income to the French banks.[38] Finally a significant motive for the interest which the French took in Russian banks was the obvious solicitude which the Russian minister of finance displayed for Russian banks during the crisis and depression. It became clear that the Russian government was prepared to go to great lengths in its endeavour to save the banks from bankruptcy, and this offered to the security minded French capitalist an excellent guarantee for the safety of the capital in Russian industrial enterprises through the medium of Russian banks. The insistence on the part of French banks that the Russian State Bank should retain a financial interest in the Russo–Asiatic Bank, founded in 1910 by the fusion of the Northern and Russo–Chinese Banks, and in the Moscow United Bank, seems to confirm this assumption and the available contracts between Russian and French banks bear it out.[39]

The second restraining factor was the influence and power of the Russian government, which could outweigh the influence of the French. The government could exercise its power by administrative intervention (*administrativnym poryadkom*), a power very real in Russian conditions. It is true that all large banks had on their boards persons of high standing, either in government departments or at court, and the government had sometimes to yield to the interests of such personalities.[40] On the whole however the banks, which like any company in Russia could have their authority to operate withdrawn by the administration at will, could not afford to quarrel with the government. Moreover the latter had very serious economic levers by means of which it could command the compliance of the banks.

In contrast to the position in contemporary Western Europe, the Russian treasury was the creditor of the Russian joint stock banks for considerable sums. The yield from the realisation of state railway loans flowed into private banks in the form of deposits. The most important item was constituted by the deposits of the resources of the treasury and State Bank maintained in the foreign branches of Russian banks. The deposits of the treasury and the State Bank in the foreign branches of Russian banks and the deposits of state railways were on 1 January of each year as shown in Table 7.1.[41]

TABLE 7.1

	Deposits in foreign branches of Russian banks	Railway deposits (m. roubles)	Total
1910	76·4	52·9	129·3
1911	155·5	154·9	310·4
1912	226·1	130·7	356·8
1913	191·5	221·5	413·0
1914	202·6	336·6	536·2

The deposits of the treasury and the State Bank were very profitable, as the banks were required to pay a 3 per cent interest only, while the official discount was 6 per cent on the average, and the private rate of discount of first-class bills even 6½–7 per cent. Moreover though these deposits were in theory short-term deposits the banks could and did keep them much longer to suit their particular requirements.

Of the special financial transactions which the ministry of finance entrusted to the banks, those consisting of purchases abroad of Russian securities and those dealing with the purchase and sale of foreign currency were the most profitable. More important than the commissions earned on these occasions, which were not negligible, were the credits for millions of roubles which were thereby granted to the banks. As the final settlement was normally effected after a considerable lapse of time and as moreover the banks tended on the date of settlement to ask for a postponement, the advance would ultimately be transformed into a long-term credit.[42]

Even more substantial were the short-term credits granted by the State Bank to the joint stock banks (see Table 7.2).

TABLE 7.2   Short-term credits granted by the State banks to the joint stock banks

1 Jan	m. roubles	% of total deposits in joint stock banks
1909	234·4	18·5
1910	217·9	16·0
1911	357·0	16·5
1912	424·8	21·6
1913	492·1	19·6[43]

In comparison with these sums, the short-term credits supplied annually by the French fade into insignificance. Even if the total foreign short-term credits granted annually to Russian banks were taken into account, they would still be substantially smaller than the total credits made available to them by the government in various forms.[44]

Thanks to this counterpoise furnished by the Russian government, the Russian banks were in a position to preserve a large degree of independence vis-à-vis their French 'masters'. This may explain the facility with which the St Petersburg private commercial banks in 1912 eliminated the influence of J. Loste et Cie, though the contract stipulated an entente for ten years.[45]

Another factor offsetting the power and influence of the French banks was the competition between them, in spite of the standing agreements for common action. Such common action was sought in order to distribute risks and to ensure the success of a particular transaction, but the banks tended to vie with one another for the lucrative privilege of forming the syndicate for a transaction on behalf of the Russian government. Moreover there was some competition between groups of banks.[46]

However, though the government could and did counterbalance the influence of the French in Russian banks, it could not have been unaware that it would be impolitic to oppose the wishes of such banks as the Banque de Paris et des Pays Bas or the Crédit Lyonnais. It realised that though the resources of the Russian banks had increased and the Russian market had widened during the period 1910–14, the placing of securities on the Russian market was still a long and laborious process, and the credits of French banks made it possible to hold these securities over until they could be conveniently disposed of. Furthermore through the channel of the French banks Russian securities could be placed on the French market without formal appeal to this market.[47]

The last and most important consideration is that the government itself could not afford to offend the susceptibilities of the largest Paris banks, as Russia's state credit, the financing of railway construction and shipbuilding, and the fate of the monetary reform depended to a large extent on the goodwill of these banks. Therefore the government favoured the influx of foreign capital other than French in order to give itself room to manœuvre and break the 'monopoly' position of the French banks. Thus Witte encouraged German capital participation in the Russo–Chinese Bank and at a later date Kokovtsov favoured the fusion of the Russo–Chinese Bank with the Siberian Bank, in order thereby to weaken the French element to some extent. Prompted by similar considerations, Kokovtsov welcomed the more sympathetic attitude of British capital, which began to take an increasing interest in Russia after the Anglo–Russian Convention of 1907.[48]

It is difficult to say however to what extent capital from other countries acted as a counterpoise to French capital. On the contrary many instances of collaboration are recorded. Such collaboration was certainly frequent between French and British capital, though the French banks were somewhat nervous that the British might receive from the Russian government favours which were denied to them.[49] There were also many instances of collaboration with German capital. Though Russian banks with foreign capital participation can be fairly distinctly divided into those of German and French orientation, there were some in which both French and German capital can be found side by side. This was even more true of short-term credits.[50] Furthermore banks of French orientation collaborated with those of German orientation in financing Russian industrial enterprises.[51] Sometimes the co-operation of French and German banks on Russian territory reflected an existing community of interests of these banks outside Russia. The Russian authority on foreign capital in Russian banks, Ronin, affirms however that behind such co-operation there was fierce competition.[52] In the French documents the references to German competition in the sphere of private investment are infrequent and nearly always reflect the concern of the French government rather than that of the French banks. If the French financiers complained of such competition at all, it was only when they desired to coax the French government into rendering them assistance *vis-à-vis* the Russian government. On occasion competing firms or groups within one firm, in asserting their point of view before the French government, used the spectre of a surrender of French national interests for the benefit of Germany.[53]

If the Russian government could not easily afford to displease the French banks, neither could these banks afford to forfeit the goodwill of the Russian government. In the relationship of creditor and debtor the position of the latter was frequently and paradoxically the stronger. Moreover the benefits accruing to a particular French bank from a position of favour with the Russian minister of finance were too considerable to be lightly dismissed. Even though a Russian minister of finance could not afford to quarrel with the French banks as a group, he had means of making his displeasure felt in relation to an individual bank, and the Société Générale had found to its cost in connection with the so-called 'Kertch affaire' during the 1900–3 crisis.[54] These considerations account for the relative calm with which the French banks received the failure of numerous projects for financial deals in Russia vetoed by the minister of finance.

Among these projects was that for the establishment of a bank in Russia providing long-term credit for railways. This bank was *inter alia* to administer the allocation of railway orders to industry. Though put forward in 1909 by the eminent Paris banker Noël Bardac and supported by E. Noetzlin of the Banque de Paris et des Pays Bas, it was vetoed by the government, which refused to guarantee the debenture capital of the bank.[55]

The most interesting case in point however was the failure of the 'Societé Russo–Française d'Entreprises Industrielles et de Travaux Publics', commonly known as *Syndicat Verneuil*, because of the initiative taken by the French *syndic de la chambre syndicale des agents de change*, Verneuil, in promoting it. On Verneuil's initiative a meeting took place in Paris in January 1907 between the main Paris and St Petersburg banks, as a result of which a company was formed for the collective financing of various Russian ventures. The Russian banks undertook to hand over to the company all new operations entrusted to them and in particular all government concessions.

The implementation of this arrangement would have deprived Kokovtsov of the possibility of manœuvring between competing firms and of his right to which he had hitherto frequently resorted of entrusting particularly profitable operations to Russian banks alone. Furthermore Verneuil had stipulated that the majority of the orders for industrial products, arising out of the transactions carried out by the new company, should be placed with French firms. Though the Russian banks made it clear that they were not in a position to enter into engagements on that point, as this was the government's prerogative, it was nevertheless obvious that the monopoly of financing all transactions would have as its corollary the compliance of the Russian minister of finance with the wishes of such an organisation.[56] However, though Verneuil was an official in whose power it was to veto the admission of securities to the Paris Bourse, and though Russia's financial position at that time was precarious and the campaign conducted by the French press against Russia made things worse, Kokovtsov was not prepared to recognise the *Syndicat Verneuil*. Thus, when the concession for the construction of the North Donetz railway was under discussion, Kokovtsov declared that he would consider offers from the *Syndicat* on the same basis as offers from other banks and firms and not otherwise, thereby expressing his refusal to accept a monopoly position on the part of the *Syndicat*. It is noteworthy that two banking groups, both members of the *Syndicat*, competed for concession.[57] As to Verneuil's reaction, the only hint of it is his short lived opposition to the admission of the shares of the Azov–Don Bank to the Paris Bourse because of the alleged hostility of its director Kamenka to the *Syndicat Verneuil*.[58]

The two projects referred to above would seem to indicate the desire of French financiers to create for themselves an influential position *vis-à-vis* the Russian government. However the fact that they did not insist when they encountered opposition from the Russian government, coupled with the observed manner of behaviour of French financial circles during that period in general, does not seem to support the view that they intended to use their position as a means of influencing policy, but had primarily in view considerations of commercial profit.[59] If conditions such as the reservation of orders for French industry were stipulated, they did not originate from the banks. Whenever the financiers appeared to depart from the pursuit of purely financial aims the French government was invariably behind it.[60]

It is true that what the French banks failed to achieve by means of a general agreement they partly achieved through penetration into individual Russian banks and by bringing about amalgamations of Russian banks. But here also the Russian government remained master of the situation and permitted fusion when it found this advisable.[61] Moreover in individual firms, whether a bank or an industrial company, the degree of French influence was not always in direct proportion to the capital invested in them. Even where a member of the management was French, which was not frequent, he did not know Russian or Russian conditions and could exercise very little real power.[62] The concern above all for profits on the part of French financiers was partly responsible for this situation. But lack of a sufficient number of Frenchmen with suitable qualifications and willing to go to Russia was an equally important factor which, among other things, accounts for the concentration of numerous directorships in the hands of one and the same person.[63] This phenomenon was to some extent also a reflection of community of interest and concentration of capital, though to a much less extent than suggested by Soviet historians, who seem to ignore the purely practical and accidental factors. The lack of suitable French personnel had led to paradoxical instances of German elements achieving influential positions in concerns with predominantly French capital, where for political or security reasons their presence was highly undesirable.

The proportion of shares of a Russian company held in France did not even always ensure to Frenchmen a place on the board. If the remaining shares were held in large blocks, an effective opposition could be put up to a French candidate, as happened in the case of the two French nominees to the board of the Siberian Bank. Furthermore even if originally, in return for assistance of French capital, French managers or directors were chosen, this did not mean that they held this position indefinitely; on the contrary the available evidence suggests that at the first opportunity they were replaced by Russians, as was the the case with French representatives on the board of the St Petersburg Private Commercial Bank and of the North Donetz Railway Company.

Finally there was the question of the hostility of Russian public opinion to foreign capital in Russian private enterprise, a feeling which had become particularly vocal since the Russo–Japanese war and the 1905 Revolution. In these circumstances the foreign entrepreneurs and financiers thought it wiser not to emphasise too blatantly the foreign character of their firms in Russia. This applied in particular to Russian companies of relatively long standing into which French capital subsequently penetrated.[64]

To summarise, the attitudes and character of the majority of financiers on the one hand, and the part played by the Russian government in the economic life of the country on the other, acted as a restraining force on the power and influence wielded by French capital in Russia. Though it may sound paradoxical from the purely economic and technical points of view, less independence on the part of the native element and more interference by the foreign investors might have been of greater benefit in the long run not only to the individual concern but to entire branches of the economy.[65]

Foreign entrepreneurship and Russian industry: Addendum to Chapters 6 and 7*

McKay's study reflects the contemporary shift of emphasis in assessing foreign investment away from the strictly financial to the *entrepreneurial* – in this context the technological and partly managerial – aspects of foreign investment. McKay argues that foreign investment in Russia up to 1900 was *direct* investment which entailed power of decision making and active business leadership by foreign firms or individuals concerned. After 1900, and more specifically after 1908, direct investment gave way to *passive* portfolio investment, entrepreneurship being provided by large, Russian owned and operated industrial companies and banks. On the whole the distinction between the two periods in the pattern of foreign investment is not new, but McKay's contribution is to see, in this substitution of native entrepreneurship for active foreign leadership in the first phase evidence of the positive role of foreign capital in calling forth Russian entrepreneurial ability.

McKay distinguishes three sources of foreign entrepreneurship. The first came from major Western European concerns which founded affiliated Russian firms, such as majority of large metallurgical companies in Russia, to whom the Western parent company usually gave technical aid, managerial know-how and portions of joint stock capital. The second type of entrepreneur was the individual promoter, more often than not a foreigner resident in Russia and active in some industry. He acted as a link between Russian property owners, bankers and government officials on the one hand and Western banks or companies on the other. He tended to be connected with less complex industries, mainly those in which contacts with their Russian owners were crucial, and he tended to have a hand in more than one enterprise. The third source of entrepreneurship consisted of interrelated strong foreign groupings coalescing round a centre, usually a large banking firm.

* Review of J. P. McKay, *Pioneers for profit. Foreign entrepreneurship and Russian industrialisation 1885–1913*, (Chicago and London, 1970). Reprinted in abbreviated form (by permission) from *Soviet Studies*, July 1972.

This last type of entrepreneur is least satisfactorily dealt with and does not really come to life in McKay's study. The difficulty may lie in the nature of the source material, for this reviewer too has not been able to find a satisfactory interpretation of one such group, the 'Omnium'. The Soviet scholar Yu. B. Solov'ev in *Monopolii i inostrannyi kapital v Rossii*,[1] published by the Academy of Sciences in 1962, adds some fascinating detail but does not quite sustain his implied thesis that these groupings were evidence of *monopoly capitalism* in the 1890s. The need for such groupings seemed to have arisen from the inability of all but the largest entrepreneurs to secure the amounts of capital needed to sustain investment in capital intensive industries in southern Russia, while the interest of banking houses in promotion seems to indicate a desire on their part not to miss out on the opportunity for profit which the popularity of Russian investment held out.

Though different in origin, McKay maintains, all these entrepreneurs shared a common investment strategy. They were convinced that Russia lagged behind on account of its obsolete technology. By bridging the technological gap, and by providing better and more honest management, they believed they could gain substantial entrepreneurial profit. The accent was on technology as they knew it in the West. There seems to be no evidence that they ever considered the need to modify the techniques they knew to suit Russia's needs. As McKay writes : 'there was simply a right way and a wrong way of doing things,' and 'Engineers in their studies and entrepreneurs in their subsequent decisions apparently assumed that the implementation and management of advanced technology was their essential function, their raison d'être.' McKay reasons that this close tie to advanced technology may explain why foreigners concentrated on new or unmodernised industries where the technological gap was greatest even if these industries did not always pay the highest rates of return.

McKay shows convincingly that foreign businessmen were on the whole successful in implanting such modern techniques as they knew, especially in metallurgy, in which their greatest achievement was the creation of the coke–steel technology, and during the 1890s when plants were most often built from scratch or extensively renovated. Foreign management on the contrary was distinctly patchy in quality, though undoubtedly more honest. The foreign engineer did poorly in appraising and securing raw materials. The manager failed dismally in his relations with the government and various social groups outside the plant. The ultimate solution was widespread use of Russian personnel under a few experienced top foreign directors. The commercial side and contacts with outside bodies were usually handled by Russians while the foreign engineer with long residence in Russia tried to assure honest direction and technical expertise. Thus after much trial and error a generally effective balance of foreign and Russian elements in a management partnership was achieved.

McKay concludes that foreign entrepreneurship played an important and positive rôle in Russia's relatively successful industrialisation, a conclusion well supported by the evidence. It is however a matter of interest to note that in his general conclusions he somewhat reverses the order of importance of the contributions of foreign entrepreneurs. He starts with the provision and mobilisation of capital, followed by the implantation and diffusion of advanced techniques in several key industries. The provision of dynamic business leadership, the infusion of a growth outlook and the creation of a pool of local entrepreneurship come last. 'It would be facetious', writes McKay, 'to suggest that the inflow of foreign capital which accounted for roughly one-half of all new investment in industrial corporations during this period, was due only to non-economic deficiencies in Russian business, government and society.' Indeed it would, and yet, because of the author's emphatic treatment of the technological aspect and the understatement of the financial, there is a real danger that the uninitiated might assume this very thing. Thus McKay argues that foreign entrepreneurs had no differential access to capital as reflected in the high interest rates they had to pay on borrowed capital after 1900. Leaving aside the fact that, as is clear from McKay's evidence, at the height of foreign investment in the 1890s capital was available to foreigners at much lower rates, there is overwhelming evidence to the effect that rates on borrowed capital in Russia were on the average much higher than in France, Belgium and even Germany. I. F. Gindin maintains that even in 1913, when the Russian money market was infinitely stronger, the cost of private credit was two to two and one-half times higher there than in the major European countries.

In discussing capital mobilisation, McKay writes that much native capital was mobilised by foreign entrepreneurs who thus performed an important function of matching savings with investment opportunities. This was certainly the case, and the student owes a debt to McKay for having identified the Russian subscribers to shares of some industrial companies. It is clear however that if one discounts resident foreigners, the proportion of the capital generated in Russia itself was not large in proportion to the total. Moreover if domestic sources of savings could be more easily tapped by foreign entrepreneurs than by Russians, this was due to the knowledge or belief that the foreigners involved were either men of substance or had solid financial backing behind them. This attitude was shared by the Russian government, which in courting foreign investment was also concerned about a net addition to the pool of capital resources and about the balance of payment.

In analysing the strategy of capital mobilisation, McKay emphasises recourse to debenture issues as a neglected element of the capital structure of foreign enterprises in Russia, which gave them a powerful leverage. This feature of the capital structure of Russian companies, which was much more pronounced in the railway companies where share capital was very insignificant and where debentures bore government guarantee, was a reflection of the difficulty of procuring risk and short-term working capital and was determined by the structure and the investing habits of bondholders abroad, in France in particular, where fixed interest securities were more easily marketed. However the ability to use debenture issues in their strategy presupposed the availability of good financial backing for the underwriting and placing of debentures among the public, overwhelmingly the foreign public.

To sum up, given the very considerable cost of installing plant in South Russia, given the high cost of raw materials, transport, the need to extend long-term customer credit, etc., the availability of large amounts of capital or of credit for the initial hardware, and confidence that more would be forthcoming as and when the need arose (at least while the boom lasted and for many foreign businesses later too), were undoubtedly a differential asset which no amount of domestic entrepreneurship could match. Few Russian firms, unless assisted by the government directly or indirectly, would have had the staying power of some of the French and Belgian companies when the slump came or when no dividends were distributed over a number of years. With the exception perhaps of a few firms affiliated to large foreign concerns which, like the French ones, were reputed to rely on self-financing, the majority of foreign enterprises in Russia, precisely because advanced technology was their *raison d'être*, needed the extensive backing of well disposed banking institutions and a wide investing public at home. The very fact that the bulk of the author's evidence comes from banking archives may be of some relevance as to the significance of the financial element, unless we assume that their interest was purely academic. The ability of foreign entrepreneurs to call forth Russian entrepreneurship may in itself be evidence that lack of business ability and failure to respond to opportunity did not figure prominently among the factors accounting for Russia's lagging behind. Finally the speed and success with which native entrepreneurship succeeded in establishing itself in industries in which fixed costs were relatively small, such as textiles and food processing, point in the same direction. However though McKay might have underrated the financial factor, he has performed an important service by drawing attention to the entrepreneurial aspect of foreign investment in Russia, hitherto ignored or denied, by this reviewer among others.

As McKay's title indicates, foreign entrepreneurs in Russia were motivated by search for profits. Those first in the field, the pioneers, undoubtedly reaped large ones in the early years and, after a lean interval, respectable ones later on. Others followed, attracted by these successes, which were well publicised both by the Russian government and the financial press. However taken as a whole, the profit record of foreign business in Russia was nothing to write home about. What therefore were the attractions of foreign business in Russia?

McKay denies that specific policies of the Russian government induced foreign capital imports. Though he is quite right to adduce Arcadius Kahan's and other evidence to show that the rôle of the Russian government in the industrialisation process has been exaggerated, he has gone too far the other way by reducing the rôle of the finance ministry under Witte to that of propagandist and advertiser of Russia's opportunities for profit making. Gindin's evidence that some of the measures of government inducement were of long standing proves little. What is significant for the period of the 1890s is that the sheer combined weight of inducements, the cumulative effect of what went before, resulting in the growing involvement of the mass of the population in a market economy, and the conjunction of measures and policies in the monetary, credit, budgetary, foreign trade and railway construction spheres had created opportunities for massive import substitution and converted what in the 1870s and 1880s was a trickle into a mighty stream of foreign profit seekers.

There is little doubt that there was an intimate connection between the high profits of the few and the preferential treatment accorded to them by the Russian government and the position of near monopoly which they had enjoyed in the early years of their existence, while, subsequently, assured government orders made it possible for them to branch out in other directions to make up for the falling profitability of their main production lines. It would be unreasonable to discount these factors as contributory to the foreign entrepreneur's investment decision.

Some large concerns risking capital in Russia had a rationale in that they looked upon the Russian enterprise as an outlet for the equipment produced by them and as consumer of their technological know-how. For others it could have been a leap in the dark, rationalisation following later. A little foolhardiness in investment decisions in underdeveloped countries, according to Hirschman, is not a bad thing: exact knowledge of the likely snags might deter would-be investors;

once the plunge is made however investment has to be sustained and difficulties overcome. The capital structure of foreign companies, so subtly described by McKay, might also explain the decision to invest in Russia. By intelligent manipulation the risk to the founder could be nullified and profits collected whatever the subsequent fate of the enterprise, the price of failure being met by the investing public.

The evidence amassed by McKay seems to be overwhelmingly in favour of his thesis that foreign entrepreneurs based their business decisions on the anticipation of profits accruing from the use of advanced technology. There is just a remote possibility that the large proportion of purely technical evidence in the banking archives may overstate the real importance of the technological aspect of foreign entrepreneurship in Russia. Technical expertise of a reputable engineering firm carried weight with financial circles and was necessary to win the confidence of the investing public. However if the technological factor was really at the basis of profit calculation, then one might argue that foreign entrepreneurs by relying to such a degree on the technocrats had neglected other elements which commonly enter into the making of investment decisions, and that the resulting choice of investment projects had negatively affected their performance from the profitability angle. Our recent experience with Rolls Royce and Lockheed may suggest that, in situations where business men convince themselves that all that matters is the technological gap, the essential purpose of capitalist business, net profit margins, can be lost sight of.

It can be argued that advanced technology was a substitute because of the foreign investor's inability to maximise output by acting in accordance with the country's factor proportions, i.e. by using labour intensive methods or by using them in a strategic combination with capital intensive technology. McKay says that the requirements for capital and labour in Russia were 'fixed' by the technology – 'fixed' in the mind of the foreign engineer. In another place he speaks of the 'rigidities' in the mind of the foreign engineer. Of course in speaking of factor proportions one has the whole of Russia in mind and one assumes perfect mobility, which was not the case. In South Russia labour was in short supply and the resort to capital intensive technology had its rationality, which does not explain why entrepreneurs in search of profits chose precisely this area or this industry, unless the previously mentioned factors connected with government policy and protected markets are also considered. Though all this was pure gain to Russia, and though there is no doubt that the impressive rates of industrial growth during the 1890s were connected overwhelmingly with industries and areas where foreign investment was most pronounced, one might speculate that with more rationality the stock of new capital applied

by foreigners could have been spread over a larger area of entrepreneurial activity or that the marginal productivity of foreign capital
in Russia could have been greater. Such speculation however may be
appropriate to a discussion on 'the theoretical entrepreneur'; here we
are concerned with what actually happened.

The section discussing relations with state and society, especially the
latter, is somewhat thin. Not much has been written on this aspect of
foreign investment, which is not attitudinising. Indeed it is a subject
for a special monograph, and would require thorough research in the
press, especially local, and a study of Russian literature from this viewpoint. The acceptance of the view of one Soviet scholar that the 'campaign of the landowners [against foreign capital] should be considered
within the context of their general struggle for the preservation of the
vestiges of a feudal society' is somewhat incongruous in a work of this
calibre. The *zemstva* in their rate levying policy displayed a distinctly
anti-foreign and, in general, an anti-industrial bias, but this was part
and parcel of their *narodnik* mentality which they shared with the
vast proportion of the Russian intelligentsia and which had nothing to
do with 'feudal vestiges'.

In discussing the reasons why foreign participation in Russian industry was mutually advantageous for entrepreneur and state, McKay
stresses the political independence of the host state as the key. This needs
amplifying, especially for pre-1914 Europe. How truly independent
was Turkey or Bulgaria, though each had a sort of political sovereignty?
McKay emphasises the need, in addition, for a coherent, however
broad, development plan by the state. In Russia's case great power
status plus the very considerable wealth and income elasticity of the
state were non-negligible assets.

More recently Fred Carstensen has widened the debate on the rôle
of foreign capital in Russia's industrialisation by drawing attention
to the fact that all studies so far relied on data on the amounts of
foreign capital in the foundation capital of industrial companies in
Russia on specific dates as calculated by P. V. Ol'. Ol' used various
criteria to estimate the proportion of foreign capital, some of which
were no more than expert guessing. Carstensen gives examples showing
that effective foreign capital investment in individual cases could be
either much less or much more than the data based on foundation
capital would indicate.

Furthermore because the data are static and do not register flows,
they are not suitable for estimating with any precision at what particular point the inflow of real resources from abroad had made an
impact on industrial growth rates. Only the construction of balance of
payments tables from year to year would in Carstensen's view make it

possible to judge with any degree of accuracy the contribution of foreign capital to Russia's industrialisation.

Finally Carstensen throws out a suggestion that the use of foundation capital data might have exaggerated the French and Belgian contribution, and understated that of the Germans and the British.[2]

8 Russia's public debt and the French market, 1889–1914: A statistical assessment[*]

The discussion of Franco–Russian financial relations has always been accompanied by much acrimony and passion. Both on the Russian and on the French side the problem has been charged with emotional overtones. On Russia's side, there has always been a feeling of humiliation at the thought that ministers of Imperial Russia like those of another Bulgaria or Turkey had to come cap in hand to ask for credit in Paris, pay what many of them considered to be usurious, crippling interest rates and dividends, and on occasion be forced to grant diplomatic or commercial concessions as a *quid pro quo* for financial assistance.

On the French side there has been a feeling that the French public had been misled into investing in Russia by unscrupulous bankers and journalists who had derived large gains from their connection with the Russian government, and by politicians who had diplomatic ends in view; that their hard won savings went to bolster up a tottering autocracy, for bribes to corrupt officials, and to buy armaments for Russia's military adventures in the Balkans and the Far East; that French industry had been starved of capital so that French money could be pumped into Russian bonds at unjustifiably low rates of return considering the risk involved.

It is not the aim of this paper to enquire to what extent these attitudes on both sides were justified; it is hoped that some of the statistical data which follow may clear the way to a more informed approach to the problem.[1]

It is well known that the French had sunk a large proportion of their savings invested in foreign securities in Russian bonds. Between 1899 and 1914 this proportion was never less than one quarter of their total foreign investments. Similarly, looked at from the Russian side,

* Unpublished paper submitted to the conference of the French Economic History Society held in Paris in October 1973.

French holdings were never less than 26 per cent of the direct Russian government debt during the period from 1 January 1893 to 1 July 1914. French investment in bonds issued by the Russian government directly, to be referred to subsequently as direct government bonds, was the principal form of French financial interest in Russia. Second in importance was French investment in bonds the interest on which was guaranteed by the Russian government. These bonds, customarily called government guaranteed bonds, consisted of bonds issued by Russian railway companies, the mortgage bonds of the Land Bank for the Nobility and the mortgage certificates of the Peasants' Land Bank. Third in quantitative order of importance was French investment in Russian private enterprise. Last came French investment in bonds issued by Russian municipalities, which did not appear on foreign bourses in significant numbers before the beginning of the twentieth century.

According to our calculations, the composition of French investment in Russia on the eve of the 1914 War was as summarised in Table 8.1.

TABLE 8.1   Composition of French investment in Russia, 1 January 1914
(thousand francs)

Direct government bonds	7,193,120[a]
Government guaranteed bonds	2,729,401[a]
Municipal bonds	583,175
Investment in joint stock companies	1,745,000[b]
ESTIMATED TOTAL	12,270,696

[a]See Table 8.2.
[b]In this study (p. 174) Ol's higher estimate is given, i.e. 1,946 million.

The figure for municipal investment is taken from the *RAPPORT* of the *Office de Biens et Intérêts Privés* of the French foreign office, based on the 1·8 million individual claims registered by 31 March 1920 and submitted to the *Président du Conseil*. The assessment of investment in joint stock companies is based on M. Aulogne, *Comment sauver nos revenus étrangers*, published in 1918.[2]

The data for direct and guaranteed bonds have been taken from Table 8.2, which attempts to trace the evolution of French holdings of Russia's direct government debt exclusive of mortgage bonds from year to year and for guaranteed bonds. No allowance has been made for amortisation, but the figures involved could not have been very large in view of the long period stipulated for the repayment of principal (eighty-one years as a rule). Moreover the tendency has been in drawing up these tables to err on the conservative side. Thus in

TABLE 8.2*a*   The evolution of French holdings of Russian[a] government and
government guaranteed bonds (thousand francs)

	Government bonds	Guaranteed bonds
Before 1889	738,000	74,000
1 Jan 1890	2,380,800	
1891	2,823,060	
1892	3,521,460	
1893	3,321,460[b]	
1894	3,530,720	
1895	4,076,560	147,000
1896	4,076,560	
1897	4,462,560	
1898	4,462,560	
1899	4,462,560	381,000
1900	4,462,560	
1901	4,462,560	531,000
1902	4,755,120	
1903	4,755,120	
1904	4,755,120	
1905	5,555,120	
1906	5,555,120	
1907	6,773,120	
1908	6,773,120	
1909	6,773,120	
1910	7,193,120	850,200
1911	7,193,120	
1912	7,193,120	
1913	7,193,120	1,086,881
1914	7,193,120	2,064,401
1 July 1914	7,193,120	2,729,401

[a]Unless otherwise specified (see Table 8.2*b*), the data referring to the
proportion of each loan held in France according to the *RAPPORT*, has been
accepted as basis for calculating French holdings of each loan at the time of
issue.
[b]The 3 per cent gold loan issued in October 1891, nominal value 500 million
francs, was originally successfully taken up in France but subsequently there
was a drastic fall in its value and the Russian government purchased on the
Paris Bourse 200 million worth of these bonds at 73 per cent of the nominal.
By January 1893 the Russian State Bank still held 49,942,250 gold roubles'
worth of these bonds equivalent of about 200 million francs. During 1893 the
State Bank was selling these bonds partly on the Paris Bourse and partly to
Russian Banks. By August 1893 the total was allegedly placed according to
the *Journal de St. Péterbourg* (Crédit Lyonnais, Historique de la Dette). However
in August 1896 the Russian Bank was observed selling 30 million francs' worth
of the 1891 Loan. (F30–332, Fin. aux Etr.)

TABLE 8.2b   Analysis of Table 8.2a (thousand francs)

	Direct government bonds		Guaranteed bonds
before 1889	4% 1867 & 1869		3% Transcaucasian
	4% 1880	738,000	74,000
1889	4% gold issue	440,000	
	Consol. 4%		
	1st & 2nd ser.	1,202,800	
1890	4% gold 2nd, 3rd		
	& 4th issues	442,260	
1891	Consol. 4% 3rd ser.	198,400	
	3% gold 1st issue	500,000	
1893	4% gold 5th issue	119,260	
1894	4% gold 6th issue	50,000[a]	Various railway bonds[a]
	3% gold 2nd issue	139,840	73,000
	3½% gold	356,000	
1896	3% gold 3rd issue	356,000	
1898			3½% mortgage bonds of[b]
			the Nobles' Bank–219,000[a]
			Transcaucasian–15,000
1900			3½% mortgage bonds of[b]
			the Nobles' Bank–150,000
1901	Consol. 4%	292,560	
1904	5% treasury bonds	800,000	
1906	5% gold loan	1,228,000[c]	
1909	4½% gold loan	1,220,000[d]	Railway bonds–319,200[e]
1912			4½% certificates of the
			Peasant Land Bank[e]
			236,681
	July 1909–Jan 1914		Railway bonds–977,520
	After 1 Jan 1914		665,000

[a]Delamotte, Inspecteur des Finances, Mission en Russie, 1 Jan 1905, F30–331.
[b]Association Nationale, Emprunts cotés à Paris, effectivement placés en France. App. G. O. Crisp, Ph.D. thesis (London, 1954) and Delamotte, loc. cit.
[c]On January 1906 French banks subscribed to short-term Russian treasury bills for 100 million roubles to be repaid out of the proceeds of the 1906 loan. F30–329, 24 Nov 1910, minute. For the loans of 1906 and 1909 the evidence is from the *Direction du Mouvement Général des Fonds*. The figures of the *Direction* are based on stamp duty for 10 November 1910. *RAPPORT* estimates the proportion of these loans held in France as 72 and 74 per cent, respectively. It is unlikely that Frenchmen were selling these bonds during 1910–14, as a considerable improvement had occurred in Russia's credit standing during this period and the return on these loans was exceptionally good. It is more likely that some selling took place during the war and perhaps immediately following the outbreak of the Revolution as these loans were resented by a section of Russian public opinion as the credits which helped autocracy to assert itself after 1905.
[d]The treasury bills of 1904 fell due in the same year so that French holdings increased by 420 million francs only.
[e]Calculated on the basis of data from *Crédit Lyonnais, Historique de la Dette*.

most cases, unless contradicted by other reliable evidence, it has been assumed that the proportion of each loan, relatively to the total in circulation, held in France was originally the same as it was in the *RAPPORT*, which is probably not a full record of French claims.[3] It has therefore been assumed that the overestimates resulting from the non-deduction of amortisation are more than compensated.

Table 8.4 uses the estimates of French holdings of government bonds to ascertain the weight of French investment relative to the total Russian direct government debt. The importance of the French market for Russian government bonds comes into relief when the proportion of French holdings is compared with the estimated proportions of total foreign holdings of these bonds (Table 8.3).

To summarise, the proportion of Russia's pre-war public nominal debt held in France was as Table 8.5 indicates.

Our figures for French holdings of Russian public stock differ substantially from the data compiled by Dr René Girault in his recent study.[4] We are almost coming into line for the last two years, i.e. 1913 and 1914.

We have no hesitation in arguing that for the period up to 1894 the lower figures suggested in our table are more acceptable. This is certainly true of the period before 1889, where our figure is close to the calculation made by French Inspector of Finances Delamotte[5] (his 820 million francs – ours 738 million). For 1 January 1894 Girault's figure is closer to Delamotte's, but we still find ours more acceptable. It is close to the findings of a study made by the Association Nationale des Porteurs des Valeurs Mobilières, based on various assessments, such as amounts issued in France, coupons paid in France, etc. of 3460 million against our 3530·7 million francs.

The acceptance of the lower figure for the period before 1 Jan 1889 would mean even a higher rate of increase of French holdings of Russian securities during the period preceding the formal conclusion of the political alliance between France and Russia than indicated by Dr Girault. Most of the funds in question were conversion loans, six of which had been issued on the French market between 1889 and 1894. Their outstanding value in 1917 was 3200 million francs.

The discrepancies in our figures up to roughly 1910 are due in our opinion to the overestimate of the early data in Girault's estimates. On the other hand Girault's figures are closer to some contemporary official and semi-official estimates, a summary of which is given in Table 8.6. In our opinion most of these estimates, especially for the period 1896–1901, were alarmist. The French finance ministry became suddenly aware of the huge volume of Russian securities which had entered French portfolios within a relatively short time. They were also embarrassed by

TABLE 8.3　Foreign holdings of direct government bonds (%)

1 Jan	Foreign holdings of direct government debt[a]	French holdings
1895	30	27·4
1899	37	27·4
1904	46	26·9
1909	46	28·8
1914	48·4	30·7

[a] *Wirtschaft und Statistik* (Berlin, 1934) no. 11.

TABLE 8.4　French holdings as proportion of Russia's total direct government debt

	Direct government debt[a]		French holdings as % of total[b]
	(million roubles)	*(million francs)*	
1 Jan 1893	4,619·4	11,287·6	29·4
1894	4,854·6	12,913·2	27·3
1895	5,588·3	14,864·8	27·4
1896	5,705·7	15,177·1	26·8
1897	6,087·2	15,191·9	29·3
1898	6,101·3	16,229·4	27·5
1899	6,102·1	16,231·5	27·4
1900	6,100·1	16,232·5	27·2
1901	6,210·5	16,519·9	27·0
1902	6,473·7	17,220·0	27·6
1903	6,629·2	17,633·6	26·9
1904	6,636·1	17,652·0	26·9
1905	7,066·4	18,796·0	29·5
1906	7,681·8	20,433·6	27·2
1907	8,456·5	22,494·3	30·1
1908	7,657·0	20,367·6	33·4
1909	8,835·7	23,502·9	28·8
1910	8,038·7	21,382·9	33·7
1911	9,015·6	23,981·5	30·0
1912	8,941·5	23,784·4	30·0
1913	8,845·6	23,529·3	30·6
1 July 1914	8,811·3	23,438·0	30·8

[a] Based on Gindin, *Russkiye kommercheskiye banki*, p. 446, and *Ministerstvo Finansov* (1904–13).
[b] See Table 8.2.

TABLE 8.5   Per cent of Russian public debt held in France

	Total 1 Jan 1914 in (millions)[a]	Estimated abroad in (millions)[b]	Estimated in France (million francs)	% of total in France[c]	% of foreign holdings in France
1 Direct government debt	8,811 roubles 23,438 francs	4,229 roubles 11,249·1 francs	7,193·1	30·7	63·9
2 Guaranteed debt	4,317 roubles 11,483·2 francs	1,726·8 roubles 4,593 francs	2,729·4	23·7	59·4
3 Municipal debt	563 roubles 1,497 francs	420 roubles 1,117·2 francs	583·2	38·8	52·2
TOTAL (million francs)	36,418·8	16,959·6	10,505·7	28·9	61·1

[a] *Wirtschaft und Statistik.*
[b] Ibid.
[c] Table 8.2.

TABLE 8.6   Summary of estimates of French holdings of Russian government and government guaranteed bonds (m. francs)

Before 1887	No. 610, Sénat, Année 1922, Annexe au procès verbal de la séance du 20 Oct 1920	over 1,500
Before 1889	Delamotte, Inspecteur des Finances, Mission en Russie, 1 Feb 1905, F30–331	over 820
1 Jan 1894	Association Nationale des porteurs des valeurs mobilières	3,260
	Association Nationale des porteurs des valeurs mobilières	3,450
	15 Jan 1894, A.N. F30–329 (total French investment in Russia both in public and private funds)	5,000
1896	Raphael George Lévy, *Revue des Deux Mondes* (March 1897)	6,000
	Cochery aux Aff. Etr., 6 July 1897, A.N. F30–334	6,000
1897, beginning of the year	Cochery aux Aff. Etr., 6 July 1897, A.N. F30–334	6,500
1898, beginning of the year	8 Mar 1898, A.N. F30–335, Finances aux Aff. Etr.	6,000–8,000
1898, Aug	9 Aug 1898, A.N. F30–334, Peytral à Delcassé	7,000
1900	A. Neymarck, Congrès International des valeurs mobilières (Paris 1900), vol. 3	7,000–8,000
1904	*Economist*, London, 13 Feb 1904	7,000–8,000
1905	A. Neymarck, in *Rentier*, 27 Mar 1905	7,700–8,000
	A. Vyshnegradsky of the Russian Credit Office, 8 Mar 1905, A.N. F30–331	7,000

TABLE 8.6—*continued*

1909	Crédit Lyonnais, 1 July 1909	8,424
	31 Dec 1909, AN. F30-332	8,638
	Arthur Raffalovich in Journal des Débats, 15 Mar 1909 (holdings in France, Belgium and Switzerland)	9,334·5
1914, beginning	Association Nationale (includes municipal bonds; only securities quoted in Paris)	8,221
1 July 1914	Crédit Lyonnais (includes municipal bonds)	10,526

the tactics used by the Russian finance minister Witte who after the introduction of the gold standard began to place Russian internal bonds unobtrusively through the medium of French banks thereby escaping the scrutiny of the French government.

The French finance minister, Cochery, began to complain that, as no end could be seen to Russia's credit requirement, the French market was exposed to a drainage of funds consequent upon Russian issues 'à jet continu'. 'En ouvrant donc nos portes à tout ce qui, de près ou de loin, pourra dépendre de l'Etat, nous courrions le risque de devenir les seuls commanditaires de toute la Russie.'[7] Cochery even began to express apprehension concerning the safety of French savings when he wrote to Delcassé on 8 March 1898, 'Est-il dès lors prudent de laisser s'accroître notre créance sur un seul pays, alors surtout que nous ne partageons cette créance avec personne et que nous serions seuls à supporter les conséquences d'une crise qui atteindrait notre débiteur?'[8] Finance Minister Caillaux went further still. He asked Delcassé to intimate to the Russian government 'qu'il est dans l'intérêt bien entendu de la Russie comme du nôtre de chercher dans l'avenir l'accès d'autres marchés financiers où il pourra effectuer les opérations de crédit que justifie la mise en valeur de ses richesses considérables et de son très vaste territoire'.[9]

One might assume that sales of Russian securities had taken place during the Russo–Japanese War and the Revolution of 1905 and subsequently repurchased, but specific evidence for this is lacking and Girault's data based on research in banking archives give no indication of such sales. On the whole there is plenty of evidence of the stability of French holdings of Russian bonds in the hands of the *public véritable*. The 1906 loan took some time to become firmly placed as it was addressed by the issuing banks to those interested in a higher yield security than Russian bonds commonly were. Some Russian securities held by Frenchmen might have been sold during the 1914 war. This is a possibility which needs investigating. However the proportions of the declared capital of each individual security on the basis of claims by

French holders seems to accord so well with all the information we have about the popularity of particular bonds as to make probable wartime sales outside France statistically insignificant.

Finally if our and Girault's tables converge so neatly by 1914 this may be partly due to his underestimate of the increase in French holdings of Russian guaranteed bonds between 1909 and 1914 by 1533·4 million francs, according to our estimates.

So far we have dealt only with nominal amounts. The effective amounts which reached the Russian treasury on account of direct government borrowing or the railway companies on account of railway bonds were usually less than the nominal : firstly because the issue price was lower and secondly because bankers' commissions and other expenditure connected with the issue were far from negligible. Naturally the rate of net yield depended on the circumstances in which an individual loan was launched, i.e. Russia's credit rating, the state of the money market at the time, etc.

Table 8.7 shows the nominal value and net yield of the principal Russian government loans floated on the French market. Only 85 per cent of the nominal value of the seventeen principal loans issued by the Russian government entered its exchequer. A portion of the 15 per cent reached Russia in the form of commissions if and in so far as Russian banks participated in the syndicates underwriting the issue, as was increasingly the case after 1900. However before 1900 this portion was not very large. Neymarck estimated that the purchase price of Russian fixed income securities to their holders had been 12½ per cent less than their nominal value. Only in the case of industrial securities which were sometimes issued at a premium did the effective capital exceed the nominal.

Table 8.9 attempts to estimate the annual interest payments made by the Russian government on account of direct and guaranteed bonds placed in France using our estimates of French effective holdings in Table 8.2. No allowance has been made for amortisation, but the amounts involved were not large. The margin of error is larger towards the end of the table. In 1914 amortisation entailed only 30 million roubles.

It has been estimated that during the five years preceding the outbreak of the war in 1914 Russia spent on the average annually 345 million roubles on interest and dividends to foreign holders of Russian securities. In 1914 these payments were made up as indicated in Table 8.8.[10]

If we apply the calculations of France's share of foreign holdings from p. 203, the estimate in Table 8.10 of the cost of servicing Russia's debt in France in 1914 emerges.

TABLE 8.7   The effective yield of the principal Russian loans floated in Paris

Loan	Nominal value	Net yield to the Russian government		Effective rate of interest to government
	(roubles)	*(roubles)*	*(%)*	*(%)*
4% gold loan 1889		166,562,500	83·5	4·98
4% consol. 1st ser.	262,500,000		86·87	4·77
4% consol. 2nd ser.	465,747,000	641,979,520	88·87	4·65
4% gold loan 1890	135,000,000	121,623,754	90·0	4·58
3rd 4% loan 1890	112,500,000	102,424,725	91·04	4·52
4th 4% gold 1890	15,661,500	14,721,807	94·0	4·40
4% consols 3rd ser.	120,000,000	114,317,271	95·3	4·297
3% gold loan 1891	112,586,625	87,748,337	76·19	4·22
5th 4% gold loan 1893	66,764,062	64,916,051	93·72	4·376
3% gold loan 1891 balance	74,913,375	58,051,866	77·5	4·14
3% gold loan 1894 2nd issue	62,437,500	46,828,125	79·0	4·044
3½% gold loan 1894	150,000,000	138,091,377	91·06	3·86
3% gold 1896 3rd issue	150,000,000	137,111,700	88·75	3·78
4% rent 1901	159,000,000	149,460,000	94·0	4·25
5% 1904	300,000,000	282,000,000	94·0	6·00
5% 1906	843,750,000	620,218,750	80·5	6·61
4½% 1909	525,000,000	448,875,000	83·0	5·42
	3,743,360,062	3,194,930,783	85	

Source: P. P. Migulin, 'Russky gossudarstvenny dolg', in P. P. Dolgorukov and I. I. Petrunkevich (eds), *Voprosy gossudarstvennogo khozyaystva* . . . (St Petersburg, 1907) pp. 52, 55; for 1906 and 1909 calculated on the basis of Tsentrarkhiv, *Russkiye finansy i yevropeyskaya birzha v 1904–1906* (Moscow–Leningrad, 1926) pp. 375–82.

TABLE 8.8   Interest and dividends payable abroad by 1914 (m. roubles)

Service of the direct government debt abroad of 4,200 million roubles	179
Service of the government guaranteed debt of 1,720 million roubles	77
Service of the municipal debt of 420 million roubles	21
	277
Dividends and interest on private investment of about 2,000 million roubles	120
TOTAL	397

TABLE 8.9 Estimate of the annual interest payments[a] made by Russia in France (m. francs)

End of year	Interest on government debt	Interest on the guaranteed debt
1889	95·2	2·22
1890	112·9	2·22
1891	135·8	2·22
1892	135·8	2·22
1893	140·5	2·22
1894	159·2	5·14
1895	159·2	5·14
1896	169·9	5·14
1897	169·9	5·14
1898	169·9	13·40
1899	169·9	13·40
1900	169·9	18·60
1901	181·6	18·60
1902	181·6	18·60
1903	181·6	18·60
1904	221·6	18·60
1905	221·6	18·60
1906	282·5	18·60
1907	282·5	18·60
1908	282·5	18·60
1909	301·4	32·96
1910	301·4	32·96
1911	301·4	32·96
1912	301·4	44·82
1913	301·4	88·82
1914	301·4	118·74
TOTAL	5,432·0	577·12

[a]Of course it is unthinkable that amounts payable should have been exactly the same to the franc over several years. There must have been variations even when the holdings remained stable. The figures are meant to show the order of magnitude rather than exact amounts.

The figure for the cost of servicing the public debt in France in 1914 (if municipal debt is excluded) in Table 8.10 is about 8 million francs more than in our estimate in Table 8.9. M. Chasles, in the *Revue Internationale Economique Belge*, no. 3 (1920), arrived at a figure of 400 million francs. The *Association Nationale* arrived at a similar figure of 397 million francs by using as a basis the advances made by the French government during the 1914–17 war for the payment of coupons on Russian loans to French nationals. The actual

TABLE 8.10   Interest and dividends payable to France in 1914 (m. francs)

Service of the direct government debt in France of 7,213·1 million francs	305·9
Service of the government guaranteed debt of 2,729·4 million francs	122·3
Service of the municipal debt of 583·2 million francs	29·2
	457·4
Dividends and interest in private investment of about 1,745 million francs	100·0
TOTAL	557·4

amount due was however higher as many Frenchmen failed to claim their interest because of war dislocation.[11] The Crédit Lyonnais calculation of 430 million which includes 30 million roubles for amortisation is also very close to our estimate.[12]

On the basis of our estimates French bondholders had earned on their investments in Russian government and guaranteed bonds during 1889–1914 the sum of around 6000 million francs, which represents about 60 per cent of the nominal value of their estimated investments (over 70 per cent if only direct government bonds are considered).

The juxtaposition of Tables 8.2 and 8.9 is interesting. It shows that during 1897–1901 some 850 million francs in interest payments entered French portfolios on account of Russian direct government bonds without any new French investment in this security. It is not surprising that there was a growing market for guaranteed bonds, which as they were not free of tax were not as favourable a form of investment as were direct bonds, though both types enjoyed the same element of security from their association with government. It is not surprising either that the Crédit Lyonnais was willing to oblige the Russian finance minister in the matter of placing Russian mortgage and other bonds without official subscription.

Similarly the period which followed the 1901 loan till 1904 entailed influx of interest payments into France of over 540 million francs on account of direct bonds without a corresponding new investment which explains the agitation at the news of a Russian loan in Germany in 1902 and the eagerness of the Paris banks to consider a loan to Russia in 1904, as soon as the war broke out.

On the Russian side the difficulty was faced during the first period by desperate attempts to open the London and New York markets for Russian bonds, by welcoming flows of capital into industrial securities, and mainly by encroaching upon the gold holdings of the Russian treasury abroad. During the early years of the twentieth century the pressure eased up because Russia's balance of payments improved, largely because the slump halted imports expansion and because of the gradual rise in grain prices. Treasury balances from budgetary and export surpluses began to accumulate and part of these was used to increase gold holdings abroad.

Table 8.12 attempts to ascertain the effective yield to the French investors of the main Russian loans issued in France. It shows that with few exceptions (1891, 1894 and 1896, and the mortgage bonds in 1898) the yield at price of issue was well above 4 per cent and from 1904 over 5 per cent.

A comparison of the rates of yield at the prices of issue shows that the average rate of Russian government bonds quoted on the Paris Bourse in February 1899 (which did not include the high interest bearing bonds of 1906 and 1909) exceeded the average rate of French bonds of a public character. The rate of Russian bonds compared also favourably with the average rate of other foreign government bonds quoted on the Paris Bourse, even if allowance is made for the low yield of Belgian and British funds of which only a fraction of the large amounts admitted to quotation was held by Frenchmen.[13]

TABLE 8.11 Per cent yield at issue price of Russian and foreign bonds

Russian government and guaranteed bonds	4·27
Other foreign government and assimilated bonds (without British and Belgian bonds)	4·10
Foreign (inclusive of British and Belgian)	3·10
Bonds of 6 main French railway companies	3·60
City of Paris	3·40
Crédit Foncier	3·30
French *Rentes*	3·13
French colonies and protectorates	3·10

The yield at price of issue of Russian bonds explains some of their popularity with the French investor as reflected in an analysis by Pierre des Essars of the portfolios of over a thousand investors who had deposited their securities with the *Banque de France*.[14] More important however, given the long standing French preference for fixed income securities emanating from or connected with the French government (by 31 December 1899 over 82 per cent of the value of French securities quoted were either directly or indirectly controlled by the French government),[15] was the short supply of this favoured form of security relative to the growing volume of annual savings. Russian government bonds offered an acceptable substitute.[16]

This brings us to the attitude of the French banking houses involved in the flotation of Russian loans on the French market. Bouvier's evidence suggests that the Crédit Lyonnais was interested in government bonds because of their security element. When considering investment in railway companies, attention was focused on the government guarantee and on the belief that 'le gouvernement tsariste ne les laissera jamais tomber en déconfiture . . .' (i.e. the railway lines).[17]

However, though undoubtedly French banking houses recommended Russian securities to their depositors because of the preference of the French investor for this type of security, the promotion of Russian government bonds offered substantial financial gains to the issuing banks.

TABLE 8.12   Yield at the price of issue of the main Russian loans issued in France (%)

		Rate of issue	Yield at issue price
1867–9	4% loans	81·60	4·9
1880	4% loan	80·0	5·0
1889	4% gold	86·45	4·62
	4% consol., 1st ser.	89·75	4·45
	4% consol., 2nd ser.	91·50	4·37
1890	4% gold, 2nd issue	92·60	4·31
	4% gold, 3rd issue	93	4·30
	4% gold, 4th issue	93	4·30
1891	4% consol., 3rd ser.	97·1	4·11
	3% gold	79·75[a]	3·76
1893	4% gold, 5th issue	94·5	4·23
1894	4% gold, 6th issue	98–98½	4·08
	3% 2nd issue	92·30[b]	3·25
	3½% gold	94·75	3·69
1896	3% gold, 3rd issue	92·30	3·25
1898	3½% mortgage bonds	98·5	3·55
1901	4% consol.	98·5	4·06
1904	5% short-term bonds	99	5·05
1906	5% gold loan	88	5·68
1909	4½% gold loan	89·25	5·04

[a]This loan was only in part taken up by the French public; the balance purchased by the Russian government at 73 per cent was subsequently placed in France in 1893 at the price of 75·5 or at a rate of 4·14.
[b]A very small sum involved.

Table 8.13 lists the rates of subscription and of purchase by the bankers of the eighteen principal Russian government bonds issued in Paris and the estimated gross rates of profit accruing to the banks. The information given by the Russian finance minister, Kokovtsov, to the rapporteur of the budget committee of the duma that the bankers'

TABLE 8.13   The rates of gross profit of the French banks on the principal Russian loans (%)

		Price *of firm purchase* *by the banks*	*Price* *of* *issue*	*Gross profits* *of* *the banks*
1889	4% gold	83·5	86·45	2·95
1889	4% consol., 1st ser.	86·7/8	89·75	3·12
1889	4% consol., 2nd ser.	[88·1/8][a]	91·50	2·87
1890	4% gold, 2nd issue	90	92·60	2·60
1890	4% gold, 3rd issue	91·04	93	1·96
1890	4% gold, 4th issue	?	93	
1891	4% consol., 3rd ser.	95·5	97·1	1·60
1891	3% gold	76·43	79·75	3·32
1893	4% gold, 5th issue	94·5	95·9	1·4
1894	4% gold, 6th issue	97–7·5	98–8·5	1·0
1894	3% gold, 2nd issue	[80][a]	92·3	12·0
1894	3½% gold	92·13	94·75	2·62
1896	3% gold	[89·75][a]	92·0	2·25
1898	3½% mortgage bonds	97	98·5–99	1·5–2
1901	4% consol.	95·3	98·5	3·2
1904	5% treasury bonds	94	99	5·0
1906	5% gold	83·5	88	4·5
1909	4½% gold	85·50	89·25	3·75

[a]Calculated by adding 1 per cent to the net yield of the loan to the Russian treasury.

commission on Russian loans varied between 1½ and 3¾ per cent was probably correct for the majority of Russian loans except for the experimental 3 per cent 1894 which involved a very small sum, the 1904 loan, which was only for short-term treasury bonds, and the 1906 loan which was launched in exceptional political circumstances.

As to net profits the rate of 1 per cent maximum admitted by the Crédit Lyonnais was applicable to a number of loans but cannot be considered an average. Kaufman gives an average net rate of commission of 2 per cent.[18] According to Kokovtsev the bankers' net profit out of a gross profit of 3·75 per cent on the 1909 loan was 1·32 per cent. This seems to be an underestimate as the Russian government had to meet the cost of stamp duty, which by then was 2 per cent.[19] The Russian government also undertook to pay $\frac{1}{8}$ per cent commission on the 1904 treasury bonds which were redeemed out of the proceeds of the 1909 loan which increased the commission by 0·0714 per cent, and another 0·446 per cent gain arose from the difference in interest payments over a fortnight before the public subscription.[20]

These fractions sound insignificant. However when one considers the vast sums involved, an increase of the commission by even a fraction of 1 per cent represented in absolute figures very substantial gains for the issuing banks. A net profit of between 1 and 1$\frac{1}{2}$ per cent, given such mammoth loans as that of 1906, would translate into millions of francs. If we apply a rate of net profit of 1$\frac{1}{2}$ per cent to three loans (4 per cent 1888, 5 per cent 1906 and 4$\frac{1}{2}$ per cent 1900) for which we know the exact share of the loans taken by French banks, net earnings of 40 million francs would be implied. On the 4 per cent treasury bonds of 1904 the three French banks – Crédit Lyonnais, Banque de Paris et des Pays Bas and Hottinger – earned 4 million francs net each.

In addition to the profits on underwriting, banking houses earned a commission of $\frac{1}{8}$ per cent on the service of Russian loans in France. They benefited from the practice of staggering remittances of the proceeds of the loans thus gaining interest, and they were entrusted with the gold balances of the Russian treasury and State Bank on which they advanced interest of only 1$\frac{1}{4}$–1$\frac{1}{2}$ per cent. They were entrusted with and remunerated for various services on behalf of the Russian government on the money and stock exchange to forestall depreciation.[21] To sum up, it was not so much the rate of profit of banking transactions with or on behalf of the Russian government which made Russian issues attractive (much higher rates could be made on Turkish, Bulgarian or South American issues) but the size of the operation which mattered.

Finally in assessing the gain from Russian bonds account must be taken of Russian expenditure on publicity which, except in the early years, was borne by Russia and Russian payments to the Bank of France on the basis of the Convention of April 1895 for its services as a depository of Russian bearer bonds. This Convention had undoubtedly added to the popularity of the Russian bonds by endowing them with an *estampille officielle*.

The above discussion of the profits of the French issuing banks does not imply that the promotion of Russian bonds by them was prompted by this consideration alone. The preference of the French public for a specific type of security and the short supply of French securities of this kind were undoubtedly points of departure for investment decisions of French banks.

In looking at the attitudes of the banking houses and the French public it may be necessary to have another look at Russia as a field of investment in the 1880s and 1890s not from our vantage viewpoint but from the point of view of a pre-1914 conservative and orthodox minded middle-class investor or financier in France. Russia's record as a debtor was very good indeed. The French had known and held Russian securities for at least fifty years before their mass influx at the end of the 1880s and had no reason to mistrust them. The Russian government was often embarrassed financially, but it never actually defaulted. With very rare exceptions was there in pre-1914 Europe any consciousness of the danger to financial stability inherent in a country with depressed standards of living for all but a few. The most thoughtful might have feared for Russia's stability on account of her autocratic government, suppression of liberty and bureaucratic abuse. However the average investor and even financier was not likely to allow this question to preoccupy him unduly as a theoretical possibility. Indeed before 1905 the conservative Frenchman might have thought that the stability of his own country was more precarious than that of Imperial Russia.

It has often been suggested that the French investing public had been misled into investment in Russia by articles extolling Russia's position in the daily and financial press heavily subsidised by the Russian government. 'La venalité de la presse a joué un rôle particulièrement important pour le succès des emprunts russes,' wrote a historian of France's economic development.[22] There is abundant evidence of the heavy toll exacted by the French press from a frequently reluctant Russian government. The letters of Russia's financial agent in Paris, Raffalovich, to the finance minister in St Petersburg, which first appeared in instalments in the French communist daily *l'Humanité* and were subsequently published as a book under the title *l'Abominable Vénalité de la Presse*, contain exact data on the amounts expended on subsidies and the names of the recipients.[23] The impression derived from reading this gruesome account is not that this procedure was effective in moulding French opinion but that the French press, having discovered the hyper-sensitivity of the Russian government to foreign criticism and its almost pathological concern for its credit standing abroad, applied a form of blackmail to coax the Russians into continuing and increasing their subsidies.[24]

The relations between the Russian government and the French press took the form of payments for the insertion of prospectuses, advertisements and lists of coupons which had been amortised, all normal and 'respectable' transactions, although the rates paid somewhat exceeded the usual ones. In addition the Russian government made payments for articles on particular aspects of Russia's economic and financial position, written or drafted by Russia's financial agent, Raffalovich, who however enjoyed a reputation in his own right as an expert in financial matters. The Russian government similarly paid for the publication of official financial or economic information concerning Russia, such as governmental decrees, budget estimates, etc.

At regular intervals agreements were concluded as to fixed sums to be paid to the press over a limited period of time especially at times when Russia was experiencing political difficulties. Upon the outbreak of the Russo–Japanese War a sum of 200,000 francs was placed at the disposal of the Banque de Paris et des Pays Bas for distribution to the press for a period of three months.[25] These payments were intended as additional to the payments assigned for the purpose of publicity by the banks issuing Russian loans. In anticipation of each Russian loan the French journals were preparing themselves for a campaign for or against the loan long before its issue in order either to win an allocation of publicity or, if they were not included among the fortunate ones, to draw the attention of the issuing banks and the Russian government to the fact that it was unwise to ignore them.[26]

The effectiveness of the publicity for Russian bonds was marred by a number of factors. Russian loans were not the only ones which were eulogised in the press. Every needy foreign government or corporation appealing to the Paris market made sure beforehand of the attitude of the press. (The Russian ambassador in Paris, Izvolsky, complained that other countries devoted much larger sums for this purpose than Russia.)[27] Faced by a flood of propaganda on behalf of all sorts of foreign securities, every one promising fabulous returns and security, the average French investor could hardly be expected to base his investment policies on the opinion of the press.

Moreover if the propaganda in favour of Russia's creditworthiness was extensive, no less strong and vocal were the voices deprecating Russia in various ways. There were the Russian political emigrés who rarely missed the opportunity to harm the government which they abhorred. There were the Jewish organisations denouncing Russia for her pogroms. There were also the socialists who in the press and on the forum of the *Chambre* expressed their hostility to Russia's political system and their criticism of loans to a 'gouvernement d'assassins'. There was the correspondence from Great Britain, where the *Times* in particular was known for its biting criticism of Russia and her finances. Finally there were various individuals, for various reasons personal enemies of the then Russian finance minister, men like E. Cyon, Sharapov, etc. who published pamphlets attacking Witte's policy.

Finally one and the same journal changed its complexion overnight either because the Russian government had discontinued its payments or because it felt that the subsidy was not large enough or because a paper hitherto unsubsidised was entered on the list of the subsidised. In these circumstances the French investor was more likely to become confused or cynical, but he certainly would not look to the press for investment guidance.[28]

However at the very beginning of the Franco–Russian financial *entente* in the late 1880s the publicity organised by E. Cyon was probably effective in raising interest in and enthusiasm for Russian bonds. This publicity was effective because it was new and because it skilfully exploited the patriotic emotions of the average Frenchman. For the first time Russia's economic and financial position was presented in a blast of propaganda as if Russia were a newly discovered land.[29]

Otherwise throughout the period under consideration the importance of the press in the matter of investments in Russian bonds was of a negative nature. Unless 'influenced' the press could aggravate the feeling of uncertainty among the public once such feeling had been aroused by important events. To calm public opinion during the Russo–Japanese War and the 1905 Revolution the press was promised substantial subsidies if they exercised restraint and refrained from publishing 'des nouvelles tendencieuses dont la répétition pourraient provoquer une panique également funeste à la Russie et a l'épargne française'. By and large this arrangement worked.[30]

Whatever the difficulties and occasional humiliations Russia encountered as a large-scale international debtor, she did on the whole receive her credit cheaply considering the high cost of capital in Russia. The Russian government had found in the French investor an ideal creditor : steady in his investing habits, not prone to panic, concerned about steady income at modest levels rather than speculative gains. Though a fairly large proportion of Russia's public debt contracted in France was used to restore military equipment lost in or financial stability affected by war, as after 1905, a much larger proportion of the total was used to strengthen the economy.[31] In any case had French credits not been forthcoming, Russia would have allocated less of her domestic resources for economic purposes, as military considerations commonly received priority.

It has been argued that the net inflow of real resources from abroad was not of a sufficiently high magnitude relative to national income to compensate for the costs of the policy of reliance on capital imports. Contemporaries were aware of the social cost involved. There were a few however who felt that reliance on foreign capital imposed upon the Russian government a set of orthodox financial policies which could be restrictive of growth.[32] This is also the view of some contemporary historians. In our view however both the government and the public needed the elements of self-scrutiny, self-discipline and education which an orthodox financial policy, and especially the gold standard, were imposing. There is no evidence that the policies pursued as a result of reliance on foreign capital infused a deflationary bias into the economy which reduced growth potential.[33] Much more will have to be known about the behaviour of prices before firm conclusions can be made on this point.

General conclusion

Though each of the essays here presented contains conclusions pertinent to its subject matter, one can make a few general points based on an impressionistic overall view of Russia's economic development since the earliest times.

The first point to be made is that, though Russian economic and social history was full of dramatic interludes, overall economic change was relatively slow and uneven, leaving large areas of the economic landscape unaffected by modern development. Poverty was too long seated and endemic, costs of development too high and the magnitude of the task too overwhelming, for even great advances to make significantly large impacts upon aggregates in the short run. Islands of modern growth were surrounded by seas of traditional or semi-traditional economies.

The task of first gaining and then sustaining great power status, though it often provided the impetus for development policies, was in the long run among the most pernicious influences upon Russia's ability to sustain an economic effort. It constituted a constant drain on resources away from productive employment, especially as much of Russian military equipment could not be produced domestically. It led to considerable public indebtedness, much of it to foreign countries, and to a legacy of monetary anarchy, which in their turn imposed upon the Russian government sets of policies (in the monetary, commercial and budgetary fields) not always consistent with achieving optimal growth rates.

Where the rôle of the state in the economy is concerned we suggest that a dynamic rather than static approach, indicating an evolving and frequently shifting balance between state policy and market forces, offers the most correct assessment of Russian historical reality. When considered statically, government policy in the economic sphere was rarely monolithic or consistent, not only because government did not speak with one voice, but because military, political and general financial interests took precedence over macroeconomic aims. Nevertheless it seems to us that under Witte there was a conjuncture of various policies, pursued with great intensity over a relatively long time and entailing a considerable volume of government expenditure, which in interaction with market forces had contributed to an industrial take-off.

Despite tariffs and various interventionist economic policies, the Russian economy evolved in interaction with the international economy; foreign trade in its widest sense was not just a residual as during the Stalinist period in the USSR but constituted a significant proportion of the GNP. Because of the uneven economic advance, Russia as a latecomer scored some advantages as so ably argued by A. Gerschenkron, but was also exposed to many disadvantages and hazards. International diplomatic and military involvements on occasion aided her and more often compounded her difficulties.

It is commonly believed that there was continuity between the industrial strategies of the 1880s and 1890s and under Stalin. While there is no denying that the economic environment and traditions made for certain common features, there was nothing in these earlier policies which in any way approximated to the Stalinist pricing and taxation policies to the detriment of the rural sector, whether as producer or consumer. Neither does the study of the structure of prerevolutionary industry confirm the alleged similarity between Russian and Soviet industrialisation patterns with the emphasis on heavy industry. Both in terms of employment and output value industries catering for the mass consumer market were the leaders in the pre-1914 industrialisation.

Though the historian's attention has been rightly focused on large-scale industry where the real drama of fast growth rates was taking place and though agriculture was advancing albeit very slowly in terms of yields and techniques, the most promising development, and one most likely to make the recurring theme of direct government involvement unnecessary in the long run, was the gradual but uninterrupted erosion of the subsistence economy and the growing involvement of the population and of the country in the market. Unlike the majority of West European countries, which had become market economies before the onset of industrialisation, in Russia the creation of a market economy was part of the process of industrialisation. It is because a market meant much more than just effective demand, or the use of money in exchange, or even good transport facilities, but also confidence in the stability of the currency, a proper credit organisation, a system of reliable and enforceable law, and knowledge which came from the experience of the operation of market forces, that the stabilisation of the currency, its convertibility into gold, the banking and fiscal policies of the state from the 1860s onwards were so important. However much one might argue that alternative sets of policies might have induced more and faster growth, infusion of confidence and the development of a business mentality were in the long run most important.

Though, as with all modern development, the balance of advantage was often with the expansion of the large concern based on advanced technology, Russian development offered still before 1914 much scope for small-scale autonomous entrepreneurship which was constantly surfacing anew and displaying great resilience. From the socio-political point of view the continuous existence and vitality of small and medium business units was a positive phenomenon in the evolution of Russia. It was however cut short by the policies of War Communism during 1918–21 and of the late 1920s when the collectivisation drive and the attack on *Nepmen* effectively removed all scope for any sizeable legal autonomous entrepreneurship.

Glossary

arshin – measure of length equal to 28 inches or 71 cm.
barshchina – labour obligation of peasants
desyatina – a land measure equal to 2·7 acres
dvor – peasant homestead
guberniya – an administrative area, province
ispravnik – local government official
kazyonnaya palata – treasury office
kopek (copeck) – a Russian coin, 1/100 of a rouble
krugovaya poruka – joint liability for taxes and dues
kustar – peasant engaged in cottage industry
ministerstvo gossudarstvennykh imushchestv – ministry of state domains
mir – peasant commune
obrok – quitrent paid by peasants in cash and kind
odnodvortsy – 'One-homesteaders'. State peasants descended from the small servitors on the southern frontiers in the sixteenth and seventeenth centuries
polovnik – share cropper
pomeshchik – fief holder, noble landowner
pomestye – until the eighteenth century a fief: later a general term for an estate owned by nobles
pood – weight equal to 36 lb.
possessional workers – workers attached to the factory not the person of factory owner
szlachta – Polish nobility
udel – land belonging to members of the Imperial family
uyezd – district, subdivision of a *gouberniya*
vedro – liquid measure equal to 3·25 gallons
versta – verst, measure of length equal to 0·66 miles
volost' – subdivision of a district, territorial commune
yassak – a tax in furs paid by non-Orthodox subjects of the Tsar
zhalovannaya gramota – charter

Notes

CHAPTER 1

1 Raymond W. Goldsmith, 'The economic growth of Tsarist Russia 1860–1913', in *Economic Development and Cultural Change*, vol. 9, pt II (1961) pp. 441–75.

2 A. Gerschenkron, 'The rate of growth of industrial production in Russia since 1885', *Journal of Economic History*, VII-s (1947).

3 A. Madison, *Economic growth in Japan and the USSR* (London, 1969) p. 104.

4 See p. 112, this study. By 1913 the weight of Russia's pig iron production in the total of five most advanced countries rose from 3·7 in 1890 to 6·5 per cent in 1913, demand for cotton from 7·8 to 12 per cent; but industrial output was not more than 3·14 of total world output.

5 J. F. Karcz (ed.), *Soviet and East European agriculture* (Berkeley, 1967) p. 250; A. Kahan, 'Natural calamities and their effect upon the food supply in Russia', *Jahrbücher für Geschichte Osteuropas*, Neue Folge, bd 16/68.

6 A. Baykov, 'The economic development of Russia', *Economic History Review*, VII (1954) pp. 137–49.

7 Even in the first three centuries there were already elements of relative backwardness. Large-scale landed property was late to emerge and only very incipient features of a feudal system were in evidence. More importantly having acquired their Christianity through the medium of Church Slavonic, not Greek, the Russians made no contact with original Byzantine written work, and there is little evidence of any body of conceptual law, of speculative thought, or political theory.

8 There is evidence too that this rigid state-organised system became necessary when massive increases in taxation burdens coupled with the lure of new lands to the east and south resulted in mass flights from the centre in the second half of the sixteenth and the early seventeenth century.

9 K. Kocharovsky, *Sotsyal'ny stroy Rossii* (Prague, 1926) p. 13.

10 J. Hicks, *A theory of economic history* (London, 1969).

11 P. G. Ryndzyunsky, 'Gorodskoye naseleniye', in M. K. Rozhkova (ed.), *Ocherki ekonomicheskoy istorii Rossii . . .* (Moscow, 1959) pp. 276–358.

12 Gerschenkron, *Europe in the Russian mirror* (London, 1970) lecture 3.

13   Ibid.
14   M. Tugan-Baranovsky, *Russkaya fabrika*, 3rd ed. (Leningrad, 1934) p. 12.
15   P. Struve, *Kriticheskiye zametki* (St Petersburg, 1904) p. 83.
16   Tugan-Baranovsky, op. cit., pp. 105 ff. and V. K. Yatsunsky in Rozhkova, loc. cit., p. 226.
17   A. Kahan, 'Continuity in economic activity and policy during the post-Petrine period in Russia', *Journal of Economic History*, vol. xxv, no. 1 (Mar 1965).
18   D. Landes, *Cambridge Economic History*, vol. vi, pt 1, p. 286. A. Kahan, 'The costs of "Westernization" in Russia', *Slavic Review*, vol. xxv, no. 1 (Mar 1966).
19   Yatsunsky, loc. cit., pp. 174 ff.
20   B. Kafengaus, *Voprosy Istorii*, no. 7 (1962) pp. 69–80.
21   On the basis of P. G. Ryndzyunsky, *Krest'yanskaya promyshlennost' v Rossii* (Moscow, 1966).
22   Tugan-Baranovsky, op. cit., p. 171.
23   Ibid., and G. von Schultze-Gaevernitz *Ocherki obshchestvennogo khozyaystva i ekonomicheskoy politiki Rossii*, from German (St Petersburg, 1901) p. 69.
24   Schultze-Gaevernitz, op. cit., p. 72; see also R. Portal, 'Industriels Moscovites: Le secteur cotonnier (1861–1914)', *Cahier du Monde Russe et Soviétique*, vol. iv, pp. 1–2, 5–46.
25   Yatsunsky, loc. cit., p. 183, and Portal, loc. cit., p. 8.
26   Yatsunsky, loc. cit., p. 196.
27   Witte's answer to gentry memorandum, *Istorichesky Arkhiv*, vol. iv (1957) p. 134.
28   Schultze-Gaevernitz, loc. cit., p. 102, and p. 22 above.
29   W. L. Blackwell, *The beginnings of Russian industrialization* (Princeton, N.J., 1968) p. 403.
30   Review of Blackwell's book in *Soviet Studies*, vol. xxi, no. 4 (Apr 1970).
31   Between 1860 and 1880 output of grain grew by 70 per cent, and exports of grain increased nearly 3·3 times.
32   *Cambridge Economic History*, vol. vi, pt ii.
33   P. G. Ryndzyunsky, 'O melkotovarnom uklade v Rossii xix v', *Istoriya SSSSR*, no. 1 (1961) p. 62.
34   Ibid., p. 68. See also Sviatlovsky (German ed.), pp. 115–16.
35   Ibid., pp. 61 ff.
36   Tugan-Baranovsky, op. cit., pp. 332–3.
37   Goldsmith, loc. cit.; Ryndzyunsky, *Krest'yanskaya promyshlennost'* . . ., op. cit., p. 47, n. 23.
38   Tugan-Baranovsky, op. cit., pp. 282–4.
39   Ryndzyunsky, *Krest'yanskaya promyshlennost'* . . ., op. cit., p. 47.
40   Ibid., pp. 233–6.
41   S. Zak, *Promyshlenny kapitalizm v Rossii* (Moscow, 1908) pp. 66–71.
42   Ibid., p. 69; Zak estimated that the industrial labour reserve on account of landless and semi-landless peasants was 9 million in the 1890s.
43   Ibid., p. 72.
44   S. Swianiewicz, *Forced labour and economic development* (London, 1965) p. 62.
45   A. and I. de Navarette, 'Underemployment in underdeveloped econ-

omies', in A. N. Agarwala and S. P. Singh, *The economics of underdevelopment* (London, 1969) p. 343.

46 *World Columbian Exposition* (St Petersburg, 1893) p. 514.

47 Zak, op. cit., p. 22.

48 H. M. Druzhinin, 'Likvidatsiya feodal'noy sistemy v russkoy pomeshchichyey derevne (1862–1882)', *Voprosy Istorii*, no. 12 (Dec 1968) p. 21.

49 Alexander III's legislation strengthening the commune was distinctly reactionary but had little negative effect on the spurt of the 1890s and was disregarded where the commune had become obsolete. The coexistence of this policy in the agrarian sector with the progressive policy in industry would suggest a lack of co-ordination between the two, and may indicate that the process of industrialisation was a less conscious one than commonly assumed, or that the connection between the two was not strikingly obvious.

50 A. E. Lositsky, 'Rasspadeniye obshchiny', *Trudy Imperatorskogo Vol'no Ekonomicheskogo Obshchestva*, vol. 1–2 (1912). The generally accepted 10 per cent peasant contribution to marketings by 1860 has been challenged by I. D. Kovalchenko, in *Yezhegodnik agrarnoy istorii vostochnoy Yevropy* (1963) pp. 481–3.

51 See our forthcoming chapter in *Cambridge Economic History*, vol. VII.

52 Schultze-Gaevernitz, op. cit., p. 269 n.

53 *Istorichesky Arkhiv*, loc. cit., p. 128 – the exact amount was 850 million roubles.

54 The effective yield was according to the gentry not more than 70 per cent. Witte maintained that the depreciation was pronounced during the decade of the 1860s, for about ten years. Ibid., p. 125.

55 Ibid.

56 S. Atava (S. Terpigirev), *Oskudneniye*, Sochineniya (St Petersburg, 1899) vol. II; Sviatlovsky, who made a study of the land market, suggests that the medium-size estate was most vulnerable.

57 A. Troynitsky, *Krepostnoye naseleniye . . .* (St Petersburg, 1861) p. 45.

58 *Istorichesky Arkhiv*, loc. cit., p. 148.

59 The 1860s were a critical period for Russia financially. It was in the 1860s that the future chancellor of the German Reich, then ambassador in St Petersburg, formed his views about Russia's financial vulnerability and tried to reap diplomatic dividends by using financial blackmail.

60 P. Migulin, *Nasha bankovaya politika (1729–1903)* (Kharkov, 1904); M. Kh. Reutern, *Biografichesky ocherk* (St Petersburg, 1910) Prilozheniya, pp. 163 ff.

61 See the present study, Chapter 5 below.

62 A. Raffalovich, *Russia, its commerce and trade* (London, 1918) pp. 230, 250.

63 See p. 97; Reutern, op. cit., p. 157. That the change in policy was dictated less by principle than by pressure of immediate contingency is clear from the fact that the protectionist measures introduced by Bunge were in sharp contrast to his professed belief in liberal commercial policy as expressed in official documents and his teachings as professor of economics.

64 Raffalovich, loc. cit., p. 230.

65 See pp. 99–100 below.
66 See the present study, Chapter 5 below.
67 O. Crisp, 'The financial aspect of the Franco–Russian Alliance', Ph.D. thesis (London, 1954) p. 283.
68 *World Columbian Exposition*, loc. cit., xii.
69 I. F. Gindin, *Gossudarstvenny bank i ekonomicheskaya politika tsarskogo pravitel'stva* (Moscow, 1960) pp. 191–299. See also his 'Russkaya burzhuazya', *Istoriya SSR*, no. 2 (1963) p. 69, and no. 3, p. 44. A. S. Lisyansky, 'Osnovaniye Yuzovskogo zavoda', *Istoriya SSR*, no. 5, p. 15.
70 Raffalovich, op. cit., p. 232. The annual average of new line was 1384 miles as against only 427 during 1879–90.
71 A. O. Hirschman, *The strategy of economic development* (New Haven, 1960) p. 72. The oil industry was an exception. It developed independently of the government but it was at first more like an 'enclave' producing mainly for export.
72 S. Zak, op. cit., p. 47.
73 Ibid., pp. 48–9.
74 Ibid., p. 50; and pp. 97, 108 below. Zak, loc. cit., p. 54; according to Verstraete in *Congrès International des Valeurs Mobilières* (Paris, 1900) vol. 4, about 778 million roubles.
75 On the basis of *Ministerstvo Finansov, 1802–1902* and *1904–1913* (St Petersburg, 1902 and 1913, respectively).
76 S. S. Khrulev, *Financy Rossii* . . . (St Petersburg, 1909) pp. 113, 117. M. Alexeyenko (chairman of the budget committee in the duma) 'Five Years of Budget Work', *Russian Review*, no. 3 (1912) pp. 14–44.
77 A. Babkov, 'National finances and the economic evolution of Russia', *Russian Review* no. 3 (1912) pp. 170–91, 180. The land tax accounted for only 2·5 per cent of ordinary revenue in 1913.
78 Schultze-Gaevernitz op. cit., p. 449.
79 Babkov, loc. cit., p. 184. Total revenue from taxation increased by 12·5 per cent during 1881–1901; out of an average annual increase of 92 million roubles in total revenue, 51 million was from taxation of which 44 million or 86·2 per cent from indirect taxes and dues, ibid., p. 175.
80 Ibid., p. 186.
81 V. K. Dmitryev, *Kriticheskiye issledovaniya o potreblenii alkoholya v Rossii* (Moscow, 1911) p. 157, estimated that consumption of vodka per head was 0·44 *vedra* of pure spirit in the countryside and 1·44 in cities.
82 Babkov, loc. cit., p. 156.
83 Below, p. 101.
84 Witte ascribed the deficit of 640 million roubles on the running of the railways 1880–94 to the downward revision of railway freights on grain in 1889 and 1893; *Istorichesky Arkhiv*, loc. cit., pp. 123–4.
85 W. Hoeffding, 'Recent financial and trade policy of Russia', *Russian Review* no. 1 (1912) p. 78.
86 V. I. Kovalevsky (ed.), *Rossiya v kontse XIX v.* (St Petersburg, 1900) p. 237, and Hoeffding, loc. cit., p. 78.
87 Zak, op. cit., p. 56.
88 Kovalevsky, loc. cit.

89 Schultze-Gaevernitz, op. cit., pp. 227–8.
90 Hoeffding, loc. cit., p. 96.
91 Ibid.; Schultze-Gaevernitz, op. cit., p. 227.
92 Tugan-Baranovsky, op. cit., pp. 352–61, 312 ff.
93 Tugan-Baranovsky, *K luchshemu budushchemu* (St Petersburg, 1910) p. 200.
94 Thus tariffs on agricultural machinery existed between 1885–97; paradoxically they were introduced by the pro-agrarian Bunge.
95 Komitet Ministrov, *Nasha zheleznodorozhnaya politika*, vol. iv, p. 272. *Svod dannykh fabrichno-zavodskoy promyshlennosti Rossii za 1897 g.*, pp. 128–9, 186. A. A. Radtsig, *Zheleznaya promyshlennost' vsego sveta* (St Petersburg, 1900) p. 66.
96 Komitet Ministrov, loc. cit., pp. 239–40.
97 Ibid., p. 242.
98 Raffalovich, op. cit., p. 107.
99 See table in Lyashchenko, op. cit., vol. ii, pp. 238–9; Rashin, op. cit., p. 56.
100 Portal, *Cahiers*, loc. cit., p. 8, and *Svod otchetov fabrichnykh inspecktorov za 1909*, viii, indicating correlation between cotton output and the fortunes of the rural sector.
101 Below, p. 101.
102 See the present study, Chapter 5 below.
103 Gindin, op. cit., pp. 191 ff.
104 See Svod otchetov, op. cit., for 1910, 1911, 1912, 1913 indicating the extent to which government orders, especially military orders, stimulated metal working industries.
105 Below, p. 136. The proportion of non-guaranteed to guaranteed railway capital actually fell from 11 per cent in 1900, to 8 per cent in 1914; L. E. Shepelev, 'Aktsyonernoye Uchreditelstvo v Rossii', in *Akademiya Nauk, Iz istorii imperyalizma* (1959) Table xii, p. 163.
106 Raffalovich, op. cit., pp. 236 n., 238.
107 G. E. Affanas'yev, *Denezhny Krizis* (Odessa, 1900).
108 On the basis of Glasgow International Exhibition, *Russia, its industries and trade* (Glasgow, 1901) pp. 82–3; A. Raffalovich, loc. cit., p. 115, and I. Gindin, 'O nekotorykh osobennostyakh ekonomicheskoy i sotsyal'noy struktury rossiyskogo kapitalizma v nachale XX v', *Istoriya SSSR*, vol. 3 (1966) pp. 48–9.
109 J. H. Bater, 'The industrial geography of St. Petersburg: 1850–1914', Ph.D. thesis (London, 1969) p. 73, reproduced with author's permission.
110 Gindin, loc. cit., p. 48.
111 See table 1.4.
112 See also P. Gregory, 'Economic growth and structural change in Tsarist Russia: A case of modern economic growth', *Soviet Studies*, vol. xxxiii (Jan 1972) pp. 418–34, especially Table 6 and Conclusion.
113 A. S. Suvorin (ed.) (St Petersburg, 1901).
114 For data on labour see our chapter in the forthcoming Cambridge Economic History, vol. vii.
115 The discussion of the labour force is based on our chapter in the forth-

coming Cambridge Economic History, vol. vii; see also G. V. Rimlinger, review of Rashin's book on the formation of the labour force in Russia, *Journal of Economic History*, xxi (June 1961).

116 See table 1.5.

117 'Numbers and reality: A critique of estimates of foreign investment in Russia'.

118 *Vestnik Finansov*, vol. 5 (1910) p. 216; World Columbian Exposition, op. cit., pp. 12, 21; Schultze-Gaevernitz, op. cit., pp. 78–96; A. N. Shcherban, *Istoriya tekhnicheskogo razvitiya ugol'noy promyshlennosti Donbassa*, 2 vols (Kiev, 1969) i, pp. 72–3, 99, 105, 106, 110.

119 Schultze-Gaevernitz op. cit., pp. 78–99.

120 K. A. Pazhitnov, *Ocherki istorii tekstil'noy promyshlennosti dorevolyutsyonnoy Rossii* (Moscow, 1958) p. 125; '*Fabrichno-zavodskaya promyshlennost'* *Yevropeyskoy Rossii v 1910–1912 gg'*, vyp. viii i ix (Petrograd, 1914) pp. 22–6.

121 M. A. Pavlov, *Vospominaniya metallurga* (Moscow, 1945); Shcherban, op. cit., p. 71.

122 *Blackwoods Magazine*, vol. 1858 (1895) p. 809.

123 D. M. Wallace, *Russia*, 2 vols (London, 1905) i, p. 17.

124 Sixth International Congress of Economic History, Copenhagen, 19–23 August 1974; Section: *Investment Strategy in Private Enterprise*.

125 A. V. Pogozhev, *Uchet chislennosti i sostava rabochikh v Rossii* (St Petersburg, 1906) pp. 51–68, Table xxvi.

126 V. I. Lenin, *Sochineniya*, vol. 3, p. 460.

127 P. Makar'yev, *Fabrichno-zavodskaya promyshlennost' Kostromskoy gubernii nakanune mirovoy voyny* (Kostroma, 1924) p. 61.

128 'Pismo iz Vladimira', *Sovremenny Mir*, vol. 4 (1911), pp. 277–8.

129 *Svod otchotov* for 1913, pp. xxiii–xxxvii.

130 Ibid., and *Vestnik Finansov*, no. 7 (1915), p. 299.

131 J. W. Leasure and R. A. Lewis, 'Internal migration in Russia in the late nineteenth century', *Slavic Review*, vol. xxvii (Sep 1968) p. 383.

132 A. J. Rashin, *Naseleniye Rossii za 100 let* (Moscow, 1946).

133 Kovalevsky, op. cit., p. 512.

134 *Ekonomicheskoye obozreniye*, no. 9 (1929) p. 114.

135 Ryndzyunsky's *Krest'yanskaya Promyshlennost'* is a very intelligent account for the period 1861–90.

136 Tugan-Baranovsky, op. cit., pp. 396 ff. Even the girls apparently favoured those who sought work in the city; parents asked why they allowed their sons to go away would mention the greater ease of life in the city. Here, i.e. in the village – they would say – you neither starve nor have enough to eat; or that in the city they had a better chance, they were more respected, spoke differently, could dance, wore city suits, etc.

137 Tugan-Baranovsky, op. cit., pp. 375 ff.

138 See p. 129.

139 Tugan-Baranovsky, op. cit., pp. 217 ff.

140 Ibid., p. 163.

141 Gindin, *Osobennosti . . . Istoriya SSSR* (1966) pp. 54 ff.

142 Ibid., and Shcherban, op. cit., p. 72.

143 A. L. Vaynshtayn, *Narodnoye bogatsvo i narodno-khozyaystvennoye, nakoplenye predrevolyutsyonnoy Rossii* (Moscow, 1960) p. 403.
144 J. H. Boeke, *Economics and economic policy in dual societies* (Haarlem, Holland, 1953) p. 404.
145 H. Myint, 'Dualism and the internal integration of the underdeveloped economies', *Banca Nazionale del Lavoro Quarterly Review*, no. 93 (June 1970) pp. 128–56.
146 L. Y. Erman, 'Sostav intelligentsii v Rossii . . .', *Istoriya SSSR*, no.1 (1963) p. 166, Tables 10 and 11, p. 174.
147 M. Kaser, in *Essays in Honour of E. H. Carr*, ed. C. Abramsky (London, 1974) pp. 236–7.
148 See p. 169 below and the forthcoming volume VII of the Cambridge Economic History.
149 H. Barkai, 'The macro-economics of Tsarist Russia in the industrialization era', *Journal of Economic History*, vol. XXXIII, 2 (June, 1973).

CHAPTER 2

1 W. Kirchner, *Commercial relations between Russia and Europe 1400–1800 . . .* (Bloomington, Ind. 1966).
2 Ibid., p. 243.
3 ibid., p. 244.
4 Kirchner, op. cit., p. 232.
5 J. T. Fuhrmann. *The origins of capitalism in Russia: Industry and progress in the sixteenth and seventeenth centuries* (Chicago, 1972).
6 V. I. Shunkov, *et al.* (eds), *Perekhod ot feodalizma k kapitalizmu v Rossii . . .* (Moscow, 1969).
7 Fuhrmann, op. cit., pp. 10–11.
8 See pp. 14–5 and 49–50.
9 See p. 189.
10 *U istokov krupnogo proizvodstva v russkoy promyshlennosti: k voprosu o genezise kapitalizma v Rossii* (Moscow, 1970).
11 *L'Oural au XVIIIe siècle. Etude d'histoire économique* (Paris, 1950), review originally published in *Slavonic and East European Review* vol. XXX (Dec 1951).
12 *Etudes industrielles sur l'Oural* (Paris, 1899).
13 *Politika russkogo samoderzhaviya v oblasti promyshlennosti (20–50-ye gody XIX v)* (Moscow, 1968).
14 In *Essays in Russian history: A collection dedicated to George Vernadsky* (Hamden, Conn. 1964).
15 Skerpan, loc. cit., p. 211.

CHAPTER 3

1 A. G. Troynitsky, *Krepostnoye naseleniye Rossii po desyatoy narodnoy perepisi* (St Petersburg, 1861) pp. 57–8, quoted by P. A. Khromov, *Ekonomicheskoye razvitiye Rossii v XIX-XX vekakh* (Moscow, 1950) p. 83.

2 Ibid. The terms 'state peasant' or 'crown peasant' can be used synonymously. Peasants who belonged to the imperial family in their capacity as landowners were known till the end of the eighteenth century as 'court peasants' (*udel'nyye*), and are here referred to as *udel* peasants.

3 *Polnoye Sobraniye Zakonov Russkoy Imperii* (subsequently referred to as *PSZ*), vii, 4533, 4538, viii, 5228.

4 P. Milyukov, *Gosudarstvennoye khozyaystvo Rossii v pervoy chetverti XVIII veka i reforma Petra Velikogo* (St Petersburg, 1905) pp. 476–7.

5 B. Sergeyevich, *Drevnosti russkogo prava* (St Petersburg, 1909) vol. i, pp. 257 ff.

6 *PSZ*, i, 79; M. Dyakonov, *Ocherki iz istorii sel' skogo naseleniya v Moskovskom gosudarstve* (St Petersburg, 1898) pp. 157–62.

7 *PSZ*, viii, 5579, ix, 7136, xxii, 16046, 16467, 26376; V. I. Semevsky, *Krest'yane v tsarstvovaniye Imperatritsy Yekateriny II*, 2 vols (St Petersburg, 1901–3) ii, pp. 721 ff.; B. V. Veshnyakov, 'Istoricheskiy obzor proiskhozhdeniya raznykh nazvaniy gosudarstvennykh krest'yan', *Zhurnal Ministerstva Gosudarstvennykh Imushchestv* (Mar 1857) quoted by N. M. Druzhinin, *Gosudarstvennyye krest'yane i Reforma P. D. Kiselyova* (Moscow, 1946) pp. 38 ff.

8 *PSZ*, iii, 1542, 1594, 1669.

9 On the basis of Semevsky, op. cit., vol. i, pp. 16–18, vol. ii, p. 12; Druzhinin, op. cit., p. 45.

10 According to P. Keppen, *Devyataya reviziya* (St Petersburg, 1857) pp. 189–92, the state peasants in 1835 represented 34 per cent of all peasants. The fall in the relative proportion of state peasants was partly due to the fact that in the census of 1796 foreign colonists and Jewish agriculturists were counted as state peasants while Keppen did not include them.

11 *PSZ*, xxi, 15724, xxii, 16611, xxviii, 21698, xxxi, 24605, xxxviii, 29343, 28863, vi, 4869, 4977, vii, 5249, 5250, ix, 6734, 7404, xii, 10390, xxxix, 29979.

12 Troynitsky, op. cit., pp. 57–8.

13 'Krest'yane', *Entsiklopedicheskiy slovar'*, ed. F. A. Brokhauz and I. A. Efron (St Petersburg, 1895) vol. xvi.

14 Druzhinin, op. cit., pp. 316, 311 ff.

15 M. Raeff, *Michael Speransky* (The Hague, 1957) p. 302; Semevsky, op. cit., ii, p. 434; M. Dyakonov, *Ocherki obshchestvennogo i gosudarstvennogo stroya drevney Rusi* (St Petersburg, 1908) p. 487.

16 *PSZ*, xiv, 10237; *Sbornik Imperatorskogo Russkogo Istoricheskogo Obshchestva*, vol. 98, 'Obozreniye upravleniya gosudarstvennykh imushchestv za poslednikh 25 let'; I. P. Rukovsky, *Istoriko-statisticheskiye svedeniya o podushnykh podat'yakh* (St Petersburg, 1862) pp. 17–34, prilozheniye vi; Druzhinin, op. cit., pp. 221 ff.

17 Ibid., p. 27.

18 *PSZ*, i, 10, 112, xxii, 16393, xxiii, 17175, xxx, 23656; Semevsky, op. cit., ii, pp. 623, 721–5; Khromov, *Ocherki ekonomiki feodalizma v Rossii* (Moscow, 1957) p. 45; *Entsiklopedichesky slovar*, loc. cit., A. Gertsen, *Byloye i dumy*, 5 vols (Berlin, 1921) i, p. 362.

Notes 231

19 'Prilozheniye k zhurnalu 16.11.1827 and 2.12.1828', Zasedaniye 16 i 19 dekabrya 1828, *Sbornik*, vol. 74.
20 I. Ignatovich, *Pomeshchichiye krest'yane nakanune osvobozhdeniya* (Moscow 1910) p. 90.
21 V. I. Semevsky, *Kazyonnyye krest'yane v tsarstvovaniye Yekateriny II*, 2 vols (St Petersburg, 1879) II, pp. 260–3; Rukovsky, op. cit., prilozheniye VI; Khromov, op. cit., p. 79.
22 During 1760–70 money rents paid by serfs amounted to 2–3 roubles per soul annually; in 1830 on the Vorontsov estates they reached up to 30 roubles (Khromov, op. cit., pp. 90–1). E. I. Indova, 'Krest'yane tsentralno promyshlennykh votchin Vorontsovykh v pervoy polovine XIX verka', *Istoricheskiye zapiski*, vol. 38 (Moscow, 1951) pp. 176–208, 192.
23 Baron von Haxthausen, *The Russian Empire*, 2 vols (London, 1856) II, pp. 316 ff.
24 *Sbornik*, vol. 98., loc. cit.
25 Haxthausen, op. cit., I, pp. 212, 472.
26 M. M. Bogoslovsky, 'Gosudarstvennyye krest'yane pri Nikolaye I', *Istoriya Rossii v XIX veke*, ed. A. I. Granat, 9 vols (St Petersburg, n.d.) I, p. 243.
27 Ibid. pp. 240 ff. Herzen recorded the muddle and inefficiency prevailing in the *palaty*. He did not know whether to laugh or to cry when perusing the files with their bizarre headings: 'The case of the loss without trace of the house of the *volost'* administration and on the eating up of its plan by mice'; 'The case of the disappearance of *twenty-two* rent producing assets of the state i.e. 15 versts of land'; 'The case of the transfer of the boy Vassily to the female sex'. Op. cit., I, pp. 359 ff.; M. Speransky, 'Zapiska o krepostnom prave', ed. Kalachev, quoted by L. M. Ivanov, 'Gosudarstvennyye krest'yane moskovskoy gubernii i reforma Kiselyova', *Istoricheskiye zapiski*, vol. 18 (Moscow, 1945) pp. 76–129, 78; Raeff, op. cit., pp. 234–5, 285–6; Haxthausen, op. cit., II, p. 212.
28 *Sbornik*, vol. 98, loc. cit.
29 Ibid.
30 Ibid., and Haxthausen, op. cit., II, p. 405 ff.
31 Ibid., and Bogoslovsky, loc. cit., p. 245.
32 Bogoslovsky, loc. cit., pp. 236 ff.; *Sbornik*, vol. 74, 'Zhurnal komiteta uchrezhdyonnogo vysochayshim reskriptom 6.12.1826; vol. 90, 'Bumaig komiteta 6.12.1826', otdel III and prilozheniya.
33 'Kiselyov, P. D.', *Russkiy biograficheskiy slovar* (St Petersburg, 1897) pp. 702–17; A. P. Zablotsky-Desyatovsky, *Graf P. D. Kiselyov i yego vremya*, 2 vols (St Petersburg, 1882) II pp. 11 ff., 148.
34 Bogoslovsky, loc. cit., pp. 250 ff.
35 Ibid., pp. 251 ff.; Druzhinin, op. cit., p. 513; Ivanov, loc. cit., p. 127, Haxthausen, op. cit, II, p. 431.
36 Gertsen, op. cit., pp. 317, 318, 330.
37 Bogoslovsky, loc. cit., pp. 255 ff.; Ivanov, loc. cit., p. 127; *Russkiy biograficheskiy slovar*, Haxthausen, op. cit., II, p. 431.
38 In the Moscow *guberniya* at the beginning of 1850, of 41,000 peasants living in towns, about 8000 lived there permanently together with their

families (Ivanov, loc. cit., pp. 81 ff.). While in 1845 in the Moscow *guberniya* over 9000 *desyatinas* of land were held in intermingled strips or in joint fields with *pomeshchik* land, by 1853 only 2500 *desyatinas* were held in this manner (ibid., pp. 85 ff.).

39 Ibid., p. 89, and Haxthausen, op. cit., I, p. 117.

40 *Statistika pozemelnoy sobstvennosti i naselyonnykh mest Yevropeyskoy Rossii,* 8 vols (St Petersburg, 1880–5) quoted in P. A. Zayonchkovsky, *Otmena krepostnogo prava v Rossii* (Moscow, 1954) p. 197.

41 *Sbornik*, vol. 98, loc. cit.; Haxthausen, op. cit., II, pp. 447 ff.; Ivanov, loc. cit., pp. 126 ff.

42 Ivanov, loc. cit., pp. 124 ff.

43 Ibid.; Haxthausen, op. cit., II, pp. 432 ff. P. G. Ryndzyunsky, in 'Dvizheniye gosudarstvennykh krest'yan v Tambovskoy gubernii v 1842–1844 gg.', *Istoricheskiye zapiski*, vol. 54 (Moscow, 1955) pp. 315–26, tries to prove that there had been peasant disturbances in the Tambov *guberniya* in reaction to Kiselyov's reform. The few cases he quotes however appear isolated and not representative of the general attitude of the peasantry. Similarly N. M. Druzhinin in 'Otvet krest' yanstva na reformu P. D. Kiselyova', *Iz istorii obshchestvennykh dvizheniy i mezhdunarodnykh otnosheniy*; *Sbornik statey v pamyat adademika Yevgeniya Viktorovicha Tarle,* Akademiya Nauk SSSR (Moscow, 1957) pp. 405–37, exaggerates the importance of peasant disturbances, which even in his account were all confined to the early 1840s. There was considerable apprehension in the state villages in connection with the land surveys undertaken by Kiselyov's ministry and rumours were rife that the peasants would be put under the administration of the *udel*. There was also some opposition to the over-zealous officials who attempted to induce peasants to cultivate potatoes, hence the term 'potato revolts'. The early 1840s were also poor harvest years.

44 Ivanov, loc. cit., p. 127.

45 *Sbornik*, vol. 98, loc. cit.; Haxthausen, op. cit., II, p. 426.

46 Bogoslovsky, loc. cit., p. 256.

47 Ivanov, loc. cit., pp. 93 ff.; N. M. Druzhinin, 'Konflikt mezhdu proizvoditelnymi silami i feodalnymi otnosheniyami', *Voprosy istorii* (Moscow, 1954) no. 7, pp. 56–76.

48 Bogoslovsky, loc. cit., p. 259; *Sbornik*, vol. 98, loc. cit.

49 Ibid.; Haxthausen, op. cit., pp. 435 ff.

50 Ivanov, loc. cit., 81; *Russkiy biograficheskiy slovar,* loc. cit.

51 Kiselyov recorded in his diaries conversations with Alexander II, the Empress Maria Aleksandrovna, the Grand Duchess Yelena Pavlovna, the Grand Duke Konstantin Nikolayevich, N. A. Milyutin, Y. F. Samarin and K. D. Kavelin on the emancipation of the serfs. In a letter of 4 March 1858 Milyutin wrote that the activity of Kiselyov's ministry had laid the foundation for the solution of the peasant question in general. See Y. T. Gerasimova, 'Arkhiv Kiselyovykh', *Zapiski otdela rukopisey*, vypusk 19, Ministerstvo Kultury RSFSR (Moscow, 1957) p. 58, 68; cf. *Sbornik*, vol. 98, 'Zapiski barona Korfa'.

52 The term 'free' is to be understood as free within the framework of a still

Notes 233

fairly stratified society and under a political system involving petty police
or bureaucratic supervision over the individual. Though the various
legal restrictions on property ownership in towns, on admission to guilds,
etc., were abolished or much eased, legally, if not in the economic sense,
the rural and the urban estates were still worlds apart. Thus any litigation
arising out of the property ownership of state peasants in towns had to be
considered in joint session of urban and rural courts; the same applied to
the property of merchants in villages. Ryndzyunsky, 'Krest'yane i gorod
v doreformennoy Rossii', *Voprosy istorii* no. 9 (Moscow, 1955) pp. 26–41,
36. Also the need to purchase a passport for leaving the district for any
length of time might have restricted mobility to some extent. Upon
settling in large towns the peasant had after 1842 to purchase a residence
certificate usually paid for by the employer. His passport was retained so
that according to the minister of the interior control could be exercised
over 'the nomadic mass of people' (ibid., p. 34).

53 Meshalin, op. cit., p. 241. A. G. Rashin, 'K voprosu o formirovanii
rabochego klassa v Rossii', *Istoricheskiye zapiski*, vol. 53 (Moscow 1954)
pp. 144–93, analyses the figures for the issues of passports to peasants in
each individual *guberniya*. In the 1850s in the industrial *guberniya* of
Yaroslav one in every twelve state peasants took out a passport as against
one in every eighteen privately owned serfs. More striking is his evidence
relating to the *guberniyas* of the black earth region where owing to the
predominance of labour services among serfs the state peasants were
practically the only ones who could move freely in search of earnings. This
obtained in the *guberniyas* of Tambov and Voronezh whence peasants
migrated for field work to the territory of the Don Army; short-term
passports were involved in the main. In the *guberniya* of Kharkov during
1854–6 about 70,000 men and women moved on the average annually in
search of work, of whom over 90 per cent were state peasants. Rashin
stresses the greater mobility since Kiselyov's reform. In the Moscow
guberniya over 90 per cent of the able bodied working population of the
state villages were connected in one way or another with outside
industrial activities. The average length of absence from the village was
eight and one-half months (Ivanov, loc. cit., p. 102). According to official
data the hired labourers of the factory industry in the Moscow *guberniya*
at the beginning of the 1850s had been recruited in the main from among
state peasants (Rashin, loc. cit., p. 156). In the *guberniya* of Arkhangel
more than a third of all state peasants sought outside earnings mainly in
St Petersburg (A. I. Rakitin, 'Krest'yanskaya promyshlennost'' v
Arkhangelskoy gubernii v 40–50e gody XIX v.', *Istoricheskiye zapiski*,
vol. 59, (Moscow, 1957) pp. 181–210).

54 Haxthausen, op. cit., i, p. 243, and Rashin, loc. cit.

55 Ivanov, loc. cit., pp. 105 ff.; Haxthausen, op. cit., i, pp. 164 ff., 178, 183.
The term 'industry' was interpreted in the widest sense: all activities which
produced money income other than the cultivation of communal and individual land, if any, were classed as 'industrial'. Thus renting of land for
the purpose of trading in agricultural produce, renting forest land in
order to trade in forestry products, cattle breeding on a large scale for

trading purposes over and above the household needs and apiculture
were classed as 'industrial activities'. *Instruktsiya dlya upravleniya
gosudarstvennykh krest'yan v denezhnykh sborakh*, Ministerstvo gosudarstvennykh imushchestv (St Petersburg, 1848) p. 163.

56   Haxthausen, op. cit., I, pp. 167, 207, 237; Ivanov, loc. cit., pp. 156.
     According to official data for 1858, over 20 per cent of the urban
     population of Russia consisted of people juridically classed as rural.
     This applied also to black earth regions (Ryndzyunsky, loc. cit., p. 33).
     There were also whole rural settlements which were *de facto* urban
     (Meshalin, op. cit., p. 140).

57   Haxthausen, op. cit., II, p. 440; V. N. Yakovtsevsky, *Kupecheskiy kapital v
     feodal'nokrepostnicheskoy Rossii* (Moscow, 1953) p. 140 and table on p. 150.
     During 1826–51 about 66,000 former *pomeshchik* serfs had become urban
     citizens as against some 726,000 from among state peasants. For the
     freed serfs the title 'free village dweller' was often more attractive than
     citizenship of a town (Ryndzyunsky, loc. cit., p. 37).

58   V. Veshnyakov, *Krest'yane sobstvenniki* (St Petersburg, 1858 Appendix I.
     In the Moscow *guberniya* state peasants by 1858 had purchased on the
     average 3·9 *desyatinas* per head, in some districts 20 *desyatinas* per head;
     67 per cent of all purchases were made after 1840 (Ivanov, loc. cit., p. 89).

59   Druzhinin, in *Voprosy Istorii*, loc. cit.

60   Yields were rarely more than four-fold. N. Shipov, *Istoriya moyey zhizni*
     (St Petersburg, 1881); Khromov, op. cit., p. 180; Ryndzyunsky, loc. cit.,
     p. 31.

61   Ivanov, loc. cit., p. 91; Haxthausen, op. cit., I, pp. 118, 148.

62   Haxthausen, op. cit., I, p. 390.

CHAPTER 4

1   Internal loans of any importance were hardly practicable before the
    1880s. The first foreign loan was issued in 1769 through the banking
    house of de Smet and Reymont of Amsterdam. By 1914 the foreign debt
    of the Russian State had reached 4229 million roubles. *Wirtschaft und
    Statistik* (Berlin, 1934) no. 11, pp. 360–3.

2   Ukaz 29 Dec 1768 O.S.; M. P. Kashkarov, *Denezhnoye Obrashcheniye v
    Rossii* (St Petersburg, 1896) pp. 11, 25.

3   The credit rouble will be henceforth referred to as 'paper rouble'. The
    reform, though bearing Kankrin's name, owed more to the initiative of
    Nicholas I. See Zapiski Barona Korfa, *Sbornik Istoricheskogo Obshchestva*
    (St Petersburg, 1896) pp. xcviii, 159–69, 175–207.

4   J. de Bloch, *Les Finances de la Russie* (Paris, 1899) II, p. 256, Kashkarov,
    op. cit., II, p. 72: the circulation of notes had increased by over
    400 million. P. Migulin, *Russkiy Gossudarstvenny Kredit* (Kharkov, 1899–
    1902) p. 1132: about 1500 million roubles were borrowed during the
    war with Turkey and its liquidation.

5   Calculated on the basis of Kashkarov, op. cit., I, pp. 170, 175.

6   During 1895–9, 226 new companies had been founded and 306·9

million gold roubles invested in joint stock companies in Russia as against only sixty-eight foreign companies and 97·8 million gold roubles of foreign capital during the entire period 1851–94; P. V. Ol', *Statistika inostrannykh kapitalov* (1899, forbidden by the censorship) quoted by St. Sharapov, *Dve Zapiski o russkikh finansakh* (Berlin, 1901) p. 66; also *Slavonic Review* (Apr 1933) p. 593 and C. T. Helfferich, *Das Geld im russisch-japanischen Kriege* (Berlin, 1906) p. 26.

7   These firms were the textile firms of Knoop, the Lodz (Russian Poland) textile firms and the southern Russian ironworks which could obtain credits in London, Berlin and Paris respectively. Schultze-Gaevernitz *Volkswirtschaftliche Studien aus Russland* (Leipzig, 1899) p. 508.

8   S. Y. Witte, *Konspekt lektsiy o narodnom i gossudarstvennom khozyaystve* . . . (St Petersburg, 1912) p. 313. The onerous terms on which private railway companies in Russia in the 1870s acquired debenture capital seems to bear out the point made by Witte, and explains why the Russian government decided to take over the bond issues from the companies at a flat rate, to float the bonds themselves as consols, and to provide the companies with resources as and when the need arose. See H. E. Fisk, *The Inter-Ally Debts* (New York, 1924) p. 294.

9   The annual service of the foreign debt required 98 million roubles in 1899. *Wirtschaft und Statistik*.

10   French Consular Reports, Paris, *Archives Nationales* (hereafter *AN*) F12, 7173, Consul de Strotz, Riga, 25 May 1891, Consul Cassas, Odessa, 30 Apr 1891, A. Sauvaire, Odessa, 15 Sep 1894 and 16 Oct 1894; also *Ministerstvo Finansov 1802–1902* (St Petersburg, 1902) II, p. 114 (official publication of the Russian ministry of finance).

11   E. Zweig, *Die Russiche Handelspolitik seit 1877* (Leipzig, 1906) p. 32, and Vyshnegradsky's memorandum to the state council of 15 Apr 1891, no. 4146, quoted by M. N. Sobolev, *Tamozhennaya politika Rossii* . . . (Tomsk, 1911) pp. 705 ff.

12   Schultze-Gaevernitz, op. cit., p. 462.

13   Ibid., p. 518.

14   P. P. Migulin, *Reforma denezhnogo obrashcheniya v Rossii i promyshelenny krizis* (Kharkov, 1902) pp. 112, 124; Witte, op. cit., p. 315.

15   The Imperial was a gold coin equal to ten gold roubles, used in the main in international settlements; its fineness had been adjusted by the decree of 17 December 1885, whereby the demi-Imperial, equal to 5 roubles, was almost interchangeable with the 20 franc piece, which was said to have facilitated the penetration of Russian securities to the French market. See E Lorini, *La Riforma monetaria della Russia* (Turin, 1897) p. 56.

16   St.O. Gulishambarov, *Vsemirnaya torgovlya v XIX veke i uchastiye v ney Rossii* (St Petersburg, 1898) p. 203. Russia's commercial relations with the countries of Asia were of relatively little importance, e.g. China accounted for 3·7 per cent, Persia for 1·7 per cent and Turkey for 1·6 per cent of Russian foreign trade turnover by the middle of the 1890s; ibid., p. 180; for the geographical distribution of Russia's grain exports, see M. V. Kasperoff, 'Commerce des céréales', in *La Russie à la fin du 19e siècle*, ed.

M. V. de Kovalevsky (Paris, 1900) (Official publication of the Russian
ministry of finance).

17 Gindin, *Russkiye kommercheskiye banki* (Moscow, 1948) p. 452; in 1883 the
Russian government undertook to pay in gold for the five odd loans which
had been concluded in silver. See Migulin, op. cit., p. 4.

18 Gulishambarov, op. cit., p. 52; M. W. de Kovalevsky, op. cit., pp.
316–18.

19 Ukaz 10 Nov 1876 O.S.

20 Kashkarov, op. cit., i, p. 190.

21 Quoted by Migulin, op. cit., p. 9.

22 E. de Montebello to Hanotaux, St Petersburg, 8 Nov 1894 (copy) *AN*,
F30, 331.

23 A. N. Gurev, *Denezhnoye obrashcheniye* (St Petersburg, 1903) pp. 190, 193.

24 1881 – abolition of the salt tax on Bunge's advice by Abaza; 1886 –
abolition of the poll tax – altogether peasant taxes reduced by nearly
one-third in relation to 1882; 1882 – Peasants' Land Bank founded; 1885
– Land Bank for the Nobility founded; Sobolev, op. cit., pp. 821 ff.

25 The deficit on the Ordinary Budget during the six years of Bunge's
administration amounted to about 230 million paper roubles – calculated
on the basis of *Ministerstvo Finansov*, ii, pp. 640–3.

26 Zweig, op. cit., p. 24.

27 C. Skalkovsky, *Les Ministres des Finances de la Russie 1802–90*, tr. from
Russian (Paris, 1891) p. 268; S. S. Khrulev, *Finansy Rossii . . .* (St
Petersburg, 1909) Table ii, p. 96; *Ministerstvo Finansov*, ii, pp. 642–3.

28 The average price for a pood of Russian wheat fell according to Russian
customs statistics from 90·1 copecks during 1871–5 to 85·1 during 1876–80
and to 76·7 during the period 1881–5; V. E. Pokrovsky (ed.), *Sbornik
svedeniy po istorii i statistike vneshney torgovli Rossii* (St Petersburg, 1902) i,
p. 12; the average volume of grain exports increased by less than 6 per
cent in comparison with the period 1876–80, on the basis of ibid., p. 105.
Note: Russian customs statistics tended to underestimate exports and
overestimate the import figures, so that the balance of trade was normally
better than warranted by Russian statistics. See A. Raffalovich, *Le marché
financier* (Paris, 1897–8) p. 410, and S. Zuckerman, *Statistischer Atlas zum
Welthandel* (Berlin, 1921) graphs and tables, Russia, p. 69.

29 For an analysis of the relation between currency fluctuations and
political events, see Kashkarov, op. cit., p. 175, and Waddington to
Freycinet, London, 10 Apr 1885, *Documents Diplomatiques Français (1871–
1914)* (hereafter *DDF*) 1st ser., vi.

30 Skalkovsky, op. cit., p. 257.

31 Zweig, op. cit., p. 24, and V. N. Lamsdorf, *Dnevnik (1886–90)* (Moscow,
1926) p. 352.

32 Migulin, op. cit., p. 13.

33 Gurev, op. cit., p. 201.

34 P. I. Lyashchenko, *Ocherki agrarnoy evolutsii Rossii* (St Petersburg, 1908)
p. 265.

35 Sobolev, op. cit., pp. 491 ff.

36 Calculated on the basis of Pokrovsky, op. cit., pp. 117, 141.

37 Crédit Lyonnais, Service des Etudes Financières, Paris. Contract made at St Petersburg, 5/17 November 1888, unpublished, and Ministère des Finances Francaises, Inspection Générale, Mission en Russie (Paris, 1892) pp. 41 ff.

38 Crédit Lyonnais, loc. cit., 'Historique de la dette consolidée russe', unpublished (1889–91).

39 *Ministerstvo Finansov*, II, p. 86, Crédit Lyonnais, loc. cit., draft of the 4 per cent loan (n.d.); B. Nolde, *L'Alliance Franco–Russe* (Paris, 1936) p. 511; Laboulaye to Spuller, St Petersburg, 15 May 1889, *DDF*, 1st ser., VII.

40 *Ministerstvo Finansov*, op. cit., II, p. 85, and A. Raffalovich, *Les méthodes employées par les états au XIX siècle pour revenir à la bonne monnaie*, p. 27, in *Congrès International des Valeurs Mobilières*, 27, no. 2, 30 Apr 1900.

41 Nolde, op. cit., pp. 488 ff., and A. S. Yerusalimsky, *Vneshnyaya politika germanskogo imperializma v kontse XIX veka*, 2nd ed. (Moscow, 1951) p. 203.

42 In January 1887 Bismarck estimated Russia's debt placed in Germany at 1200 million roubles representing about 2000 million marks, according to E. Ibbeken, *Das aussenpolitische Problem Staat und Wirtschaft in der deutschen Reichspolitik 1880–1914* (Schleswig, 1928) p. 108; the *Kreuzzeitung* estimated German holdings of Russian securities at 1500 million marks.

43 Lamsdorf, op. cit., p. 137.

44 Herbert v. Bismarck to Fuerst v. Bismarck, 11 Oct 1887, *Die Grosse Politik der Europaeischen Kabinette, 1871–1915*, vol. V; Laboulaye to Flourens, 8 Aug 1887, *DDF*, 1st ser., VI, and Schultze-Gaevernitz op. cit., p. 552.

45 Skalkovsky, op. cit., p. 297.

46 French Consul General at Warsaw, (copy) Warsaw, 25 January 1896, *AN*, F30, 330. The Italian *rente* which stood at 102 in October 1887 fell to 80 in October 1893, Schultze-Gaevernitz op. cit., p. 553.

47 G. Martin, 'Histoire économique et financière', p. 452 in vol. X of G. Hanotaux, *Histoire de la nation française* (Paris, 1927), also E. V. Tarle, *Evropa v epokhu imperializmu 1071–1919* (Moscow Leningrad, 1928) p. 33.

48 Verstraete to Delcassé, St Petersburg, 31 Mar 1898, (copy) *Formation de l'encaisse or et balance économique*, *AN*, F30, 331; estimates of travellers' expenditure abroad differed widely; an official computation put it at 40 million on the average annually during 1888–91.

49 No exact figures on the balance of payments are available; according to an official computation the surplus on the balance of payments during the period 1888–91 was about 70 million gold roubles annually, Verstraete to Delcassé, 31 Mar 1898, loc. cit. See also R. Girault, *Emprunts russes et investissements français en Russie* (Paris, 1973) p. 95.

50 *Yezhegodnik Ministerstva Finansov 1869–1913* (St Petersburg, 1892) p. 76.

51 Verstraete to Delcassé, 31 Mar 1898, loc. cit.

52 Bompard to Ribot, 22 July 1895, (copy) *AN*, F30, 331.

53 Lamsdorf, op. cit., p. 338.

54 Verstraete to Delcassé, 31 Mar 1898, loc. cit.

55 Kashkarov, op. cit., pp. 1, 175.

56 S.N. v. Propper, *Was nicht in die Zeitungen kam; Erinnerungen des Chefre-*

dakteurs der 'Birschewyja Vedomosti' (Frankfurt, 1929) p. 258, and Schultze-Gaevernitz op. cit., p. 476.

57 'Credit loans' were loans issued and payable in 'paper roubles', whilst 'metallic loans' were loans issued in gold or silver or currencies based on these metals.

58 For the history of the Berlin Bourse as the market for Russian currency see Schultze-Gaevernitz, op. cit., pp. 450–524.

59 Copy of the report of the French chargé d'affaires at St Petersburg, De Vauvineux, 4 Nov 1891, *AN*, F30, 328, and Consul in Odessa, 20 Nov 1893, loc. cit., F12, 7173, also *Ministerstvo Finansov*, II, p. 311.

60 Propper, op. cit., p. 150; M. Bogolepov, *Obshchestvennoye dvizheniye v Rossi v nachale, XX veka* (St Petersburg, 1909) I, p. 158.

61 Delamotte, Inspecteur des Finances, *Mission en Russie*, 1 Feb 1905, *AN*, F30, 331, and Khrulev, op. cit., Table XXII.

62 Pokrovsky, op. cit., p. 6.

63 Lamsdorf, op. cit., p. 350.

64 Zweig, op. cit., pp. 38 ff

65 Waddington to Ribot, 11 May 1891, *DDF*, 1st ser., VIII; Herbette to Ribot, (copy) *AN*, F30, 332; D'Estornelles de Constant to Ribot, 1 October 1891 and *Doc. Dip. Fran.*, 1st ser., IX.

66 An exposition of Witte's principles can be found in his 'The national economy and Frederic List', in his *Konspekt*, and in his annual memoranda to the Emperor which accompanied the budget.

67 Witte, *Konspekt*, pp. 141, 207, 215.

68 Witte's memorandum to the state council of 14 Mar 1896, quoted by Migulin, *Reforma*, pp. 112–22.

69 Ukaz 29 Mar 1893, ukaz 8 July 1893.

70 Propper, op. cit., p. 230; A. Sauvaire, consul in Odessa, to G. Hanotaux, 29 Oct 1894, (copy) *AN*, F12, 7173; Schultze-Gaevernitz op. cit., p. 526.

71 For German reaction to Witte's *coup de force*, see M. de Chalmes, French Consul General at Warsaw to G. Hanotaux, 31 Oct 1894, (copy) *AN*, F30, 329.

72 Kashkarov, op. cit., pp. 1, 170.

73 Verstraete to Delcassé, 31 Mar 1898, loc. cit.

74 *Ministerstvo Finansov*, II, p. 410 and ukaz of 8 May 1895.

75 *Yezhegodnik* (1898) report on the budget for 1897. The most important of these were those of 3 January 1897, 29 August 1897 and 14 November 1897.

76 The first method would have meant postponing reform for many decades and required favourable political and economic conditions during this period; the second would have increased the country's foreign indebtedness beyond the safe margin; the third proved impracticable during 1881–7 when it proved impossible to withdraw the war issues.

77 Schultze-Gaevernitz op. cit., p. 472.

78 Russia's state and state guaranteed 'credit debt' amounted to 3330·3 million paper roubles by 1 January 1896 (Gindin, op. cit., p. 452). The service of this debt amounted to about 144 million paper roubles annually

Notes 239

by 1 January 1896. See French Consul General Bogard, at Warsaw, 17 Dec 1897, (copy) *AN*, F30, 330.

79 Kashkarov, op. cit., I, p. 170. E. de Montebello to Berthelot, St Petersburg, 12 Jan 1896, (copy) *AN*, F30, 330; I. K. Ozerov, *Osnovy finansovoy nauki* (Moscow, 1908) p. 265.

80 The average length of commercial bills in Russia was 137 days during 1889–94; Gindin, op. cit., p. 266. Their amount was limited and there were numerous protests; V. T. Sudeikin, *Gossudarstvenny bank* (St Petersburg, 1891) p. 427.

81 I. K. Ozerov, *Die Finanzpolitik*, in *Die Russen ueber Russland*, ed. J. Melnik (Frankfurt, 1906) pp. 231 ff. See also Chapter 5 below.

82 P. V. Ol', in Sharapov, op. cit., p. 66.

83 Cochery to Hanotaux, 11 June 1897, (draft) *AN*, F30, 335; Crédit Lyonnais, note on sales of 4 per cent *Rente Intérieure Russe* during Feb–July 1899, unpubl.

84 Kashkarov, op. cit., I, p. 226. Included is the gold which went into circulation.

85 Ibid.

86 Ibid.

87 Zweig, op. cit., pp. 156 ff.

88 According to M. Tugan-Baranovsky, *Russkaya Fabrika*, 6th ed. (Moscow, 1934) p. 265, the value of industrial output increased by 1104 million roubles during the period 1893–7, mining industries showing the largest increase. Imports increased from an annual average of 399·19 million paper roubles during 1887–91 to 534·98 during 1893–7, calculated on the basis of Pokrovsky, op. cit., p. 141.

89 Lyashchenko, op. cit., pp. 269–70.

90 During 1893–7, 52,900 quarters of grain and 15·7 per cent of the annual harvest had been exported on the average annually against only 40,700 quarters representing 14·3 per cent of the average annual harvest during 1887–92 (1 Russian quarter of wheat equalled about 360 lb.; the other grains were somewhat lighter). Calculated on the basis of Pokrovsky, op. cit., p. 6.

91 The average value of grain exports, despite the increased volume, fell from 366·7 million paper roubles per annum during 1887–91 to 337·8 million during 1893–7, and the export surplus fell from an average of 311·2 to 140 million paper roubles. Calculated on the basis of ibid., pp. 105, 117, 141.

92 According to P. V. Ol' the deficit on the balance of payments amounted to 96·4 million gold roubles, quoted by Verstraete in his report to Delcassé of 31 Mar 1898, loc. cit.; also Girault, op. cit., p. 95.

93 Verstraete to Delcassé, 30 Mar 1899, *AN*, F30, 332; 1 rouble equalled about 2·66 francs after 1897.

94 Ibid.; the figures given by P. V. Ol', quoted by Sharapov, op. cit., p. 66, were twice as high as those given by Verstraete; in 1898 the British had been particularly active mainly in the oil industry and had invested 88·75 million francs out of a total of 359 million.

95 M. Verstraete, *Les capitaux étrangers engagés dans les Sociétés industrielles* (Paris, 1900) p. 6.
96 *Mirovyye ekónomicheskiye krizisy 1848–1935*, p. 517.
97 Helfferich, op. cit., p. 14.
98 Capr vi to Kaiser Wilhelm II 10 Nov 1894, *Grosse Politik*, v, and *Bulletin Russe de Statistique Financière et Législation* (St Petersburg, 1898) p. 433.
99 A phrase employed in an unsigned and undated note placed with the correspondence relating to the 3½ per cent gold loan, 1894. *AN*, F30, 332.
100 Tugan-Baranovsky, op. cit., p. 267; the French consul-general in Warsaw, in his report of 3 March 1897 quoted above, estimated that out of Russia's foreign debt of 3500 million roubles (over 9000 million francs) about 7000 million francs were placed in France.
101 Out of a total of over 2075 million francs of foreign capital in Russian joint stock companies, French capital accounted directly for 692·3 million and for another 100 million on account of Belgian capital which represented French investment. Verstraete, op. cit.
102 A phrase employed by the financial agent of the Russian government in Paris, Arthur Raffalovich, when reporting on subventions paid to the French Press.
103 The rôle of the treasury's foreign balances and the techniques employed by the Russian finance minister are fully described in a report of Verstraete to Delcassé of 18 June 1900. *AN*, F30, 335.
104 *Report of the Minister of Finance to H.M. the Emperor on the Budget of the Empire for 1898* (St Petersburg, 1898) p. 12.
105 Verstraete to Delcassé, Delcassé, St Petersburg, 15/28 Mar 1902, *Notes sur les finances de la Russie. AN*, F30, 329.

CHAPTER 5

1 See table 5.1.
2 A. Gerschenkron, 'The Rate of Growth of Industrial Production in Russia since 1885', loc. cit., p. 149.
3 S. N. Prokopovich, 'Ueber die Bedingungen der industriellen Entwicklung Russlands', *Archiv für soziale Gesetzgebung und Statistik, Ergänzungshaft*, 10 (1913) p. 25.
4 N. D. Kondrat'ev (ed.), *Mirovoye khozyaystvo 1913–1925* (Moscow, 1926) p. 168.
5 S. G. Strumilin, *Ocherki sovetskoy ekonomiki* (Moscow–Leningrad, 1926) p. 69.
6 Shepelev, 'Aktsyonernoye uchreditel'stvo v Rossii', loc. cit., p. 156; see also the present study p. 36 above.
7 According to P. A. Khromov 'small industry' accounted for 32 per cent of the total value of industrial output in 1913; *Ocherki ekonomiki Rossii perioda monopolisticheskogo kapitalizma* (Moscow, 1960) p. 60. The larger firms of non-corporate character were known as 'mercantile houses'. By 1 January 1914 there were 7980 mercantile houses, with a capital of 390·3 million roubles. Most of them (77·6 per cent of the number, 57·2

per cent of the capital) were engaged in commerce only. Of the 42·8 per cent of the capital that went into industry as well, 19·2 per cent went into food processing.

8 Shepelev, 'Aktsyonernoye uchreditel'stvo v Rossii', loc. cit., p. 135, n. 6.

9 See p. 37. In addition, debenture capital was 238·7 million roubles on 1 January 1914. Shepelev, 'Aktsyonernoye uchreditel'stvo v Rossii', loc. cit., Table 6A.

10 See p. 39 above.

11 For a recent detailed but analytically disappointing history, see S. Y. Borovoy, *Kredit i banki v Rossii, 1650–1861* (Moscow, 1958) See also A. P. Pogrebinsky, *Ocherki finansov dorevolyutsyonnoy Rossii* (Moscow, 1954); P. Migulin, op. cit., p. 92. Shepelev, 'Arkhivnyye fondy aktsyonernykh bankov', loc. cit., pp. 58–105; M. K. Rozhkova (ed.), *Ocherki ekonomicheskoy istorii Rossii pervoy, poloviny XIX veka* (Moscow, 1959). Garvy maintains that our study understates the rôle of state owned banks in promoting industrialisation before 1860. However what Garvy demonstrates is that governments tried to use banking facilities to activate the economy but not the effectiveness of such measures. Moreover he is more concerned to show that there was continuity between Imperial Russian and Soviet banking policies than about the actual achievements of pre-Soviet banking; G. Garvy, 'Banking under the Tsars and the Soviets', *The Journal of Economic History*, vol. xxxii (Dec 1972).

12 Pogrebinsky, op. cit., pp. 42–5; Migulin, op. cit., pp. 91–2.

13 A memorandum of the finance ministry, published 1 September 1859, stressed the need for a 'correct credit organisation as the most vital condition of national development. The urgency of a suitable credit organisation is most pressing because of the revival of industrial entrepreneurship, anticipated construction of railways and other improved means of communication, and in view of the great economic reform under consideration for the majority of the agricultural population.' Borovoy, op. cit., p. 279.

14 Gossudarstvenny Bank, *Kratkiy ocherk deyatel'nosti s 1860 po 1910 g.* (St Petersburg, 1910) pp. 105–6. The liquidation of the old banking institutions absorbed 60 million roubles annually on the average.

15 Mukoseyev, 'Money and credit' in A. Raffalovich (ed.), *Russia: Its trade and commerce* (London, 1918) pp. 362–3. See Table 5.9, based on Gindin, op. cit., pp. 442–3.

16 The debt of the treasury on this account was 480 million roubles on 1 January 1880, 350 million in 1882; only in 1888 was it finally liquidated. Pogrebinsky, op. cit., pp. 120–1.

17 Mukoseyev, loc. cit., pp. 363–4.

18 Based on ibid., p. 373 and Gindin, op. cit., pp. 45, 189.

19 See Table 5.10, based on *Ocherki istorii Leningrada*, ii, p. 84.

20 Migulin, op. cit., p. 101.

21 Akademiya Nauk SSSR (ed.), *Istoriya Moskvy*, iv, p. 208.

22 Shepelev, 'Arkhivnyye fondy aktsyonernykh bankov', loc. cit., p. 18.

23 Ibid., pp. 61–2.

24 Gindin and Shepelev, 'Bankovskiye monopolii v Rossii nakanune velikoy

oktyabrskoy sotsyalisticheskoy revolyutsii', *Istoricheskiye zapiski*, vol. 66
p. 21.
25 Ibid.
26 Ibid.
27 See table 5.11. The Volga–Kama Bank and the Moscow Merchant
    Bank, though they took sixth and eighth place by size of assets, are here
    listed separately to emphasise the different nature of their activities as
    compared with the rest, in which contacts with foreign banks and issues
    on behalf of industrial concerns played a large part.
28 The first of these banks was founded in 1809.
29 Mukoseyev, loc. cit., p. 385.
30 See tables 5.4–5.8.
31 M. S. Atlas, *Natsyonalizatsiya bankov v SSSR* (Moscow, 1948) p. 17.
32 Mukoseyev, loc. cit., p. 383. The first society was founded in 1864.
33 See table 5.7.
34 Atlas, op. cit., p. 17.
35 The assets and liabilities of the bourse banks are not included in our
    tables on the evolution of the commercial credit banks. *Ministerstvo
    Finansov, 1802–1902* (St Petersburg, 1902) ii, p. 77.
36 Atlas, op. cit., p. 18.
37 Ibid. See also Shepelev, 'Aktsyonernoye uchreditel'stvo v Rossii', loc.
    cit., p. 162. Shepelev gives a list of the bourse banks with dates of
    foundation and capital (pp. 174–6). The majority, judging by the names,
    seem to have been Jewish firms; most had a rather small capital.
38 Atlas, op. cit., p. 22; Mukoseyev, loc. cit., p. 386.
39 Atlas, op. cit., p. 22.
40 *Ocherk razvitiya deyatel'nosti gosudarstvennykh sberegatel'nykh kass* (St Peters-
    burg, 1912) p. 41.
41 Of the credits granted in 1913, 21·6 per cent were for the purchase of
    cattle, 19·3 per cent for renting land, 6·8 per cent for buying land, 11·2
    per cent for buildings, 5·5 per cent for the purchase of seeds, 3·4 per cent
    for agricultural equipment, 3 per cent for the hire of labour, and 22·6 per
    cent for various other purposes. Atlas, op. cit., p. 22. An item of 6·6 per
    cent seems to be missing.
42 S. S. Katzenellenbaum, *Kommercheskiye banki i ikh torgovo-kommissyonnyye
    operatsii* (Moscow, 1912) p. 7.
43 G. A. Dikhtyar, *Vnutrennyaya torgovlya v dorevolyutsyonnoy Rossii* (Moscow,
    1960) pp. 159–60.
44 Mukoseyev, loc. cit., p. 386.
45 Atlas, op. cit., p. 23.
46 Ibid., p. 22.
47 Dikhtyar, op. cit., p. 163.
48 Mukoseyev, loc. cit., p. 38.
49 *Ministerstvo Finansov, 1802–1902*, ii, pp. 53–5; Pogrebinsky, op. cit.,
    pp. 121–3.
50 *Otchety gosudarstvennykh sberegatyel'nykh kass*, p. 16.
51 *Ocherk razvitiya deyatel'nosti gosudarstvennykh sberegatel'nykh kass*, p. 34.
52 Ibid., p. 39.

53 Ibid., pp. 36–7.
54 For example, on 1 January 1901, from the total balance of 752 million roubles, 637 million were invested in government bonds of which 37 per cent were government guaranteed railway bonds. Lyashchenko, *Istoriya narodnogo khozyaystva SSSR*, II, p. 155; *Ocherk razvitiya deyatel'nosti gosudarstvennykh sberegatel'nykh kass*, pp. 44–5; Mukoseyev, loc. cit., p. 390.
55 Atlas, op. cit., p. 21.
56 Mukoseyev, loc. cit., p. 387.
57 Atlas, op. cit., p. 21.
58 Gindin, 'Neustavnyye ssudy gosudarstvennogo banka i ekonomicheskaya politika tsarskogo pravitel'stva', *Istoricheskiye zapiski*, vol. XXXV, p. 90; Pogrebinsky, op. cit., pp. 125 ff.
59 A special committee under the chairmanship of Witte sat from 1892 to discuss means of reforming the policy of the State Bank in the direction of more active credits to industry. *Ministerstvo Finansov, 1802–1902*, II, p. 48; Pogrebinsky, op. cit., p. 177.
60 T. H. von Laue, 'A secret memorandum of Sergei Witte on the industrialisation of Imperial Russia', *Journal of Modern History*, vol. XXVI, no. 1 (Mar 1954).
61 *Ustav gosudarstvennogo banka po offitsyal'nomu izdaniyu 1895 g.*
62 Gindin, op. cit., p. 91, and Mukoseyev, op. cit., p. 362.
63 Crisp, 'The Financial Aspect of the Franco–Russian Alliance', unpublished Ph.D. thesis (London, 1954) pp. 356–83; B. V. Anan'ich, 'Uchetno-Ssudnyy bank Persii v 1894–1907 g.', in M. P. Vyatkin (ed.), *Monopolii i inostranny kapital v Rossii* (Leningrad–Moscow, 1962) pp. 274–315.
64 Mukoseyev, op. cit., pp. 367–8, 371.
65 Ibid., p. 372; *Ocherki istorii Leningrada*, III, p. 88.
66 Gindin, op. cit., p. 93.
67 Verstraete to Delcassé, Paris, 19 June 1900, *AN*, F30, 335.
68 Gindin, op. cit., p. 93.
69 See Table 5.15, based on 'Gossudarstvenny Bank Otchot za 1916 g.' (Petrograd, 1917) pp. 54–5.
70 Mukoseyev, op. cit., p. 359. On 1 January 1912 the quantity of coins and notes in circulation was only 34 francs *per capita* in Russia, as against 75 in Germany and 230 in France; E. Epstein, *Les Banques de commerce russes* (Paris, 1925) p. 45. However, Epstein estimated that in 1907 the deposit transfer operations of Russian banks meant a saving of 400 million roubles in monetary tokens; ibid.
71 Mukoseyev, op. cit., p. 378.
72 Based on ibid., pp. 359–60.
73 Based on Atlas, op. cit., p. 17; Gindin, op. cit., p. 271.
74 Epstein, op. cit., p. 16.
75 By 1900 58 per cent of the factory workers were concentrated in the St Petersburg and Moscow regions. Lyashchenko, op. cit., II, p. 159.
76 A point which needs investigating is the extent to which large banking corporations, interested as they were mainly in corporate industry, had the effect of draining funds away from the provinces and small towns, and from local industries.

77   Epstein, op. cit., p. 32.
78   Ibid. According to Gindin, 'Russkiye kommercheskiye banki', loc. cit.,
     p. 274, banking credits covered 46 per cent of the value of bills of
     exchange in circulation in 1901, 49 per cent in 1908, and 70 per cent in
     1914.
79   While in the whole commercial credit system discount and loan opera-
     tions and advances against goods had increased in the same proportion
     as other assets during 1908–14, i.e. 2·5 times, in the joint stock banks
     discounts and goods advances increased only 2·5 times while total assets
     rose 2·8 times. On the other hand in the provincial branches the relative
     weight of credits against bills and goods had risen.
80   See table 5.11.
81   E. Agahd, Grossbanken und Weltmarkt (Berlin, 1914) pp. 112 ff.
82   Katzenellenbaum, op. cit., p. 81. In 1909 one-third of all grain exports
     from Nikolayev was handled by banks directly, viz. the St Petersburg
     International, the Northern, and the Bank for Foreign Trade. The
     banking houses built stores, branch lines, etc. Similar activities were
     followed in the ports of Odessa and Kherson. Southern branches of joint
     stock banks traded in coal and exported cocoons to Italy and France,
     viz. the Russian Bank for Foreign Trade, the Russo–Asiatic, the Bank of
     Siberia and the Azov–Don. The Russian Bank for Foreign Trade and the
     St Petersburg International concentrated in their hands almost the entire
     sugar export. The shortcomings of the commercial sector may also
     account for the tendency of large firms to diversify their activities and to
     handle their own marketings, which in turn led to the large size of
     industrial units. See pp. 43–4.
83   This is the view expressed by Epstein; Gindin maintains that until well
     into the 1890s even the so-called 'commercial' bill was more in the nature
     of a promissory note, in which what mattered was the ultimate solvency
     of the debtor, not prompt repayment. Bills tended to be renewed
     repeatedly upon expiry. They represented in fact a type of extended
     credit, not necessarily self-liquidating.
84   Akademiya Nauk SSSR (ed.), Istoriya Moskvy, IV, p. 213.
85   Ibid., p. 215.
86   Ibid. Out of 12·4 million roubles lent in 1890 against securities, only
     150,000 were credits against industrial shares.
87   Ibid.
88   Anan'ich 'Uchetno-Ssudny bank Persii v 1894–1907 g.' loc. cit.
89   Akademiya Nauk SSSR (ed.) Istoriya Moskvy, IV, p. 216. The Moscow
     banks were also reluctant to join the 'Red Cross of the Bourse'. Gindin,
     'Moskovskiye banki v period imperializma (1900–1917)', Istoricheskiye
     zapiski, vol. 58, p. 41.
90   Gindin, Istoricheskiye zapiski, vol. 58, pp. 41, 43.
91   Ibid., p. 43.
92   Ibid., p. 44.
93   Table 5.16 is based on Gindin, Kommercheskiye banki, Table 34.
94   The State Bank had encouraged investments in industry by the joint
     stock banks in this respect. Gindin, Istoricheskiye zapiski, vol. 35, p. 88.

95 *Ocherki istorii Leningrada*, III, p. 95.
96 Gindin, *Kommercheskiye banki*, p. 195.
97 Gindin, *Istoricheskiye zapiski*, vol. 35, pp. 95 ff. The wording of the Imperial Consent to this effect (12 Nov 1899 O.S.) was that the State Bank could 'accept as security and also acquire with special permission in each case, in departure from the Statutes, the unrealised debenture capital of such joint-stock companies, whose viability is beyond doubt . . .'. This meant in effect aid to leading metallurgical and machine building concerns which might be in difficulty because of the cessation of foreign credits. 'Unrealised' meant usually 'not realised abroad'.
98 Ibid., p. 116.
99 Thus in 1898 in the St Petersburg International Bank one-quarter of all securities held were shares and bonds of industrial concerns; in the Discount and Loan Bank the proportion was 53·3 per cent and in the Commercial and Industrial Bank as much as 62·2 per cent. *Istoriya Leningrada*, III, p. 95.
100 For example steam horsepower in the factory industries in St Petersburg grew from 69,949 hp in 1894 to 134,634 in 1908 and to 216,835 in 1913. Ibid., p. 13.
101 Gindin, *Istoricheskiye zapiski*, vol. 35, gives a detailed analysis of infrastatutory credits to industry. He makes it quite clear that Russian liberals had completely misunderstood Witte's policy in this respect, seeing in it simply a manifestation of autocratic and bureaucratic arbitrary intervention; ibid., p. 124. Other Soviet historians see in Witte's policy simply a manifestation of an 'alliance between Tsarist autocracy and monopoly capitalism'.
102 See pp. 171, 182.
103 Banque de l'Union, 'Procès verbal de l'Assemblee Générale . . . du 8–4–1910', *AN*, F30, 336; S. Ronin, *Inostranny kapital i russkiye banki* (Moscow, 1926) pp. 67, 70.
104 See table 5.17.
105 'Reconstruction de la Banque de Commerce Privée de St Petersburg, 26–12–1909', *AN*, F30, 336.
106 E. Agahd, *Grossbanken und Weltmarkt* (Berlin, 1914) p. 113; A. M. Solov'yova, 'K voprosu o roli finansovogo kapitala v zheleznodorozhnom stroitel'stve Rossii nakanune pervoy mirovoy yoyny', *Istoricheskiye zapiski*, vol. 69, p. 199.
107 Ibid., pp. 177, 183.
108 Ibid., p. 183; K. F. Shatsillo, 'Formirovaniye finansovogo kapitala v sudostroitel'noy promyshlennosti Yuga Rossii', in Vyatkin, op. cit., pp. 26–56.
109 See p. 172; Solov'yova, op. cit., p. 184. Gindin and Shepelev, op. cit., p. 271.
110 Solov'yova, op. cit., p. 185.
111 Ibid.
112 Ibid., p. 191. For example, Kakhetya, North Caucasus, Fergana, Armavir–Toapse.
113 Shepelev, 'Aktsyonernoye uchreditel'stvo v Rossii,' 145.

114 Solov'yova, op. cit. p. 200.
115 Epstein, op. cit., pp. 31–2. By 1914 64 per cent of the demand for raw cotton was met from domestic sources.
116 Gindin, *Kommercheskiye banki* pp. 294 ff. In all projects for the setting up of special banks to grant credits to particular industries or regions, there is invariably a clamour for government assistance whether by way of direct participation or by way of subsidies (ibid., p. 314–15), an indication that either private initiative was lacking or that such special banks did not promise sufficient net return for would-be promotors. The tendency of large corporate firms to absorb small concerns with lower unit costs but limited access to capital may indicate the need for special credit for small units. See p. 42.
117 Gindin, *Kommercheskiye banki*, pp. 294 ff.
118 Ibid., p. 245.
119 The relatively limited growth of deposits in savings banks in the latest period was connected with the increased investment by peasants in agriculture and also the preference of small savers for petty credit institutions, especially co-operatives.
120 Ibid. During 1912–13 the average rate paid by joint stock banks on current account deposits was 3·87 in St Petersburg, 4 per cent in Moscow, and 4·64 per cent in the provinces. The average yield of the 4 per cent government *Rente* was only 4 per cent nominal.
121 See p. 183.
122 See table 5.4.
123 *Vestnik finansov*, no. 6 (1928) The figures given here differ slightly from those given in this study p. 183. A more recent work by A. I. Bukovetsky, 'Svobodnaya nalichnost'' i zolotoy zapas,' in M. P. Vyatkin, op. cit., p. 365, gives somewhat different figures again.
124 See table 5.4.
125 Ibid. Bourse banks with 88 million roubles' deposits are not included.
126 Epstein, op. cit., p. 74. On the other hand, Epstein shows how, under the influence of a wide network of bank branches and of improved means of transportation, the bill of exchange penetrated gradually to the small commercial firm, and how its tenor gradually diminished.
127 Ibid., p. 50.
128 Of the twenty-eight types of shares of metallurgical and construction works quoted in Paris, twenty-five were among the most active; of these only fourteen were quoted in St Petersburg. The shares of coal mines in the Donetz Basin and the Dombrova Basin in Russian Poland had dealings in Paris only. Of the seventeen types of securities of metallurgical firms quoted in Brussels, only seven were also quoted in St Petersburg. Brussels had a practical monopoly of dealings in shares of tramcar transport in Russian towns. The London stock exchange was gaining importance during 1909–13, in connection with oil, copper, and gold mining. The Berlin Bourse continued to maintain its role in dealings in shares of electrical and chemical concerns. The Amsterdam Bourse was important for Russian government stock. The Moscow Bourse dealt mainly in bonds issued by the government, railway companies, and

Notes
247

mortgage bonds. The shares of the Moscow textile firms were not quoted on the bourse.

129 The total increase in the value of securities held domestically during 1908–14 was 3687 million roubles; of these only 1175 million represented shares and bonds of joint stock companies. Foreign holdings increased by 1373 million, of which 990 million or 72 per cent of the total were shares and bonds of companies. Based on Ol', op. cit.

130 Based on Gindin, *Kommercheskiye banki*, Tables 38 and 39. See also p. 203.

131 Agahd, op. cit., p. 111.

132 Nevin, *Capital Funds in Underdeveloped Countries: The Role of Financial Institutions* (London, 1961) pp. 40–4.

133 See Table 5.18.

134 Nevin, op. cit., pp. 34–5.

135 This also applies to the contemporary situation: '. . . agricultural credit cannot be judged by economic standards alone.' Ibid., pp. 83–4.

136 Before the 1890s, when the joint stock banks were still weak, raising a mortgage was a fairly common means of obtaining credit for fixed capital, or even for operating purposes, e.g. the Bryansk Company. See also Epstein, op. cit., p. 44.

137 Nevin, op. cit., pp. 39–40.

CHAPTER 6

1 On the basis of P. V. Ol', *Inostrannyye kapitaly v Rossii* (Petrograd, 1922).

2 J. H. Clapham, *The economic development of France and Germany, 1815–1914* (Cambridge, 1923) p. 397.

3 E. Théry, '*Les valeurs mobilières en France*', *Congrès International des Valeurs Mobilières*, vol. II (Paris, 1900).

4 P. Leroy-Beaulieu in *L'Economiste Français*, 8 Dec 1900, 28 Apr 1900.

5 M. Verstraete, *Les capitaux étrangers engagés en Russie dans les sociétés industrielles* (Paris, 1900) p. 6.

6 See Chapter 1 above.

7 B. F. Brandt, *Inostrannyye kapitaly: ikh viliyaniye na ekonomicheskoye razvitiye strany*, 3 vols (St Petersburg, 1898–1901), II, p. 68. See also p. 174, below.

8 On the basis of Verstraete, op. cit. Table III. Total foreign capital according to Verstraete amounted to 2075·2 million francs, which represented 36 per cent of the joint stock capital in Russia. Verstraete did not include foreign capital invested in commercial and railway companies, and the actual proportion of foreign capital was higher. Lyashchenko estimated it at half of the total by 1900 as against one-third in 1890; Lyashchenko, op. cit., II, p. 156.

9 Ibid., p. 158, and Gindin, op. cit., p. 82.

10 Verstraete op. cit., Table III.

11 Directeur de la Banque du Nord à Dorizon, 12 June 1902, *AN*, F30, 343; Hanotaux à Cochery, 9 July 1897, F30, 328.

12 'Le régime legal des sociétés anonymes en Russie', *Moniteur officiel du Commerce*, 27 Jan 1898.

13 *AN*, F30, 343, Ministère des Finances, Note. 16 Sept 1901, *AN*, FO 30, 343.

14 Cochery à Hanotaux, 16 June 1897, *AN*, F30, 328; 'Les intérêts privés français en Russie et leur protection', *Association nationale des porteurs des valeurs mobilières* (Paris). German capital favoured this form of investment in Russia to an even greater extent than the French. Out of an estimated total of over 261 million francs of German capital in 60 companies, nearly 80 per cent went into forty-eight companies incorporated in Russia. Political factors were probably the cause of this practice, as about 65 per cent of German capital went into Russian concerns in Congress Poland and the Baltic provinces, where the laws of the 1880s aimed at restricting property rights and economic activity of the Germans. This was less true of British and Belgian capital. Verstraete, op. cit., Tables vii, ix, iv, v, xix.

15 P. V. Ol', op. cit., p. 10; the debenture capital of railway companies is not included. By 1914 the French held over 2500 million francs of Russian railway bonds. Crisp, op. cit., p. 27.

16 *Moniteur Officiel du Commerce*, loc. cit.

17 Verstraete, op. cit., Table iii.

18 N. Vereshchagin, 'Ocherki gornoy promyshlennosti Tsarstva Polskogo', *Vestnik Finansov*, no. 41 (1897); B. F. Brandt, op. cit., ii, p. 33.

19 It is difficult to determine to what extent the naturalisation of German capital was genuine and how far it was a simple stratagem facilitated by the German law of double nationality, issued in response to Russian legislation of the 1880s. Among the most important French concerns in this region was the Sosnowice Company based on Russian statutes, and the Huta Bankova incorporated in France. The three collieries of the Sosnowice Company accounted in 1895 for 43 per cent of the coal output of the Dombrowa Basin. By 1910 it employed some 7000 workmen. The Huta Bankowa, with its three large blast furnaces, ten Martins furnaces, five rolling mills, etc. employed 2800 workers; B. F. Brandt, op. cit., p. 122; B. Ischchanian, *Die ausländischen Elemente in der russischen Volkswirtschaft* (Berlin, 1913) pp. 144–5; Consul de France à Varsovie, M. de Coppet aux Affaires Etrangères, 18 Feb 1911, *AN*, F30, 340.

20 Ischchanian, op. cit., p. 146; Brandt, op. cit., ii, pp. 43 ff.; Gindin, op. cit., p. 40, n. 4.

21 Brandt, op. cit., ii, pp. 50, 54, 61.

22 Ibid. Among the outstanding French concerns was the Société des Forges et Aciéries du Donets, founded in 1891 with a capital gradually raised to 7·7 million roubles (1 rouble equalled 4 francs before the currency reform). Among its founders was a group of eminent French financiers, the same who founded the Huta Bankowa in Poland. The Crédit Lyonnais had close financial ties with both. The company had its own mines, two blast furnaces, a Bessemer plant, a rail rolling and trimming plant, and coke furnaces. The French had also a controlling interest (about 90 per cent of the capital in 1902) in the Russian Bryansk Company founded in 1873 for the production of rolling stock from imported pig iron. French interest dated from 1893 when new capital was required for a second blast

furnace and for the purchase of coal mines. In 1913 the company produced some 76 million poods of ore, over 66 million poods of coal, and 25 million poods of pig iron. Association Nationale, 'Sociétés constituées avec des capitaux français exploitant en Russie'; *AN*, F30, 340. Note confidentielle, 4 Mar 1902; Sté Générale, cabinet du Directeur, 14 May 1902; Delcassé à Caillaux, 18 Feb 1900, *AN*, F30, 343; minutes of shareholders' meetings, *AN*, F30, 343.

23 Brandt, op. cit., ii, pp. 116–17; Aff. Etr. à Cochery, 8 May 1897, *AN*, F30, 328; on the basis of P.V.Ol', op. cit., 14 n.

24 'La métallurgie russe', 19 Oct 1897, *AN*, F30, 340; M. Verstraete-Hanotaux, 14 Feb 1898, *AN*, F30, 328; A. Matveyev, *Zheleznoye delo Rossii v 1898 godu* (Moscow, 1899) pp. 2–5. Verstraete, *Etudes industrielles sur L'Oural* (Paris, 1899) 20–4.

25 Finances aux Aff. Etr., 4 Mar 1901, *AN*, F30, 343; Finances au Syndic de Faillite, 1 Apr 1901, and note 2 Apr 1901; Aff. Etr. aux Finances, 31 Dec 1902; Ambassade Impériale de Russie au Ministre des Finances, 6 Apr 1902; Witte à Caillaux, n.d., Witte à Montebello, 2 Apr 1902, F30, 340.

26 Out of twenty-six Belgian metallurgical concerns with an aggregate capital of about 200 million, eight were declared bankrupt and liquidated, four continued after they had written off a loss of sixteen million; many others led a very meagre existence; Panafieu à Pichon, 22 Sep 1909, *AN*, F30, 340.

27 On the other hand the Crédit Lyonnais was reported to have called in ruthlessly all medium and short-term credits, a policy which this bank was known to have pursued also in France during recession. It was apparently this attitude of some French banks which, among other things, had forced industrial concerns in France to rely on their own resources and to refrain from resort to bank credit. M. Verstraete à Caillaux, 29 Oct 1901, *AN*, F30, 337; S. Ronin, *Inostrannyye kapitaly i russkiye banki* (Moscow, 1926) p. 45.

28 According to P.V. Ol', op. cit., p. 10, French capital in Russian companies amounted to 731·7 million roubles or 1946·3 million francs.

29 It is estimated that 60 million roubles of French capital had entered Russian concerns producing military stores during 1900–15, which represented a 400 per cent increase. Gindin, op. cit., p. 379.

30 Association Nationale, 'Tableau des biens des principales industries françaises établi sur les déclarations des intéréssés en Russie, 29.2.1922', 'Renseignements sur les intérêts français dans les sociétés pétrolifères exploitant à Baku et Grozny'; D. I. Shpolyansky, *Monopolii ugolno-metallurgicheskoy promyshlennosti yuga Rossii* (Moscow, 1953) p. 109.

31 L'attaché commercial en Russie, 'Les Stés. anonymes étrangères en Russie' (1914), *AN*, F30, 335.

32 See p. 181.

33 In 1900 each metallurgical plant in southern Russia employed on the average 1841 men with an annual output of over 3 million poods of pig iron as against only 136,000 in the Urals; for discussion of the question of size see p. 38 ff.

34 'Aux fourneaux presque plus d'ouvriers . . .', wrote M. Lauwick,

L'industrie dans la Russie Méridionale, Rapport présenté à M. le Ministre de l'Industrie et du Travail de Belgique (Brussels–Paris, 1907) p. 181, to emphasise the high degree of mechanisation; See also P. A. Khromov, *Ekonomicheskoye razvitiye Rossii v XIX–XX vekakh, 1800–1917* (Moscow 1950) p. 327.

35 Even during the recession years 1900–9 the hp per plant in southern Russia had risen from 6159 to 9986. In 1912 the output per blast furnace in southern Russia was 3·15 million poods as against 1·5 million for the country at large. J. Glivits, *Zheleznaya promyshlennost' Rossii* (St Petersburg, 1911) pp. 111–14.

36 In 1913 the output of iron ore per miner per year was 16,400 poods in Krivoy Rog and 6100 in the Urals. Khromov, op. cit., p. 348; on the other hand side by side with high technology went very primitive methods and practices making for a type of dualism, see p. 40.

37 L. E. Hubbard, *Soviet labour and industry* (London, 1942) p. 205.

38 E.g. Société d'industrie houillère de la Russie Méridionale, Relevé des comptes de leur établissement, 1 Jan 1894, *AN*, F30, 345. This company founded in 1872 became French owned in 1892, and in 1894 an outlay of about 60 million roubles was made for the construction of houses for workers and employees, and 3·6 million for communal baths. Similar outlays were made in the French financed companies of Bryansk and Makeyevka. In the Polish region, where it was not, as a rule, necessary to provide accommodation because the works were situated in closely populated areas and the labour force was local, the Cie. Franco-Italienne had on its coal mine sites eighty-five houses for 660 workers with their families, 2318 persons in all.

39 Lauwick, op. cit., p. 147; Brandt, op. cit., ii, p. 293.

40 Briansk, Etat des dividendes payées par la Société des Usines de Briansk depuis sa fondation jusqu'en 1899, *AN*, F30, 344; Brandt, op. cit., ii, p. 236; Lauwick, op. cit., pp. 80–3.

41 George Louis à Rouvier, 3 Mar 1903, *AN*, F30, 340.

42 Lauwick, op. cit., p. 131.

43 Verstraete, op. cit., p. 161.

44 Verstraete, *La Russie*, p. 9.

45 Ibid., p. 85.

46 Ibid., pp. 13 ff.; Volga–Vishera, Verstraete à Delcassé, 25 Mar 1901, *AN*, F30, 343.

47 Verstraete, *L'Oural*, p. 46.

48 Verstraete, *La Russie*, pp. 13 ff.

49 1 Jan 1904, *AN*, F30, 343.

50 Ibid., 24 Oct 1901, F30, 340.

51 E.g. Briansk distributed 6 and 8 per cent dividends in 1911 and 1912, respectively, on preference and ordinary shares; Oural–Volga after an eclipse of a whole decade distributed in 1911 and 1912 dividends of 6 and 10 per cent, respectively. Aff. Etr. aux Finances, 28 Nov 1913, F30, 343.

52 E.g. in the Huta Bankova only 4 per cent of workers were French in 1897; by 1911 only 2 per cent, but there were thirty-seven French foremen

against twenty Russian ones; M. de Coppet, French consul in Warsaw 18 Feb 1911, *AN*, F30, 340.

53   Briansk, Bompard aux Aff. Etr., 30 Nov 1906, *AN*, F30, 344.

54   Lauwick, op. cit., pp. 136–140; According to the information collected by the Association Nationale . . . from twenty-three companies in Russia the aggregate number of Frenchmen whom they had employed was 328, or fourteen per company. The figure would require upward revision as the data were collected during the war when Frenchmen were called up into the forces, and the figures did not include the Polish region where the number of Frenchmen exceeded the average; F30, 340, M. de Coppet, *AN*, F30, 340.

55   Brandt, op. cit., ii, p. 271; In 1897 there were 1113 Frenchmen resident in Russia connected with industry; their families numbered 2094. However there were many more Germans than French in Russian industry even if only the Reichs-Germans are considered.

56   Ischchanian, op. cit., p. 96.

57   It has been estimated that 50 per cent of French investment by 1897 was due to initiative from the Lyons area. Report of the director of the Société Générale, *AN*, F30, 328.

58   Agahd, op. cit., p. 54.

59   Gindin, *Russkiye Kommercheskiye banki*, pp. 94, 102; Verstraete's report of 21 Oct 1901, *AN*, F30, 337.

60   Gindin, in *Istoricheskiye zapisky*, loc. cit.; Banque de l'Union, 'Procès verbal de l'Assemblée Générale . . . 8 Apr 1910, *AN*, F30, 336.

61   Ibid., 'Reconstruction de la Banque de Commerce Privée de St Petersburg, 26.12.1909'; Ronin, op. cit., pp. 67, 70, see also p. 149 above.

62   Ronin, op. cit., p. 127.

63   Based on Ol', op. cit., pp. 146–250 and Gindin, *Russkiye kommercheskiye banki*, pp. 371–2; see also table 5.17.

64   Ronin, op. cit., p. 128.

65   Gindin, op. cit., pp. 360 ff.

66   See p. 148.

67   See p. 149.

68   Panafieu à Pichon, 31 Aug 1909, *AN*, F30, 337; Société Générale au Ministère des Finances, 29 June 1909. While in St Petersburg the private rate of discount fluctuated between 7 and 5 per cent in 1911, in Paris it fluctuated between $3\frac{1}{2}$ and $2\frac{1}{8}$ per cent. Cf. Gindin, op. cit., p. 251.

69   By January 1913 the foreign balances of the Russian government amounted to 651 million roubles. In normal times about 60 per cent were deposited with French banks. Aff. Etr. aux Finances, 23 Feb 1913, *AN*, F30, 329, and *Novoye Vremya* 4/17 Feb 1913.

70   H. D. White, *French International Accounts 1880–1913* (Cambridge, Mass., 1933) p. 279.

71   Bonds represented only 25 and 35 per cent, respectively, of Germany's and Great Britain's portfolio; in France the proportion was well over 75 per cent and consisted largely of government bonds. White, op. cit., p. 110.

72   On 1 July 1914 French holdings amounted to 12,452 million francs of

which 7193·1 million went into government bonds, 2719·4 million into guaranteed bonds, 583·2 million into municipal bonds, representing a total of 10,505·7 million francs of investment in bonds of a public nature; only 1946 million went into dividend bearing Russian securities. Calculated on the basis of various data from the *AN*, the Crédit Lyonnais, etc., see p. 198.

73 Crisp, op. cit.

CHAPTER 7

1 Calculated on the basis of data from the Archives Nationales, Direction du mouvement général des fonds (here referred to as *AN*), the Crédit Lyonnais, Service des études financières, etc; see p. 198.

2 According to M. Aulagnon, *Bulletin d'informations russes*, no. 7, 20 July 1925, published by the commission générale pour la protection des intérêts français en Russie, and Ol', op. cit.

3 Calculated on the basis of Ol', op. cit., pp. 9–10, 8, 11, 15.

4 On the basis of Ol', op. cit., pp. 14, 18n.

5 Gindin, *Russkiye kommercheskiye banki*, op. cit., pp. 371–2.

6 On the basis of ibid. and Ol', op. cit., pp. 146–250; see also p. 148.

7 Lyashchenko, op. cit., II, p. 316. Lyashchenko's chapter on the syndicates, though displaying the understandable bias of a Soviet historian of capitalist institutions, is nevertheless an independent and valuable contribution based on new material. See also the same author's article in *Istoricheskiye zapisky*, vol. 20 (Moscow, 1946).

8 Note pour le M. de France à St Peterbourg, 22 Feb 1902, *AN*, F30, 340.

9 *AN*, F30, 340. 'Procès verbal de la réunion des délégués des usines métallurgiques de la Russie Méridionale en date du 6/19 fevrier 1902'. 'Sté Générale des hauts fourneaux, forges et aciéries en Russie (Makeevka) a M. Bénac, Directeur du Mouvement Général des Fonds au M. des Finances "Tableau des pourcentages attribués à chaque usine" . . . et Note confidentielle', 4 Mar 1902.

10 *AN*, F30, 340. Stés adhérentes à l'Union au point de vue du placement des titres; Société Générale à Bénac, 14 May 1902; Montebello à Delcassé, 9 May 1902; Vice-Consul Rabut at Kharkov to Delcassé, 1 July 1904, 12 July 1904, F30, 343; Aff. Etr. aux Finances, 9 Aug 1904; Confidential report of the Board of Golubovka and Berestovo–Bogoduk-hovo Companies, Kharkov, 15/28 Apr 1904.

11 Lyashchenko, op. cit., II, pp. 303 ff.

12 'Produgol', *Krasny Arkhiv* (hereafter referred to as *KA*), vol. 18 (1926).

13 Agence Nationale, 26 Nov 1909.

14 'Report of the French Consul General in Warsaw, de Persan, of 18 December 1902', *Moniteur official du commerce*, and Veillet.

15 The large commercial costs account *inter alia* for the lower dividends distributed by industrial companies as compared with commercial companies. The following table of average dividends distributed by companies producing and trading in metallurgical products respectively during the height of the boom throws an interesting light on this point

and, incidentally, bears out Tugan-Baranovsky's generalisation to that effect:

	1895	1896	1897	1898	1899
Metallurgical companies	8·8	5·6	5·0	9·45	6·7
Companies for commerce in metallurgical products	10·0	11·3	15·1	14·18	14·0

(expressed as percentages of the nominal share capital)

Calculated on the basis of *Yezhegodnik* . . ., for the years 1899–1902; Tugan-Baranovsky, op. cit., pp. 4, 285–6.

16 Lyashchenko, op. cit., II, p. 323.

17 *Novoye Vremya*, 2/14 Mar 1899, copy; Witte, op. cit., pp. 137 ff., 'Dokladnava zapiska Witte Nikolayu II, Fevral 1900', *Istorik Marksist*, no. 2/3 (1935) pp. 130–9; 'A secret memorandum of Sergei Witte on the industrialization of Imperial Russia', published by T. H. von Laue, in *Journal of Modern History*, XXVI, no. 1 (Mar 1954).

18 *AN*, F30, 340: Verstraete à Caillaux, 1/14 Dec 1901, Bompard à Caillaux, 13 Dec 1901, Delcassé à Caillaux, 24 Mar 1902, Boutiron à Delcassé, 24 Oct 1901; 'S. Y. Witte, Frantsuzskaya pechat i russkiye zaymy', *KA*, vol. 10 (1925).

19 Delcassé à Caillaux, 8 Oct 1901, *AN*, F30, 340.

20 Kergall, *Une enquete sur les finances russes* (Paris, 1902); Verstraete à Caillaux, 9/22 Nov 1901 (personal), 24 Nov/7 Dec 1901, *AN*, F30, 340; Bompard à Caillaux, 31 Dec 1901, *AN*, F30, 340.

21 Veillet Dufreche, consul in Moscow, to Delcassé, 19 Mar 1903, *AN*, F30, 340.

22 Ibid.

23 Ibid.

24 Ibid.

25 Though the Bryansk Company, in which the Société Générale was interested, was among the six selected enterprises and accounted for 18 per cent of the total state orders for rails, these orders absorbed only a portion of its production.

26 Ibid.

27 Note pour le M. de France à St Petersbourg, 22 Feb 1902, *AN*, F30, 340. Indeed the 'national' industry of the Urals organised the syndicate 'Krovlya' for the same reason and purpose.

28 *Vestnik Finansov*, no. 14, 7/20 April 1913: industrial prices grew much more slowly than agricultural prices during the boom of 1909–14. More importantly prices of goods from syndicated industries grew at a slower rate than industrial prices in general.

29 Bompard à Pichon, 24 Dec 1907, *AN*, F30, 340; Donets–Yur'yev Company, extraordinary meeting of shareholders, 12 May 1908, *AN*, F30, 344.

30   *AN*, F30, 329: Aff. Etr. aux Finances, 25 July 1910, Côte de la Bourse et de la Banque, 4 Aug 1913.

31   The industrial syndicates displayed 'liberal' tendencies in that they favoured recognition of trade unions, though when the question of wage increases arose, their support for labour ceased.

32   Lyashchenko, *Istoriya*, ii, op. cit., pp. 310 ff.

33   A similar position existed between the 'foreign' textile industries of the Polish region and the Moscow textile industry.

34   Verstraete's report communicated to Delcassé (Aug 1901), *AN*, F30, 340.

35   As an interesting illustration we may cite here the long and passionate struggle with the Prodameta of an entrepreneur in the Moscow metallurgical region whose most favoured argument was the necessity of defending national interests against foreign inroads. It transpired that the entrepreneur in question was a certain Jules Goujon, a Frenchman by nationality. Cf. Verstraete's report of 6/19 July 1902, *AN*, F30, 337; Report on the Nizhny Novgorod Exhibition, 5 Jan 1897, *AN*, F30, 328.

36   Verstraete, *L'Oural*, p. 24.

37   The French consul in Moscow, Panafieu, emphasised the eagerness with which the directors of the Russo–Chinese Bank waited for the projected amalgamation with the Bank of Siberia, which entailed a commission of the order of 4 million roubles. Panafieu à Pichon, 31 Aug 1909, Société Générale au Ministère des Finances, 29 June 1909, *AN*, F30, 337.

38   See p. 212.

39   Banque Sino-Russe, 'Projet de fusion', 12 Oct 1909, *AN*, F30, 337; Banque de l'Union, 'Procès verbal de l'Assemblée Générale des actionnaires de la Banque de l'Union', 8 Apr 1910, *AN*, F30, 336; 'Reconstitution de la Banque de Commerce Privée de St. Peterbourg', 26 Dec 1909.

40   A case in point was the suspension, under such pressure, of a law limiting the number of directorships which could be held by one person, such pluralism being considered detrimental to the efficiency of companies.

41   Ronin, op. cit., p. 90; see also *Vestnik Finansov*, no. 6 (1928), and p. 152 above.

42   Ibid.

43   Ibid. The figures quoted above from *Vestnik Finansov* are somewhat different from those reproduced here from Ronin, see p. 152.

44   *Vestnik Finansov*. Short-term foreign credits to Russian banks were, in million roubles, on 1 January each year, as follows: 1911 268; 1912 446; 1913 500; 1914 546. See p. 152.

45   Note confidentielle (Crédit Français, formerly J. Loste et Cie), Paris, 27 May 1913, *AN*, F30, 336.

46   Bompard à Pichon, 25 Jan 1908, *AN*, F30, 340; Verstraete à Caillaux, 16/29 Oct 1901, *AN*, F30, 337.

47   The Russian banks earned a commission from their participation in issues of securities in Paris for which there was no market in Russia, frequently without actually having to advance the capital.

48   B. A. Romanov, *Rossiya v Manchzhurii* (Leningrad, 1928) pp. 48, 91, 96, 481–3; and *AN*, F30, 331, Panafieu à Pichon, 18 Sep 1909.

49   Kokovtsov to Cochery, 19 Sep/2 Oct 1909, *AN*, F30, 331.

50 Ronin, op. cit., pp. 131–2.
51 See, for numerous examples of such collaboration, N. Vanag, op. cit.
52 Ronin, op. cit., p. 132.
53 Makeyevka à l'Ambassadeur français à Petrograd, 12/25 June 1916, *AN*, F30, 342.
54 Société Générale à Bénac, 14 Oct 1902, *AN*, F30, 343.
55 Ronin, op. cit., p. 136.
56 Société Russo–Française d'entreprises industrielles et de travaux publics, Procès-verbaux, communiqués par M. Verneuil, 28 Jan 1907, *AN*, F30, 340.
57 Bompard à Pichon, 20 Feb 1907, *AN*, F30, 340. In the contract between the North Donetz Railway Company and the banking houses, signed in St Petersburg on 7/20 June 1908, the Société Russo–Française d'entreprises industrielles et de travaux publics forms part of the issuing syndicate contributing 13½ per cent of the total capital. Cf. Nord Donetz. *AN*, F30, 339.
58 Azoff-Don, B. Kamenka to Verneuil, 9 June 1912, sous plis Sté Marseillaise à Luquet, 11 July 1912, *AN*, F30, 336.
59 Agahd, op. cit., p. 109.
60 Moreover the banks ostensibly complied with the wishes of the French government while it was in the power of the government to prevent their participation in a given transaction. As soon however as the government's consent was obtained, the banks were always in a position to find excuses for the failure to keep their promises. They successfully evaded the undertaking made on the occasion of the introduction to the Paris Bourse of Russian railway bonds that the material for the construction of these lines would be ordered exclusively from enterprises in which the French were interested. See numerous examples: *AN*, F30, 340.
61 Ronin, op. cit., p. 117.
62 The Shanghai branch of the Russo–Chinese Bank was a case in point.
63 Ol', op. cit., pp. 22–3. As in the Putilov armament works and in the Russo–Chinese Bank. Boutiron aux Aff. Etr., 5 May 1906, Finances, Cabinet du Directeur, Banque Sino-Russe, 29 Sep 1909, *AN*, F30, 337.
64 Dorizon à Dir du Mouvement Gén. des Fonds, 3 Dec 1907, *AN*, F30, 344.
65 Russian financial authorities were well aware of the character of French activity in Russia. An article in the official weekly of the Russian ministry of finance, dated 22 September 1913, declared that 'the bearers of French capital in Russia are Belgian and German entrepreneurs who superimpose on the enterprise they direct their own national stamp', and that French capital, unlike German, did not penetrate deep into the economic life of the country, that it played a passive rather than an active part. Cf. *Vestnik Finansov*, no. 38 (1913)

ADDENDUM TO CHAPTERS 6 AND 7

1 'Peterburgsky Mezhdunarodny Bank i frantsuzsky finansovy kapital v gody pervogo promyshlennogo pod'yoma v Rossii . . .'.
2 Carstensen, loc. cit.

CHAPTER 8

1   R. Girault's *Emprunts russes et investissements français en Russie 1887–1914*
    (Paris, 1973), which discusses in depth Franco-Russian financial relations
    within the framework of international relations, goes a long way towards
    a balanced understanding of the nature of the relationship.

2   *Bulletin d'informations russes*, no. 7, 20 July 1925.

3   *Association Nationale des Porteurs des Valeurs Mobilières*, 10 Feb 1921, estimated
    that one-eighth of French holdings of direct and guaranteed Russian bonds
    had not been declared; R. Girault, op. cit., p. 72, n. 2.

4   Girault, op. cit., p. 84.

5   Delamotte, Inspecteur des Finances, Mission en Russie, 1 Feb 1905, *AN*,
    F30, 331.

6   See *Summary of Estimates*.

7   Note pour le Ministre, 16 Feb 1897, Minute du 9 Juin 1897, Analyse,
    AN, F30, 334; Cochéry à Hanotaux 11 June 1897, 6 July 1897, *AN*, F30,
    335; Cochéry aux Aff. Etr., 17 Aug 1897, *AN*, F30, 334.

8   Finances aux Aff. Etr., 8 Mar 1898, *AN*, F30, 334.

9   'Dicté par Caillaux . . .', 18 July 1901, *AN*, F30, 334.

10 *Wirtschaft und Statistik*.

11 Association Nationale, *Les intérêts privés français en Russie et leur protection*,
    10 Feb 1921.

12 *Historique de la dette*.

13 Calculated on the basis of Decoudou, 'Les valeurs mobilières admises à la
    cote officielle de la Bourse de Paris', in *Congrès international des valeurs
    mobilières. Documents, mémoires et notes monographies*, 5 vols (Paris, 1900) p. 2.

14 E. Théry, 'Les valeurs mobilières en France', in *Congrès international*, vol. 2.

15 Idem.

16 See Table 8.12.

17 S. Bouvier, *Le Crédit Lyonnais de 1863 à 1883: la formation d'une banque de
    dépôts*, 2 vols (Paris, 1963) I, p. 743; see also Bouvier, 'L'installation du
    Crédit Lyonnais en Russie Tsariste et la préhistoire des emprunts russes',
    Revue d'histoire économique et sociale, XXXIX, no. 1 (1961) p. 88.

18 M. E. Kaufman, *Das Franzoesische Bankwesen* (Tuebingen, 1910) p. 122.

19 The stamp duty for government securities was raised from the rate of 1 per
    cent introduced in 1898 to 2 per cent in 1909.

20 *Tsentrarkhiv*, p. 382.

21 See p. 183.

22 H. Sée, *Histoire économique de la France* (Paris, 1942) pp. 358–9.

23 A. Raffalovitch, *L'abominable vénalité de la presse* (Paris, 1931).

24 Strange as it may seem, the Russian government emerges from the account
    in a less ignoble, though more pathetic, light than the editors probably
    intended to present it.

25 Tsentrarkhiv, op. cit.; Raffalovitch to Kokovtsov, 31 Mar/13 Apr 1904.

26 A. Raffalovitch, op. cit., p. 36; *KA*, vol. 10, op. cit.

27 *Un Livre Noir*, 2 vols (Paris, n.d.) II.

28 Raffalovitch, op. cit., pp. 36 ff.; Raffalovitch to Kokovtsov, 11/24 Apr
    1904, *Tsentrarkhiv*.

29 E. de Cyon, *L'alliance franco-russe*, 2nd ed. (Lausanne, 1895) pp. 337 ff.
30 Bompard à Delcassé, 11 Mar 1905, 13 Mar 1905, *DDF*, 2, vɪ; Nelidov to
    Lamsdorf, 10/23 Mar 1905, 17 Feb/2 Mar 1906, *Tsentrarkhiv*.
31 Chambre des Députés, doc. 6830, session de 1936, séance 5 Mar 1936.
32 P. Kh. Shvanebakh, *Denezhnoye preobrazovaniye i narodnoye khozyaystvo* (St
    Petersburg, 1901) pp. 27 ff.
33 Barkai, loc. cit., p. 364.

Bibliography

PRIMARY SOURCES

Unpublished

Archives Nationales, Paris, Consular Reports, F12, 7172 ff.
Archives Nationales, Paris, Ministère des Finances, Direction du Mouvement Général des Fonds, F30, 328–F30, 345.
Association nationale des porteurs des valeurs mobilières, Paris.
Crédit Lyonnais, Service des Etudes Financières, Historique de la dette consolidée russe, Paris.

Published

Documents Diplomatiques Français (1871–1914).
Krasny Arkhiv, ed. *Tsentrarkhiv*.

Official publications

France, Office de Biens et Intérêts Privés, Rapport à Président du Conseil, 31 Mar 1920.
Gossudarstvenny Bank, *Otchot za 1916 g.* (Petrograd, 1917).
Ministerstvo Finansov, *Vestnik finansov, promyshlennosti i torgovli*, weekly (St Petersburg, 1883–1914).
——, *Yezhegodnik Ministerstva Finansov* (St Petersburg, 1869–1913).
Ministerstvo Vnutrennikh Del, *Pervaya vseobshchaya perepis naseleniya Rossiyskoy Imperii 1897* (St Petersburg, 1899).
——, *Tsentral'ny Statistichesky Komitet, Yezhegodnik Rossii 1904–1907* (St Petersburg, 1905–8).
Ocherk razvitiya deyatel'nosti gossudarstvennykh sberegatel'nykh kass (St Petersburg, 1912).
Otchoty gossudarstvennykh sberegatel'nykh kass.
Ustav Gossudarstvennogo banka po ofitsyal'nomu izdaniyu, 1895.

SECONDARY WORKS

Affanas'yev, G. E., *Denezhny Krizis* (Odessa, 1900).
Alexeyenko, M., 'Five Years of Budget Work', *Russian Review*, no. 3 (1912).

Anan'ich, B. V., 'Uchotno-ssudny bank Persii v 1894–1907 g.', in M. P. Vyatkin (ed.). *Monopolii i inostranny kapital v Rossii* (Leningrad–Moscow, 1962).

Atava, S., [Terpigorev, S.], *Oskudneniye*, Sochineniya (St Petersburg, 1899) vol. II.

Atlas, M. S., *Natsyonalizatsiya bankov v SSSR* (Moscow, 1943).

Babkov, A., 'National finances and the economic evolution of Russia', *Russian Review*, no. 3 (1912).

Barkai, H., 'The macro-economics of Tsarist Russia in the industrialisation era', *Journal of Economic History*, vol. XXXIII, 2 June 1973.

Bater, J. H., 'The industrial geography of St. Petersburg: 1850–1914', Ph.D. thesis (London, 1969).

Baykov, A., 'The economic development of Russia', *Economic History Review*, 2, VII (1954).

Blackwell, W. L., *The beginnings of Russian industrialization* (Princeton, N.J., 1968).

Bloch, J. de, *Les Finances de la Russie* (Paris, 1899).

Boeke, J. H., *Economics and economic policy in dual societies* (Haarlem, Holland, 1953).

Bogolepov, M., *Obshchestvennoye dvizheniye v Rossi v nachale XX veka* (St Petersburg, 1909).

Bogoslovsky, M. M., 'Gosudarstvennyye krest'yane pri Nikolaye I', *Istoriya Rossii v XIX veke*, ed. A. I. Granat, 9 vols (St Petersburg, n.d.).

Borovoy, S. Ya., *Kredit i banki v Rossii* (Moscow, 1960).

Bouvier, J., *Le Crédit Lyonnais de 1863 à 1883: la formation d'une banqe de dépôts*, 2 vols (Paris, 1963).

——, 'L'installation du Crédit Lyonnais en Russie Tsariste et la préhistoire des emprunts russes', *Revue d'histoire économique et sociale*, XXXIX, no. 1 (1961).

Brandt, B F., *Inostrannyye kapitaly; ikh vhiyaniye na ekonomicheskoye razvitiye strany*, 3 vols (St Petersburg, 1898–1901) II.

Brokhauz, F. A., and Efron, I. A. (eds). 'Krest'yane', *Entsiklopedicheskiy slovar'*, vol. XVI (St Petersburg, 1895).

Bukovetsky, A. I. 'Svobodnaya nalichnost i zolotoy zapas', in M. P. Vyatkin (ed.). *Monopolii i inostranny kapital v Rossii* (Leningrad–Moscow, 1962).

Carstensen, F., 'Numbers and reality: a critique of estimates of foreign investment in Russia', paper presented to a conference of the French Economic History Society in Paris (Oct 1973).

Clapham, J. H., The economic development of France and Germany, 1815–1914 (Cambridge, 1923).

Confino, M., *Domaines et seigneurs en Russie vers la fin du XVIIIᵉ siècle* . . . (Paris, 1963).

Congrès International des valeurs mobilières, *Documents, mémoires et notes monographies*, 5 vols (Paris, 1900).

Crisp, O., 'The financial aspect of the Franco-Russian Alliance', Ph.D. thesis (London, 1954).

Cyon, E. de, *L'alliance franco-russe*, 2nd ed. (Lausanne, 1895).

Decoudu, M., 'Les valeurs mobilières admises à la cote officielle de la Bourse de Paris', in *Congrès des valeurs*, vol. 2.

Dikhtyar, G. A , *Vnutrennaya torgovlya v dorevolyntsyonnoy Rossii* (Moscow, 1960).

Dmitryev, N. K., *Kriticheskiye issledovaniya v potreblenii alkoholya v Rossii* (Moscow, 1911).

'Dokladnaya zapiska Witte Nikolayn II, Fevral' 1900', *Istorik Marksist*, no. 2–3 (1935).

Druzhinin, N. M., *Gosudarstvennyye krest'yane i Reforma P.D. Kiselyova* (Moscow, 1946).

——, 'Konflikt mezhdu proizvoditelnymi silami i feodalnymi otnosheniyami', *Voprosy Istorii*, no. 7 (1954).

——, 'Likvidatsiya feodal'noy sistemy v russkoy pomeshchichyey derevne (1862–1882)', *Voprosy Istorii*, no. 12 (1968).

Druzhinin, N. M., 'Otvet krest'yanstva na reformu P.D. Kiselyova', *Iz istorii obshchestvennykh dvizheniy i mezhdunarodnykh otnosheniy: Sbornik statey v pamyat adademika Yevgeniya Viktorovicha Tarle*, Akademiya Nauk SSSR (Moscow, 1957).

Dyakonov, M., *Ocherki iz istorii sel'skogo naseleniya v Moskovskom gosudarstve* (St Petersburg, 1898).

——, *Ocherki obshchestvennogo i gosudarstvennogo stroya drevney Rusi* (St Petersburg, 1908).

Epstein, E., *Les banques de commerce. Leur rôle dans l'évolution économique de la Russie* (Paris, 1925).

Erman, L. Y., 'Sostav intelligentsii v Rossii' . . .', *Istoriya SSSR*, no. 1 (1963).

Falkus, M. E., *The industrialization of Russia, 1700–1914: studies in economic history by the Economic History Society* (London, 1972).

——, 'Russia's National Income, 1913: a re-evaluation', *Economica* (1968).

Fishlow, A., *American railroads and the transformation of the ante-bellum economy* (Cambridge, Mass., 1965).

Fisk, H. E., *The Inter-Ally Debts* (New York, 1924).

Fogel, R. W. *Railroads and American Economic Growth* (Baltimore, Md, 1964).

Fuhrmann, J. T., *The origins of capitalism in Russia: Industry and progress in the sixteenth and seventeenth centuries* (Chicago, 1972).

Garvy, G., 'Banking under the Tsars and the Soviets', *Journal of Economic History*, vol. xxxii (Dec 1972).

Gerasimova, Y. T., 'Arkhiv Kiselyovykh', *Zapiski otdela rukopisey*, vypusk 19, Ministerstvo Kultury RSFSR (Moscow, 1957).

Gerschenkron, A., 'Agrarian policies and industrialization, Russia 1861–1917', Chapter viii in *Cambridge Economic History*, ed. M. Postan and H. J. Habakkuk, vol. vi, pt 2.

——, *Economic backwardness in historical perspective*, (Cambridge, Mass., 1962).

——, *Europe in the Russian mirror. Four lectures in economic history* (Cambridge, 1970).

——, 'The rate of growth of industrial production in Russia since 1885', *Journal of Economic History*, vii–S (1947).

Gindin, I., *Gossudarstvenny bank i ekonomicheskaya politika tsarskogo pravitel'stva* (Moscow, 1960).

——, 'Moskovskiye banki v period imperializma (1900–1917)', *Istoricheskiye zapiski*, vol. 58 (1956).

Gindin, I., 'O nekotorykh osobennostyakh ekonomicheskoy i sotsyal'noy struktury rossiyskogo kapitalizma v nachale XX v', *Istoriya SSSR*, vol. 3 (1966).
——, *Russkiye kommercheskiye banki* (Moscow, 1948).
—— and Shepelev, L. E., 'Bankovskiye monopolii v Rossii nakanune velikoy oktyabrskoy sotsyalisticheskoy revolyutsii', *Istoricheskiye zapisky*, vol. 66 (1960).
Girault, R., *Emprunts russes et investissments français en Russie 1887–1914* . . . (Paris, 1973).
Glasgow International Exhibition, *Russia, its industries and trade* (Glasgow, 1901).
Glivits, J., *Zheleznaya promyshlennost Rossii* (St Petersburg, 1911).
Goldsmith, R. W., 'The economic growth of tsarist Russia 1860–1913', in *Economic Development and Cultural Change*, vol. 9, pt II (1961).
Gregory, P., 'Economic growth and structural change in Tsarist Russia: a case of modern economic growth', *Soviet Studies*, vol. 3 (1972).
Gulishambarov, St. O., *Vsemirnaya torgovlya v XIX veke i uchastiye v ney Rossii* (St Petersburg, 1898).
Gurev, A. N., *Denezhnoye obrashcheniye* (St Petersburg, 1903).
Haxthausen, Baron von, *The Russian Empire*, 2 vols (London, 1856).
Helfferich, C. T., *Das Geld im russisch-japanischen Kriege* (Berlin, 1906).
Hicks, J., *A theory of economic history*, (London, 1969).
Hirschman, A. O., *The strategy of economic development* (New Haven 1960).
Hoeffding, W., 'Recent financial and trade policy of Russia', *Russian Review*, vol. 1 (Jan 1912).
Hubbard, L. E., *Soviet labour and industry* (London, 1942).
Ibbeken, E., *Das aussenpolitische Problem Staat und Wirtschaft in der deutschen Reichspolitik 1880–1914* (Schleswig, 1928).
Ignatovich, I., *Pomeshchich'ye krest'yane nakanune osvobozhdeniya* (Moscow, 1910).
Indova, E. I., 'Krest'yane tsentralno-promyshlennykh votchin Vorontsovykh v pervoy polovine XIX veka', *Istoricheskiye zapiski*, vol. 38, (1951).
Instruktsiya dlya upravleniya gosudarstvennykh krest'yan v denezhnykh sborakh, Ministerstvo gosudarstvennykh imushchestv (St Petersburg, 1848).
Ischchanian, *Die auslandischen Elemente in der Russischen Volkwirtschaft* (Berlin, 1913).
Kahan, A., 'Continuity in economic activity and policy during the post Petrine period in Russia', *Journal of Economic History*, vol. xxv, 1 (Mar 1965).
——, 'The costs of "Westernization" in Russia', *Slavic Review*, vol. xxv, 1 (Mar 1966).
——, 'Natural calamities and their effect upon the food supply in Russia', *Jahrbücher für Geschichte Osteuropas*, Neue Folge, Bd 16/68.
Karcz, J. F. (ed.), *Soviet and East European agriculture* (Berkeley, Calif., 1967).
Kaser, M., Education in Tsarist and Soviet development', in C. Abramsky (ed.), *Essays in honour of E. H. Carr* (London, 1974).
Kasperoff, M. V., 'Commerce des céréales', in *La Russie à la fin du 19ᵉ siècle*, ed. M. V. de Kovalevsky (Paris, 1900).
Katzenellenbaum, S. S., *Kommercheskiye banki i ikh torgovo-kommissyonnyye operatsii* (Moscow, 1912).
Kaufman, M. E., *Das Franzoesische Bankwesen* (Tuebingen, 1910).
Keppen, P., *Devyataya reviziya* (St Petersburg, 1857).

Khromov, P. A., *Ekonomicheskoye razvitiye Rossii v XIX-XX vekakh* (Moscow, 1950).

——, *Ocherki ekonomiki Rossii perioda monopolisticheskogo kapitalizma* (Moscow), 1960).

Khrulov, S. S., *Finansy Rossii, v svyazi s ekonomicheskom polozheniyem eyo naseleniya* (St Petersburg, 1909).

Kinyapina, N. S., *Politika russkogo samoderzhaviya v oblasti promyshlennosti (20-50-ye) gody XIXv.*, (Moscow, 1968).

Kirchner, W., *Commercial relations between Russia and Europe 1400–1800 . . .* (Bloomington, 1966).

Kocharovsky, K., *Sotsyal'ny stroy Rossii* (Praga, 1926).

Kocka, J., 'Investment strategy in private enterprise,' *Sixth International Congress of Economic History* (Copenhagen, 19–23 Aug, 1974).

Komitet Ministrov, *Nasha zheleznodorozhnaya politika*, 4 vols. (St Petersburg 1902).

Kondratiev, N D. (ed.), *Mirovoye Khozyaystvo 1913–1925* (Moscow, 1926).

Kovalchenko, I. D., *Yezhegodnik agrarnoy istorii vostochnoy Yevropy*, 1963.

Kovalevsky, V. I. (ed.), *Rossiya v kontse XIX v.* (St. Petersburg, 1900).

Landes, D., 'Technical change and development in Western Europe 1750–1914'. *Cambridge Economic History*, vol. VI, pt 1.

Laue, T. H. von, 'Factory inspection under the "Witte System" ', *American Slavic and East European Review*, XIX (1960).

——, 'Russian peasant in the factory, 1892–1904', *Journal of Economic History*, XXI (1961).

——, (ed.) 'A secret memorandum of Sergei Witte on the industrialization of imperial Russia', *Journal of Modern History*, XXVI (Mar 1954).

——, *Sergei Witte and the industrialization of Russia* (New York and London, 1963).

Lauwick, M., *L'industrie dans la Russie Meridionale . . .* (Bruxelles–Paris, 1907).

Leasure, J. W., and Lewis, R. A., 'Internal migration in Russia in the late nineteenth century', *Slavic Review* vol. XXVII, September 1968.

Lenin, V. I., *Sochineniya*, izdaniye 3-oye, vol. 3, 1930.

Léon, P., Crouzet F., and Gascon, R. (eds.), *L'industrialisation en Europe au XIXe siècle*, publ. Centre National de la Recherche Scientifique (Paris, 1972).

Lisyansky, A. S., Osnovaniye Yuzovskogo zavoda, *Istoriya SSR*, No. 5.

Un livre noir: 'Diplomatie d'avant guerre d'après les documents des archives russes, novembre 1910–julliet 1914', 2 vols (Paris, n.d.).

Lorini, E., *La Riforma monetaria della Russia* (Turin, 1897).

Lositsky, A. E., 'Rasspadeniye obshchiny', *Trudy Imperatorskogo Vol'no Ekonomicheskogo Obshchestva*, 1912, vol. 1–2.

Lyashchenko, P. I., 'Iz istorii monopoliy v Rossii', *Istoricheskiye zapiski*, vol 20. (1946).

——, *Ocherki agrarnoy evolutsii Rossii* (St Petersburg, 1908).

McKay, J. P., *Pioneers for profit: Foreign entrepreneurship and Russian industrialization, 1885–1913* (Chicago and London, 1970).

Makar'yev, P , *Fabrichno-zavodskaya promyshlennost' Kostromskoy gubernii nakanune mirovoy voyny* (Kostroma, 1924).

Martin, G., 'Histoire économique et financière', vol. X of G. Hanotaux, *Histoire de la nation française* (Paris, 1927).

Matveyev, A , *Zheleznoye dele Rossii v 1898 godu*, (Moscow, 1899).
Metzer, J , 'Some economic aspects of railroad development in Tsarist Russia', Ph.D. dissertation (Chicago, 1912).
Migulin, P., *Nasha bankovaya politika, 1729–1903* (Kharkov, 1904).
——, *Reforma denezhnogo obrashcheniya v Rossii i promyshlenny krizis, 1893–1902* (Kharkov, 1902).
——, *Russkiy gossudarstvenny kredit* (Kharkov, 1899–1902).
——, *Voyna i nashi finansy* (Kharkov, 1905).
Miller, M. S., *Economic development of Russia 1905–1914* (London, 1926).
——, *The economic development of Russia 1905–1914*, 2nd ed. (London, 1967),
Milyukov, P., *Gosudarstvennoye khozyaystvo Rossii v pervoy chetverti XVIII veka i reforma Petra Velikogo* (St Petersburg, 1905).
Mukoseyev, V. A., 'Money and credit', in A. Raffalovich (ed.), *Russia: Its trade and commerce* (London, 1918).
Myint, J., 'Dualism and the internal integration of the underdeveloped economies', *Banca Nazionale del Lavoro Quarterly Review*, no. 93 (June 1970).
Nevin, E., *Capital funds in underdeveloped countries: the role of financial institutions* (London, 1961).
Navarette, A. and I. de 'Underemployment in underdeveloped economies', in A. N. Agarwala and S. P. Singh, *The economics of underdevelopment* (London, 1969).
Nolde, B., *L'Alliance Franco-Russe* (Paris, 1936).
Ol', P. V., *Statistika inostrannykh kapitalov* (St Petersburg, 1899).
Ozerov, I. K., 'Die Finanzpolitik', in *Die Russen ueber Russland*, J. Melnik ed. (Frankfurt, 1906).
——, *Osnovy finansovoy nauki* (Moscow, 1908).
Pavlov, M. A , *Vospominaniya metallurga* (Moscow, 1945).
Pazhitnov, K. A., *Ocherki istorii tekstil'noy promyshlennosti dorevolyutsyonnoy Rossi* (Moscow, 1958).
Pintner, W. M., *Russian economic policy under Nicholas I* (New York, 1967).
Pogozhev, A. V., *Uchot chislennosti i sostava rabochikh v Rossii* (St Petersburg, 1906).
Pokrovsky, V. E. (ed.), *Sbornik svedeniy po istorii i statistike vneshney torgovli Rossii*, 2 vols (St Petersburg, 1902).
Portal, R., 'The industrialisation of Russia', Chapter IX in M. Postan and H. J. Habakkuk (eds), *Cambridge Economic History*, vol. VI, pt 2.
——, 'Industriels Moscovites: Le secteur cottonier (1861–1914)', *Cahier du Monde Russe et Soviétique*, vol. IV.
——, *L'Oural au XVIIIᵉ siècle. Etude d'histoire économique* (Paris, 1950).
'Prilozheniye k zhurnalu 16.11.1827; 1.12.1828', *Sbornik Istoricheskogo Obshchestva*, vol. 98.
Prokopovich, S. N., 'Über die Bedingungen der industriellen Entwicklung Russlands', *Archiv für soziale Gesetzgebung und Statistik*, Ergänzugsheft 10 (1913).
Propper, S. N. v., *Was nicht in die Zeitungen kam: Erinnerungen des Chefredakteurs der 'Birschewyja Vedomosti'* (Frankfurt, 1929).
Radtsig, A. A., *Zheleznaya promyshlennost' vsego sveta* (St Petersburg, 1900).
Raeff, M., *Michael Speransky* (The Hague, 1957).
Raffalovitch, A., *L'abominable vénalité de la presse* (Paris, 1931).

Raffalovitch, A., *Le marché financier* (Paris, 1897–8).
——, '*Les méthodes employées par les états au XIX siecle pour revenir à la bonne monnaie*', in *Congrès International des Valeurs Mobilières* no. 2 (30 Apr 1900, Paris).
——, *Russia, its commerce and trade* (London, 1918).
Rakitin, A. I., 'Krest'yanskaya promyshlennost' v Arkhangelskoy gubernii v 40–50e gody XIX v.', *Istoricheskiye zapiski*, vol. 59 (1957).
Rashin, A. G., *Naseleniye Rossii za 100 let* (Moscow, 1946).
——, 'K voprosu o formirovanii rabochego klassa v Rossii', *Istoricheskiye zapiski*, vol. 53, (1954).
——, *Formirovaniye rabochego klassa Rossii* (Moscow 1958).
Reutern, M. Kh., *Biograficheskiy ocherk* (St Petersburg, 1910).
Rimlinger, G., 'Autocracy and the factory order in early Russian industrialization', *Journal of Economic History*, vol. xx (1960).
——, 'The Expansion of the labour market in capitalist Russia, 1861–1917', *Journal of Economic History*, xxi (1961).
——, 'The management of labour protest in Tsarist Russia, 1870–1905', *International Review of Social History*, vol. v (1960).
Romanov, B. A., *Rossiya v Manchzhurii* (Leningrad, 1928).
Ronin, S., *Inostranny kapital i russkiye banki* (Moscow, 1926).
Rozhkova, M. K. (ed.), *Ocherki ekonomicheskoy istorii Rossii pervoy poloviny XIX veka* (Moscow, 1959).
Rukovsky, I. P., *Istoriko-statisticheskiye svedeniya o podushnykh podat'yakh* (St Petersburg, 1862).
Russkiy biograficheskiy slovar' (St Petersburg, 1897): 'Kiselyov, P. D.'
Ryndzyunsky, P. G., 'Dvizheniye gosudarstvennykh krest'yan v Tambovskoy gubernii v 1842–1844', *Istoricheskiye zapiski*, vol. 54 (1955).
——, 'Gorodskoye naseleniye' in M. K. Rozhkova (ed.) *Ocherki ekonomicheskoy istorii Rossii* . . . (Moscow 1959).
——, 'Krest'yane i gorod v doreformennoy Rossii' *Voprosy istorii* no. 9 (1955).
——, *Krest'yanskaya promyshlennost' v Rossi* (Moscow 1966).
——, 'O melkotovarnom uklade v Rossii xix v' *Istoriya SSSR* no. 1 (1961).
Schultze-Gaevernitz G., *Ocherki obshchestvennogo khozyaystva i ekonomicheskoy politiki Rossii* trans. from German (St Petersburg, 1901).
——, *Volkswirtschaftliche Studien aus Russland* (Leipzig, 1899).
See, H., *Histoire économique de la France* (Paris, 1942).
Semevsky, V. I., *Krest'yane v tsarstvovaniye Imperatritsy Yekateriny II*, 2 vols (St Petersburg, 1901).
Sergeyevich, B., *Drevnosti russkogo prava* (St Petersburg, 1909).
Shatsillo, K. F., 'Formirovaniye finansovogo kapitala v sudostroitel'ney promyshlennosti Yuga Rossii', in M. P. Vyatkin (ed.), *Monopolii i inostranny kapital v Rossii* (Moscow–Leningrad, 1962).
Shcherban, A. N., *Istoriya tekhnicheskogo razvitiya ugol'noy promyshlennosti Donbassa*, 2 vols (Kiev, 1969).
Shepelev, L. E., 'Aktsyonernoye uchreditelstvo v Rossii', in M. P. Vyatkin (ed.), *Iz istorii imperializma* (Moscow–Leningrad, 1959).
——, 'Arkhivnyye fondy aktsyonernykh bankov' in *Problemy Istochnikovedeniya*, vol. vii (1959).

Shipov, N., *Istoriya moyey zhizni* (St Petersburg, 1881).

Shpolyansky, D. I., *Monopolii ugol'no-metallurgicheskoy promyshlennosti yuga Rossii* (Moscow, 1953).

Shunkov, V. I. *et al.* (eds), *Perekhod ot feodalizma k kapitalizmu v Rossii . . .* (Moscow, 1969).

Shvanebakh, P. Kh., *Denezhnoye preobrazovaniye i narodnoye khozyaystvo* (St Petersburg, 1901).

Sixth International Congress of Economic History (Copenhagen, 19–23 Aug 1974), section: 'Investment Strategy in Private Enterprise', paper by J. Kocka.

Skalkovsky, C., *Les Ministres des Finances de la Russie 1802–90*, trans. from Russian (Paris, 1891).

Skerpan, A. A., 'National economy and emancipation', in A. D. Ferguson and A. Levin (eds), *Essays in Russian history: a collection dedicated to George Vernadsky* (Hamden, Conn., 1964).

Sobolev, M. N., *Tamozhennaya politika Rossii . . .* (Tomsk, 1911).

Solov'yova, A. M., 'K voprosu o roli finansovogo kapitala v zheleznoderozhnom stroitel'stve Rossii nakanune pervoy mirovoy voyny', *Istoricheskiye zapiski*, vol. 69 (1961).

Statistika pozemelnoy sobstvennosti i naselyonnykh mest Yevropeyskoy Rossii 8 vols (St Petersburg, 1880–5).

Strumilin, S. G., *Ocherki sovetskoy ekonomiki* (Moscow–Leningrad, 1926).

Struve, P., *Kriticheskiye zametki* (St Petersburg, 1904).

St Sharapov, *Dve zapiski o russkikh finansakh* (Berlin, 1902).

Sudeikin, V. T., *Gossudarstvenny bank* (St Petersburg, 1891).

Swianiewicz, S., *Forced labour and economic development* (London, 1965).

Svyatlovsky, V. V., *Der Grundwechsel in Russland (1861–1908)* (Leipzig, 1909).

Tarle, E. V., *Evropa v epokhu imperializma 1871–1919* (Moscow–Leningrad, 1928).

Théry, E., 'Les valeurs mobilières en France', *Congrès International des valeurs Mobilières* vol. II (Paris, 1900).

Troynitsky, A. G., *Krepostnoye naseleniye Rossii po desyatoy narodnoy perepisi* (St Petersburg, 1891).

Tsentrarkhiv, *Russkiye finansy i yevropeyskaya birzha v 1904–1906* (Moscow–Leningrad, 1926).

Tugan-Baranovsky, M., *K luchshemu budushchemu* (St Petersburg, 1900).

——, *The Russian factory in the 19th century* trans. from 3rd Russian ed. A. Levin and C. S. Levin under the supervision of G. Grossman (Homewood, Ill., 1970).

——, *Russkaya fabrika*, 3rd ed. (Leningrad, 1934).

Vanag, N., *Finansovy kapital v Rossii nakanune mirovoy voyny* (Moscow, 1925).

Vaynshtayn, A. L., *Narodnoye bogatsvo i narodno-khozyaystvennoye nakoplenye predrevolyutsyonnoy Rossii* (Moscow, 1960).

Verstraete, M., *Les capitaux étrangers engagés en Russie dans les Sociétés industrielles* (Paris, 1900).

——, *Etudes industrielles sur l'Oural* (Paris, 1899).

Veshnyakov, B. V., 'Istoricheskiy obzor proiskhozhdeniya raznykh nazyaniy gosudarstvennykh krest'yan', *Zhurnal Ministerstva Gosudarstvennykh Imushchestv* (Mar 1857).

——, *Krest'yane sobstvenniki* (St Petersburg, 1858).

Wallace, D. M., *Russia*, 2 vols (London, 1905).

White, H. D., *French international accounts 1880–1913* (Cambridge, Mass., 1933).

Witte, S. Y., *Konspekt lektsiy o narodnom i gossudarstvennom khozyaystve* . . . (St Petersburg, 1912).

World Columbian Exposition (St Petersburg, 1893).

Yakovtsevsky, V. N., *Kupecheskiy kapital v feodal'no krepostnicheskoy Rossii* (Moscow, 1953).

Yatsunsky, V. K., 'Krupnaya promyshlennost Rossii v 1790–1860 gg' in M. K. Rozhkova (ed.), *Ocherki ekonomicheskoy istorii Rossii pervoy poleviny XIX veka* (Moscow, 1959).

Yerusalimsky, A. S., *Vneshnyaya politika germanskogo imperializma v kontse XIX veka*, 2nd ed. (Moscow, 1951).

Zablotsky-Desyatovsky, A. P., *Graf P. D. Kiselyov i yego vremya*, 2 vols (St Petersburg, 1882).

Zak, S., *Promyshlenny kapitalizm v Rossii* (Moscow, 1908).

Zapiski Barona Korfa, *Sbornik Istoricheskogo Obshchestva* (St Petersburg, 1896).

Zayonchkovsky, P. A., *Otmena krepostnogo prava v Rossii* (Moscow, 1954).

Zuckerman, S., *Statistischer Atlas zum Welthandel* (Berlin, 1921).

Zweig, E., *Die Russiche Handelspolitik seit 1877* (Leipzig, 1906).

Index

DATE DUE